THE ATTACHMENT-BASED FOCUS GENOGRAM WORKBOOK

The Attachment-Based Focused Genogram Workbook is a hands-on guide for clinicians looking to integrate attachment research and family systems theory into their practice, with particular attention to intergenerational transmission processes.

The book introduces a range of relationship mapping and timeline tools, grounded in the use of focused genograms and the Intersystem Approach. Examining the importance of the therapeutic bond within a variety of client-systems, the book outlines a new methodology for identifying childhood attachment patterns, adult attachment styles, family scripts and attachment narratives, and contextual social bonds. Exercises are also included throughout to encourage reflective thinking and to consolidate key concepts.

Utilizing genograms as an essential tool in systemically focused family practice, this workbook will help therapists at all levels to apply and strengthen systemic considerations for clinical practice and research. The text also complements the revised edition of *Focused Genograms*, which uniquely applies attachment research for individuals, couples, and families in contextual clinical settings.

Rita DeMaria, PhD, Licensed Marriage and Family Therapist (LMFT), is an American Association of Sexuality Educators, Counselors, and Therapists (AASECT) certified sex therapist and an American Association for Marriage Family Therapy (AAMFT) approved supervisor with extensive expertise in systemic applications of attachment theory within a comprehensive focused genogram methodology, and with a unique focus on disorganized attachment.

Briana Bogue, Marriage and Family Therapist (MFT), PhD Candidate, is a couple and family therapist and trauma researcher. She has dedicated her research and clinical work to understanding how individuals, couples, families, and larger systems experience trauma and access resilience.

Veronica Haggerty, MA, Registered Nurse (RN), MFT, is a couple and family therapist and a victim advocate committed to helping individuals, families, and couples navigate a pathway to healing.

"*The Attachment-Based Focused Genogram Workbook* offers a detailed, practical learning experience for clinicians who want to expand the traditional use of the genogram, applying attachment and systems theory to assessing and designing interventions for clients. The authors present useful, theory supported exercises and visual processes, helping clinician and client to collaborate in understanding complex systemic, intergenerational patterns. As an added bonus the workbook contains exercises, aiding new and experienced clinicians in self-discovery, facilitating the all-important therapeutic alliance."

Theresa A. Beeton, PhD, LCSW, co-author of
Assessing Family Relationships: A Family Life Space Drawing Manual

"*The Attachment-Based Focused Genogram Workbook* is useful for any therapist interested in using visual tools to gain a focus on treatment. This workbook instructs clearly the process of determining the interconnectedness that is part of any systemic treatment. Moving beyond a summary of those simply involved in treatment, the Focused Genogram leads the clinician in a step-by-step manner into a case conceptualization that incorporates a sophisticated link to attachment theory. All students and practicing clinicians could benefit from the workbook in that it helps take copious information, and allows one to gain precise understanding of multiple dimensions in a visual format. Following the procedure laid out by Dr. Rita DeMaria, et al., will assist a therapist to reduce the complexity of clinical work and create a method to explore the dynamics of any case."

Scott Browning, PhD, ABPP, professor, Department of Professional
Psychology, Chestnut Hill College, Philadelphia

"This workbook is a useful guide for our Couples and Family Therapy programs' practicum and internship. The authors have written in a way that engages a new generation of students and therapists, as well as clinical supervisors and researchers. The workbook provides helpful assessment tools such as the Focused Genograms, which are based predominantly on Attachment Theory and Bowen Family Systems Theory. I am confident that my students will find this required workbook beneficial as they use it alongside the textbook *Focused Genograms* in our Couple and Family Therapy graduate programs."

Jay E. Oh, PhD, president and professor, Southern California School
of Couples and Family Therapy at Daybreak University

"To help couples and families develop healthier ways of relating in the here and now, clinicians must competently guide them through a journey into their past—not only the past of their relationship and of their families of origin, but also of the multiple generations that preceded them and from whom they inherited their physical and personal traits and their interactional tendencies. *The Attachment-Based Focused Genogram Workbook* is the essential guidebook to help therapists unmask and dissect that deeper past, bringing about understanding of the historical forces that underlie their clients' present relationship problems and thereby making liberation from those difficulties possible. No therapist should attempt the demanding work of couple or family therapy without it!"

Mo Therese Hannah, PhD, professor of psychology, Siena College; advanced
clinician in Imago Relationship Therapy; New York State licensed psychologist

THE ATTACHMENT-BASED FOCUSED GENOGRAM WORKBOOK

Expanding the Realms of Attachment Theory

Rita DeMaria, Briana Bogue, and Veronica Haggerty

Routledge
Taylor & Francis Group

NEW YORK AND LONDON

First published 2020
by Routledge
52 Vanderbilt Avenue, New York, NY 10017

and by Routledge
2 Park Square, Milton Park, Abingdon, Oxon, OX14 4RN

Routledge is an imprint of the Taylor & Francis Group, an informa business

Library of Congress Cataloging-in-Publication Data
A catalog record for this title has been requested

ISBN: 978-1-138-03853-0 (hbk)
ISBN: 978-1-138-03854-7 (pbk)
ISBN: 978-1-315-17700-7 (ebk)

Typeset in Interstate
by codeMantra

MIX
Paper from
responsible sources
FSC
www.fsc.org   FSC™ C013985
Printed in the United Kingdom
by Henry Ling Limited

To Gerald Weeks, who developed one of the most significant integrative theoretical and clinical models, the *Intersystem Approach*, which provides a thoroughly developed application of theory and practice for systemic practice. I am forever grateful that Gerald was willing to collaborate with me to integrate attachment theory as part of his lifetime of published works.

–Rita DeMaria

To my clients, my greatest teachers.
For my family and my love.

–Briana Bogue

To those whom I have been able to help, to those whom I hope to be of help, and to those who are grateful … may they pass it on to the next generation. And to my family and mentors who believed in me and invested in my potential, I am eternally grateful.

–Veronica Haggerty

CONTENTS

FIGURES

TABLES

EXERCISES

ABOUT THE AUTHORS

Rita DeMaria, PhD, LMFT, Certified Sex Therapist (CST), is affiliated with Council for Relationships, Philadelphia, Pennsylvania, where she provides clinical services, training, and supervision in the combined Thomas Jefferson–Council for Relationships Master's Program in Couple and Family Therapy as well as the Post-Graduate Certificate Program in Couple and Family Therapy. DeMaria began her work with families after three important experiences. First, she enrolled in an introductory social work practice course that provided the "Helping Relationships" text which set her upon her path to helping others with their relationships. Next, she was introduced to Conjoint Family Therapy by a professor who learned of her interest in social work and family therapy. The professor suggested that she might find a role model in Virginia Satir. The third experience was provided by her practicum supervisor in 1973 when she was provided the opportunity to participate in a training by the Philadelphia Child Guidance Clinic. Her career spans over four decades and she can be considered among the firsts of the second generation of "family therapists." DeMaria developed the concepts of focused genograms in 1995 with specific intentions to integrate an attachment-based approach to clinical assessment and treatment. She has developed an attachment focused therapeutic bond known as Therapeutic Posture (TxP). With the development of the *Attachment-Based Focused Genogram Work* and the forthcoming publication (and the companion *Focused Genograms: Intergenerational Assessment of Individuals, Couples, and Families*, 2nd edition), she hopes that others will contribute to a comprehensive and systemic approach to helping our clients develop more secure bonds and loving relationships.

Dr. DeMaria is a licensed Marriage and Family Therapist in Pennsylvania, an AASECT certified sex therapist and has been an Approved Supervisor for the American Association for Marriage Family Therapy (AAMFT) for over 30 years. She is also a member of the Society for Sex Therapy and Research (SSTAR). She has immersed herself in studying attachment theory in the early 1980s and her conceptual and clinical work addresses the complexity of an intergenerational framework. She has published, authored, and coauthored several books and journal articles in the field of couple and family therapy, including the subfield of couple relationship education. She is on the editorial board of the *Journal of Couple and Relationship Therapy* and is a reviewer for the *Journal of Sexual and Relationship Therapy: International Perspectives on Theory, Research and Practice.* Dr. DeMaria coauthored a book with Readers' Digest, *The 7 Stages of Marriages,* with Sari Harrar. Most recently, she has coauthored an encyclopedia entrance with Maureen Hannah, PhD, *The PAIRS Enrichment Program; Encyclopedia of Couple and Family Therapy* (2019), Springer International Publishing.

Briana Bogue, MFT, is a trauma-informed, attachment-focused Couple and Family Therapist at Council for Relationships in Philadelphia, Pennsylvania. She is also a PhD candidate at Bryn Mawr College, Graduate School of Social Work and Social Research. Her research and clinical work are centered in resilience, particularly on intergenerational processes of attachment and of adaptation to trauma. Bogue works clinically with individuals, couples, and families, to build on their existing strengths and add to their coping strategies collaboratively.

Veronica Haggerty, MA, RN, MFT, is currently a Marriage and Family Therapist affiliated with Council for Relationships, Philadelphia, Pennsylvania, where she provides clinical services. She began her professional career helping people as a registered nurse and progressed from the physical aspect to the psychological and emotional aspects of helping others, in pursuing a Masters in Counseling degree. She acquired a depth of knowledge in marriage and family therapy using the Intersystem Approach and attachment theory. She brings this knowledge, experience, and skills set to this workbook to help future clinicians understand the intricacies of relationships and thereby use the *Attachment-Based Focused Genogram Workbook* as their guide in helping them navigate a path that will assure effective treatment planning.

CONTRIBUTING AUTHOR

Markie Louise Christianson, (L. C.) Twist, PhD, (she/her/they/them) is the Program Coordinator of the Graduate Certificate in Sex Therapy Program and Professor in the Human Development and Family Studies Department and Marriage and Family Therapy Program at the University of Wisconsin-Stout. Dr. Twist is a Licensed Marriage and Family Therapist (IA, NV) and Mental Health Counselor (IA), an AAMFT Clinical Fellow and Approved Supervisor, and an AASECT Certified Sexuality Educator and Certified Sexuality Educator Supervisor. She is the coauthor of the books, *The Internet Family: Technology in Couple and Family Relationships* and *Focused Genograms: Intergenerational Assessment of Individuals, Couples, and Families* (2nd edition), and the coeditor of the book, *Eco-Informed Practice: Family Therapy in Age of Ecological Peril*. Dr. Twist also serves as the Editor-in-Chief of *Sexual and Relationship Therapy: International Perspectives on Theory, Research and Practice*.

ACKNOWLEDGMENTS

I have had the good fortune to work with two very special people on this *Focused Genogram Workbook* (FGW), Briana Bogue and Veronica Haggerty. We are friends, colleagues, and kindred spirits who have the primary goal to help others and advance clinical knowledge and practice. We each have our own unique Clinical Mind Maps as we develop a unique therapeutic relationship with each of our clients. I also acknowledge Markie L. C. Twist for her contributions for the Basic Genogram and the Addictions Focused Genogram in this FGW. Bill Coffey who graciously reviewed the Addictions Focused Genogram contributed his knowledge and expertise regarding addictions and emotionally focused therapy. Nina Fortuna, LMFT, participated in reviewing and making contributions in both the FGW and *Focused Genograms, 2nd Edition*. I have been very grateful for her suggestions, support, and participation.

My purpose for writing the second edition of *Focused Genograms: Intergenerational Assessment of Individuals Couples and Families* and the companion *The Attachment-Based Focused Genogram Workbook* is to help practitioners learn to dialectically and systemically explore intergenerational transmission of attachment, while simultaneously creating a therapeutic alliance that will provide a foundation of trust, compassion, emotional support and development, mindful living, and ideally, a path that will provide personal, relational, and all other benefits of knowing oneself and loving others.

Rita DeMaria

I would like to thank my friends and family for constantly cheering me on as I move through the clinical and academic worlds. To Rita, thank you for your unending teachings and patient investment in me from the very beginning; you have certainly helped me to grow into the opportunities you have given me. To Dylan, thank you for being my steady source of strength and inspiration.

Briana Bogue

I want to thank all those who wanted more of me, especially my husband Dennis, for understanding my commitment to this work. It is because of the knowledge I have acquired and the vast experiences I have had reading, writing, and working with Rita that I have come to this time in my life and career. It has been a long and treasured journey, for which I know, how really blessed I am, in having a caring and kind family who understands and values commitment, loyalty, and love.

Veronica Haggerty

ABBREVIATIONS

AAI	Adult Attachment Interview
AdFG	Addictions Focused Genogram
AVT FG	Abuse, Violence, Trauma Focused Genogram
BD	Bipolar disorder
BG	Basic Genogram
CIM	Couple Interaction Map
CF	Case Formulation
CMM	Clinical Mind Map
DD	Disorganized/Disoriented
DSM	Diagnostic and Statistical Manual of Mental Disorders
ESFT	Ecosystemic Structural Family Therapy
FCM	Family Connections Map
FG	Focused Genogram(s)
FG2	Focused Genograms: Intergenerational Assessment of Individuals, Couples and Families, 2nd Edition (DeMaria, Weeks, & Twist, 2017)
FOO	Family of origin
G0	Present Generation
G1	First Generation
G2	Second Generation
G3	Third Generation
G4	Fourth Generation
GFG	Gender-Focused Genogram
IA	Intersystem Approach
IMM	Internal Models Map
IWM	Internal Working Model
The Loop	Couple Interaction Infinity Loop
MFS	My Mothers, My Fathers, My Self Focused Genogram
OCSB	Out-of-control sexual behavior
SBE	Social Bonds Ecomap
SoT	Self-of-the-therapist
TxP	Therapeutic posture
WAI	Working Alliance Inventory

Introduction

The Intersystem Approach Meets Focused Genograms

An Intergenerational Systemic Attachment-Based Approach to Assessment and Treatment

We developed this *Focused Genogram Workbook* (FGW) because we identified a gap in the application of genograms that did not match the way we were utilizing them in clinical practice. Our intention behind developing the FGW is to provide you with a guide to understanding how all the tools combine to influence your conceptualization of the case, as well as your use of attachment-focused therapeutic posture (TxP). The combination of the components you will learn in the FGW will help guide you to foster a unique integrative treatment approach for each client-system within the context of the therapeutic alliance. No matter how experienced you are as a therapist, as you gain more knowledge and competence using this integrated approach, your mind-set and your skills will be strengthened. Finally, you will gain greater mastery for clinical problem-solving and processing while your clinical expertise expands.

The overarching goal in this book is to help students, therapists, and supervisors expand their ability to conceptualize any given client-system systemically and dialectically. The *Focused Genograms* text (FG2, 2017) and this companion FGW provide a roadmap for developing an integrative methodology for assessment and intervention with client-systems. Incorporating attachment theory throughout the Intersystem's four domains is a guide for developing an attuned, responsive, and modulated attachment focus for clinical practice. In each chapter, we provide figures and tables to help you learn how to use this approach. The overarching aim of our approach to case formulation and the therapeutic alliance is to establish and enhance TxPs for any given client-system.

The FGW contains the newest applications of the attachment-based FGs, in particular, the Clinical Mind Map (CMM), along with the Basic Genogram (BG), the Addictions FG, and the comprehensive IA Case Formulation (CF).

- The CMM, introduced in Part I Chapter 2, helps practitioners visually conceptualize complex systemic applications to individuals, couples, families, and larger systems.
- TxP in Part II Chapter 3 includes a description of the phases for TxP. Part II also includes a new FG (based on the Gender Genogram) which is named My Mothers, My Fathers, My Self (MFS). The MFS FG is used for practitioners who want to explore their own unique individual, couple, family, and contextual domains through the lenses of attachment theory.
- The CF, in Part III Chapter 9, was proposed by Weeks in his earliest text describing the IA (1986). The CF provides a structured process for gathering pertinent and detailed information about the client-system to determine applicable intervention strategies.
- The updated BG, Part IV Chapter 10, has been expanded and included in this workbook.
- The Addictions Focused Genogram (AdFG), Part IV Chapter 11, has become a prominent FG because of the importance of assessing for addiction during the early assessment period. The opioid crisis has had a devastating impact on generations. The AdFG allows for the assessment of addictions of all types and their effects on the domains.

Part I: Foundations of the Focused Genogram Applications of Attachment Theory

Systemic thinking is also creative thinking. We have developed graphics and tables to guide you as you enhance your ability to think systemically. The tools in this book will guide you as you begin to conceptualize ways you can explore your clinical practice. The IA and the Intergenerational Transmission of Attachment (Figure 1.1) and The FG Roadmap (Figure 1.2) show how the IA and FG tools have integrated attachment and mapping into a holistic assessment. Two additional tables, The Intersystem Domains, Attachment Terms, and FG Tools (Table 1.2) and Mapping Attachment in the Four IA Domains (Table 1.3), contribute to this illustration. Finally, the CMM (in Chapter 2) is a new tool that provides a visual way of helping the readers expand their own ways of thinking and apply the various tools that we have developed.

Chapter 1 begins with attention to a systemic attachment-based approach using a variety of genograms. The theme of the chapter is exploring an intergenerational systemic attachment-based approach to assessment and treatment. FGs are thematic with four topical considerations along with additional timelines. Chapter 2 introduces the CMM and a pictorial perspective on helping therapists, clinicians, and others who work systemically with the clients, patients, students, and others. The CMM fosters a more expansive view of any particular client-system. Our term, client-system, provides a comprehensive perspective of individuals, couples, families, and larger systems.

Part II: Foundations of Therapeutic Posture

TxP and the Keys to Therapeutic Style in Clinical Practice

Chapter 3 is a keystone to developing an all-inclusive methodology for a unique focus on developing a collaborative therapeutic alliance, in particular, the therapeutic bond. The therapeutic bond has been termed "'Therapeutic Posture," to designate that a practitioner can utilize different therapeutic styles to accommodate and respond to clients and patients. We also introduce a model for addressing the progression of TxP over time through a series of phases.

Chapter 4 describes an attachment-based Self-of-the-Therapist (SoT) project, which features the My Mothers, My Fathers, My Self (MFS) Genogram. This particular chapter has been used in the Council for Relationships (CFR) Post Graduate MFT Training Program, titled "The Intersystem Approach to Relationship Therapy." CFR has uniquely been able to stand the test of time as an independent and free-standing clinical, teaching, and research center with a comprehensive focus on relationships. In addition to the SoT project, the postgraduate interns develop more than five other variations of genograms and personal and professional genograms, leading them to become sophisticated, systemic, and dialectical practitioners for treatment of individuals, couples, families, and community programs. The inclusion of an attachment-based exploration of personal relationships with individuals, couples, and families provides a secure foundation for clinical practice. Learning how to explore attachment experiences through the therapeutic alliance, and particularly the therapeutic bond, sets a foundation for developing TxP.

Part III: Applications in the Four Intersystem Approach Domains

The Individual, the Couple, the Family, and the Community

Chapter 5 describes the application of attachment theory using the Internal Models Map (IMM). The IMM identifies an internal state of mind that includes the key parental and caregiver persons from birth to age 10. The most significant attachment experiences take place within the first four years of an infant/young child's life. Traumatic events in infancy, preverbal, and early childhood stages of development can have a significant impact on a child's ability to form healthy physical and emotional bonds. The Individual Timeline is an important tool for assessing key events. The IMM is a key for developing TxP and uses the mapping symbols for childhood attachment patterns.

Chapter 6 highlights the couple domain and the Couple Interaction Map (CIM), which we consider the heart of the family system. The CIM explores the interplay of Childhood Attachment Patterns and Adult Attachment Styles that provide for a unique emotional duality as a couple relationship forms over time. The CIM depicts the ten steps that lead to disconnection, distress, and loneliness, and those that lead to empathy, compassion, and vulnerability. The Relationship Experiences Timeline begins around 14 years of age, as adolescents begin to explore their own relationship experiences. The most significant years for developing long-lasting relationships are often influenced by adolescence and young adulthood into early adulthood. Bowlby's attachment theory highlights the resiliency for establishing secure attachment bonds during later adolescence and adulthood. The couple dynamic can be considered the most potent for untangling negative emotional interaction patterns and establishing more secure adult attachment bonds. We have also created a Couple Flow Map to guide clinicians through the CIM leading to enhanced connection, vulnerability, and empathy. A clinical example that provides a detailed application of the CIM is provided.

Chapter 7 explores the Basic Family Map which was developed during the earliest days of the family therapy pioneers. Various people in the field used and applied adaptations and symbols for the use of the family map. A clinical example of an individual's basic family is included. A new symbol also illustrates a broader use of gender diversity.

The Family Connections Map (FCM) is a new and unique tool that is based on Olson's (2011) FACES IV Circumplex Model. As the FG2 evolved, the use of the Circumplex Model resulted in the development of the FCM. The FCM has several important functions: (1) following Byng-Hall's (1998) suggestions, we include family attachment scripts and family attachment narratives; (2) Olson's (2011) model revealed four uniquely different disorganized family styles and also established a process for identifying each family member's individual adult attachment style; (3) mapping symbols for family systems typically include both childhood attachment patterns and adult attachment styles.

Chapter 8 presents the fourth domain of the IA (the contextual domain), which explores the Social Bonds Ecomap (SBE). Each of the concentric circles in the SBE illustrates another dimension of a client-system's social bonds within the community and elsewhere. A clinical case example is included.

Chapter 9 provides a clinical case formulation that has been a foundation for developing a holistic assessment of a clinical case. The FG2 incorporated attachment-based methods and tools within the *Attachment-Based Focused Genogram Workbook*. A blank CF form is included in the chapter with an illustration using a fully developed, attachment-based, clinical example of a couple case. The tables and figures address each domain along with the attachment-focused TxP.

Part IV: The Evolving Focused Genograms

Chapter 10 explores the updated BG that includes attachment-focused questions. As part of the *Focused Genograms: Intergenerational Assessment of Individuals, Couples, and Families* (1999, 1st edition), the authors have continually improved and advanced the application of attachment theory within the topics and questions. Another important consideration is to maintain focus on contextual and clinical aspects of the BG along with additional attention to contemporary issues surrounding race, ethnicity, and immigration factors.

Chapter 11 introduces the basics of assessment for the AdFG, which is a new addition and explores a complex array of challenges around addictions. The AdFG provides an additional companion to both the updated BG and the Attachments Focused Genogram (FG2, 2017). These three genograms together provide a unique window into the devastating impacts on individuals, couples, families, and communities due to alcohol, drugs, behavioral addictions, and all other variations that can be identified. Addiction presents unique challenges for facilitating treatment for insecure and disorganized individuals, couples, and families. These challenges include difficulty in maintaining emotional connections with others, establishing emotional self-soothing, and many other challenges. The AdFG is a significant FG for practitioners to learn and apply in clinical practice, particularly with the biological, psychological, and relational aspects of addiction.

References

Byng-Hall, J. (1998). Evolving ideas about narrative: Re-editing the re-editing of family mythology. *Journal of Family Therapy, 20*(2), 133-142.

DeMaria, R., Twist, M. L. C., & Weeks, G. R. (2017). *Focused genograms: Intergenerational assessment of individuals, couples, and families*. New York, NY: Routledge.

Olson, D. (2011). FACES IV and the circumplex model: Validation study. *Journal of Marital and Family Therapy, 37*(1), 64-80.

Part I
Foundations of the Focused Genogram Applications of Attachment Theory

1 Attachment-Based Focused Genograms

The Intersystem Approach and Applications of the Attachment Theory Construct

Overview

Welcome to the *Attachment-Based Focused Genogram Workbook* (FGW). The purpose of the FGW is to provide a guide for students, therapists, clinical supervisors, and researchers in using the attachment-focused genogram (FG) assessment tools. FGs allow clinicians to explore intergenerational transmission of attachment bonds and narratives that influence beliefs, attitudes, behaviors, emotional functioning, illnesses, trauma, and more – for individuals, couples, and families. The application of the attachment-based FG maps, in particular, fosters and establishes the formation of a therapeutic alliance and a thorough and well-integrated treatment plan.

The overarching goal of this FGW is to provide you with a new way to develop your Case Formulations (CFs). Each chapter begins with objectives and provides guided instructions to help you gain mastery over developing goals, tasks, and a therapeutic bond with your client-system. The Intersystem Approach (IA) influences the therapist's selection of techniques and strategies that are the best fit for the client-system. The client-system is likely to experience greater confidence in treatment because of the therapist's immediate attention to the problem, via a thorough assessment and flexibility in beginning treatment and establishing an attachment-focused therapeutic alliance. While the body of literature on the use of genograms in clinical training is extensive, it is based predominantly on Bowenian Family Systems Theory. Unfortunately, most Bowen-oriented articles are older and none of them reference the FG. The extant literature focuses on the clinical application of a broad-based genogram or specific (topical) genograms (McGoldrick, Gerson, & Petry, 2008). The ideas in these articles are often very general and could be applicable to any prototype of a very basic and traditional genogram despite the multicultural focus. In addition, the articles and books do not stress integration, theory, or training. The most recent edition of *Focused Genograms: Intergenerational Assessment of Individuals, Couples and Families* (2017) along with this new *Attachment-Based Focused Genogram Workbook* provides an integrated method for exploring individual, couple, family, and community intrapersonal and interpersonal dynamics. Further, the concept of therapeutic posture (TxP) has been defined, described, and detailed as an application to strengthen the therapeutic alliance within this workbook, a new and unique consideration within the context of genograms. The inclusion of attachment theory as a primary relational construct using various genograms, CFs, maps, and timelines for all four domains of the IA, along with a differentiated attachment-focused clinical approach when working with client-systems, provides a comprehensive and systemic approach in clinical practice.

Each chapter starts with objectives and contains background information and exercises to help you learn the concepts and apply the tools. The objectives of this chapter are as follows:

Objectives

1 List the ways you can use the FG Roadmap to describe the IA for the four domains (Exercise 1.1).
2 Describe how using the IA, FGs, and attachment-based mapping and timelines might help you in your ability to conceptualize a case (Exercise 1.2).

The IA and the Attachment-Based FGs

The IA is an integrative dialectical and systemic approach to assessment and treatment. Dialectics provide a logical methodology for developing a meta-theory of change, a meta-theory of human development and relationships, and a dialectical conceptual process that allows for an understanding of the dynamic relationships among systems (DeMaria, Weeks, & Twist, 2017). Dialectical thinking is the process by which clinicians can hold conceptions of both the individual and the intergenerational family system simultaneously. This remarkable method for case conceptualization works for even the most complex multi-person client-system cases.

FGs provide an attachment-based, multidimensional infrastructure that provides a way of thinking integratively among the IA's four domains: the individual, the couple, the family, and the contextual, which encompasses the sociocultural-geopolitical climate of the client-system. In *Focused Genograms*, 2nd edition, we developed a new set of FGs that provide useful tools for clinicians. These tools include the mapping and timeline tools that have been expanded and infused with attachment theory. Using the FG tools (FGs, maps, and timelines) helps the practitioner conceptualize the client-system holistically integrating the IA's four domains. This workbook includes the application and uses of all the FG mapping and timeline tools. We also provide a compendium of FG questions, from both editions of the FG books (DeMaria, Weeks, & Hof, 1999; DeMaria et al., 2017), which will help guide the assessment of your clients as you explore and address the various FGs.

Attachment theory has been integrated into each domain such that the attachment terms for each domain are pictured within it. For example, the individual domain addresses childhood attachment experiences and lists the childhood attachment patterns of secure, anxious-avoidant, anxious-ambivalent, and disorganized. The adult and family/intergenerational domains are similarly listed. The interactional construct of the self in a relationship is part of the original dialectical meta-theory of the IA and includes intrapsychic elements of the self and interpersonal elements of relationships with others. Finally, the outer domain, or the fourth domain, is the contextual domain. It includes cultural, religious, political, and natural elements.

Figure 1.1 incorporates the inner and outer dialectics with all the domains, the FG maps and timelines, and includes four generations (labeled G0-G4) illustrating the intergenerational transmission of attachment bonds within the overall approach. The outer dialectic creates a boundary around the intergenerational family system and incorporates numerous aspects of the contextual domain.

Within each FG, clinicians can develop maps and timelines for each of the four domains. The individual domain maps the childhood attachment patterns with parental figures using the Internal Models Map (IMM).

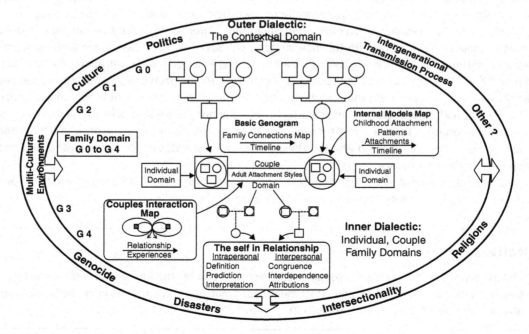

Figure 1.1 The IA and Intergenerational Transmission of Attachment Bonds.

The couple domain uses the Couple Interaction Map (CIM), which provides a guide for identifying adult attachment-style interaction patterns as well as other aspects of couple interactions. The Family Connections Map (FCM) provides a guide for exploring family-of-origin (FOO) attachment-focused family dynamics through the attachment lens. The Social Bonds Ecomap (SBE) provides a guide for exploring social bonds within and among all the domains.

A timeline accompanies each map to track the events that have taken place in each domain that influence the presenting problem.

Parallel to the FG maps, the FG timelines correspond to each IA domain. Adding to the richness of relational mapping, the timelines capture developmental information and life events on a continuum. Their subjects include the following:

- Exploring childhood attachment experiences and developmental struggles, abuse, or trauma.
- Intergenerational patterns of fairness and entitlement that impact secure/insecure attachment for individuals, couples, and families.
- Intimate relationship experiences through adolescence and adulthood.
- Family-life traumas and tragedies, along with patterns of intimate family violence during the client/couple/family life cycle.
- Multigenerational contextual and community impacts for individuals and families.

Timelines provide an important tool to assist the student and practitioner to understand a client – feedback, clarification of life experiences, relationship and contextual information that help formulate diagnoses, and treatment plans.

Table 1.1 visually represents the FG Roadmap, a conceptual framework for using the FG tools as part of the IA case formulation. The attachment-based tools provide specific mapping tools and timeline tools for each domain.

Table 1.1 The FG Roadmap

Domains	Maps	Maps and Timelines
Individual	IMM	Attachment Experiences — Timeline →
Couple	CIM	Relationship Experiences — Timeline →
Intergenerational	FCM	Family Experiences — Timeline →
Contextual	SBE	Domains; Close Networks; Environment Change Over Time; Institutions; Culture

Exercise 1.1 FG Roadmap Worksheet

Directions: After reviewing the IA and the intergenerational transmission of attachment bonds (Figure 1.1) and the FG Roadmap (Table 1.1), in the space below, enter the four domains (Individual, Couple, Intergenerational/Family, and Contextual) under the heading. Then using the other two headings, list the attachment-based FG maps and timeline experiences belonging to each of those domains.

Domains	Maps	Timelines

Expanding Your Clinical Perspective and Skills

Integrative thinking is a more commonly applied term than dialectics and incorporates systemic thinking as well. The IA is an important integrative approach that has been developed and enhanced over 35 years. The IA is a dialectical meta-theory with two key integrational constructs: attachment theory and interactional theory. These constructs provide practitioners a systemic approach to assessment and intervention. Consequently, you will learn to think in an integrative way about clients, which will also enhance your ability to engage with each person within the client-system. Kallio (2011) suggests that using the term integrative thinking captures the potential evolution of adult cognitive development. This is supported by Seigel's (2004) ideas about the human brain's development of complexity as it ages, with a healthy brain maintaining flexibility. Also, Hill (2015) suggests that an integrated mind and body are goals of therapeutic healing. Therefore, practitioners who focus their attention on the development of systemic assessment will also lead to integrative thinking, which may further yield to wisdom over time in clinical practice. Although further discussion of the adult capacity to think integratively is beyond this brief description; therapists, who continually explore using the combined IA and FG and their related foci, will likely enhance their therapeutic relationships with individuals, couples, families, and communities.

We propose that using the FG tools (FGs, maps, and timelines) help develop the practitioner's ability to conceptualize the client-system systemically. The key characteristic of systemic thinking is the ability to hold the four domains in mind while addressing the complexity of the contrasts and contradictions that exist among the individuals within the various relational systems. The introduction of a comprehensive Clinical Mind Map (CMM) in Chapter 2 provides a visual conception of the strategies and techniques the therapist chooses to use. A client-system is likely to experience greater connection and confidence in treatment because of the therapist's comprehensive and holistic approach to the presenting problems.

Table 1.2 highlights the attachment terms and FG tools that belong to each IA domain. For example, the individual domain uses the IMM to show the childhood attachment patterns with the parental figures.

Table 1.2 The Intersystem Domains, Attachment Terms, and FG Tools

Domains	Attachment Terms	FG Tools
Individual (childhood)	Attachment patterns	IMM – depicts the parental attachment figures and childhood attachment patterns
Couple (adult)	Attachment styles	CIM – depicts the adult attachment interaction styles which often intensify and ultimately trigger emotional reactions based in childhood attachment patterns

Domains	Attachment Terms	FG Tools
Intergenerational/family	Family scripts (Byng-Hall), family legacies (fairness genogram), and family attachment narratives	FCM – a graph with 16 options for a range of secure, preoccupied, dismissive, and disorganized family narratives. These narratives reflect predictable patterns that reveal behaviors, emotions, and repetitive cycles of intergenerational relationships
Contextual	Social bonds (attachment based)	SBE – a design of four concentric circles that provide unique spheres of influence upon and resources for a client-system

The IA: Intergenerational Transmission of Attachment Bonds

The attachment construct incorporated into the IA applies to each of the IA domains: the individual, the couple, the family, and the contextual. The contextual domain incorporates sociocultural and political-geographic environment (Keitaibl, 2012) as well as other features. The four mapping tools – the IMM, the CIM, the FCM, and the SBE – are useful in tracking the complexity of the attachment styles, patterns, and scripts within the client-system and help the therapist establish a multi-directed and systemic approach to TxP for each person in the client-system. Mapping a client's attachment styles, patterns, scripts, and social bonds across all domains of the IA is crucial as part of clinical practice.

Each domain can be explored through attachment patterns and styles and their widespread relational impact throughout the client-system. Vetere and Dallos (2008) also highlight the clinical importance of developing family-focused, attachment narratives. Consequently, the use of the various FGs in this text will also enhance, strengthen, and deepen the therapist's understanding of the social bonds, family scripts and narratives, the couple interaction patterns that support or constrain movement toward secure attachment, and the internal working models (IWMs) that guide attachment beliefs and behavior.

Understanding a coordinated method for exploring, understanding, and learning how to apply the various attachment terms that are found in the literature is a crucial knowledge base for systemically focused clinicians. Practitioners often question (and are sometimes confused by) the differences in the terminology of attachment patterns and styles for children and adults (see Table 1.1). Many articles, books, and book chapters describe the various terms used to describe attachment and provide the history of how these terms or categories were developed, but they do not provide a practical way to apply this information in an integrative fashion. In subsequent chapters, specific mapping tools (see Table 1.1) also provide guidance for developing your understanding of the terms and applications for the attachment-based assessments.

In Table 1.3, attachment terminology is matched with each of the unique mapping tools along with the timeline tools for all the four domains.

Table 1.3 Mapping Attachment in the Four IA Domains

IA with the Four Domains	Individual	Couple	Family	Cultural/Contextual
Mapping attachment behaviors across the four domains	Childhood attachment patterns: Internal working models	Adult attachment styles: adult interaction patterns	Family scripts, legacies, and family narratives	Social bonds
Integrating the attachment timeline	Individual: childhood events ages 4–10 years; adolescence ages 11–17 years	Relationship experiences: older adolescents; young adults, adulthood	Family/intergenerational	Spheres of influence include extrafamilial supports, community connections and services, and institutional providers

Therapeutic Posture

The new attachment-based FG tools integrate attachment-focused assessments that help the therapist develop the therapeutic bond within the therapeutic alliance from the initial interview. The TxP is finely attuned to the attachment patterns, styles, scripts, and narratives of the individual or the relational unit.

Within the cohesive FG Roadmap, the therapeutic alliance (an evidence-based aspect for therapeutic change) is guided by three factors: goals, tasks, and the therapeutic bond (Bordin, 1980, 1994). Goals are collaboratively developed between the practitioner and the client-system. Tasks are developed to address the presenting problems the client-system brings into treatment using a variety of emotionally focused, cognitive, and behavioral strategies. The therapeutic bond has an overarching purpose that is to foster a facilitating therapeutic relationship that strengthens emotional attunement between therapist and client-system. This approach is also supported by the neurobiological research on attachment and bonding (Fosha, Siegel, & Solomon, 2009; Hill, 2015).

DeMaria (1999) identified and further developed a specifically focused therapeutic bond that is called therapeutic posture (TxP). TxP is defined as an attachment-focused therapeutic bond within the therapeutic alliance. The clinician's TxP vis-à-vis the client(s) is determined by "where the client is"[1] at the start of treatment. Consequently, the clinician must learn how to assess and foster a congruent TxP with the client-system in order to establish a sense of safety, security, and stability for the client. Clinical research has established that clients with insecure attachments at intake have poorer outcomes than those with secure attachments at intake. Specific relational styles provide a model for strengthening the therapist–client reparental therapeutic alliance. TxP is formulated based on the assessment of each client's IWMs of attachment, which are then depicted using the IMM, and then will be addressed throughout this workbook.

The Four Domains and the Attachment-Focused Maps

The IA provides an integrative framework and a method that helps the therapist keep two dimensions in mind. These include the clients' intrapersonal internal experiences and the clients' interpersonal relational experiences, especially for romantic relationships. Attachment theory uniquely applies to relationship quality within the self and with significant relationships within the client's system of interpersonal experiences. In order to meet the particular needs of the many client-systems that enter treatment with insecure attachments, the IMM is a tool for understanding the individual's childhood attachment experiences. The IMM is foundational to understanding how childhood experiences impact and influence adult attachment styles (individual), couple interaction patterns (couple), and family narratives and scripts (family). In addition, the IMM provides the foundation for the practitioner to use TxP with the individuals, couples, or families in a variety of clinical settings. TxP provides a method and process for therapists to establish an attuned relationship with the client based on the clinician's understanding of the client's IWMs of parental figures.

The CIM focuses on adult attachment interactions which reinforce or modify the expression of childhood attachment experiences, particularly insecure attachments. Childhood attachments are not static. New romantic relationships have the potential to help each partner develop a secure base that provides each person support, comfort, care, and sexual opportunities. Assuming a romantic bond that includes sexual attraction, adult attachment styles provide a foundation for exploring and enhancing a sexual relationship.

When partners are in conflict, adult attachment styles often intensify and, ultimately, trigger childhood attachment patterns within the couple relationship bond. We use the term first-order change to characterize surface level change. First-order change aims to stabilize the couple's relationship with one another, typically using a cognitive and/or behavioral approach to treatment. When we use the term *second-order change*, the focus of treatment is on changing the partners' perceptions of themselves with their partners, not for or against each other. Qualitative changes in each person's mind and spirit toward the relationship are crucially important in order to prevent reverting back to typical relational "loops." In addition to exploring and identifying the emergence of the negative emotional infinity loop, partners will seek a variety of couple therapies emphasizing cognitive, behavioral, emotional, and narrative methods. These approaches all aim to help couples develop more secure cognitive, emotional, physical, and sexual bonds through improvements in healthy relationship skills and habits.[2] However, the goal of the CIM is to help the clinician guide the couple through a process with three key elements – empathy for one's partner, willingness to be vulnerable, and compassion that minimizes activation and hyperactivation during emotional distress – in order to move above continual negativity and emotional allergies (which are described in Chapter 6).

The CIM is a tool that helps therapists examine the links between the clients' childhood attachments and their parental attachments to their children, if present. Adult attachment patterns rest on early life experiences and ultimately become the expression of the intergenerational family attachment scripts and narratives (Cowan & Cowan, 2005, 2009; Cowan, Cowan, Pruett, & Pruett, 2007). Adult attachment patterns are also predictive for parental bonding behaviors with their infants and children (Bernier & Dozer, 2003; Karavasilis, Doyle, & Markiewicz, 2003; Schneider, Gurman, & Coutts, 2005). Another very important aspect of the couple relationship is the role of the relationship to moderate the couple's intimate relationship interaction loops (Dinero, Conger, Shaver, Widaman, & Larsen-Rife, 2011).

The parental bonding behaviors are a primary factor in the intergenerational transmission of both secure and insecure attachment styles, patterns, and scripts as childhood attachment experiences are recreated within the family system. Within the parenting dynamic, both the adult attachment interaction loop and each partner's childhood attachment patterns, which we describe as IWMs – a term given by Bowlby (1969), have bearing on each parent's parenting style. Consequently, parenting styles experienced by each member of the couple are played out repeatedly in the couple relationship resulting in family scripts that are central to transmission of attachment styles throughout the family system (Byng-Hall, 1995). The CIM reveals the couple's current adult attachment interaction loops, which will then reveal the internalized patterns of couple dynamics with their individual parental figures. As the couple continues to replay their own unique negative interaction patterns within their relationship as well as their internalized experiences of their parents' relationship, the couple begins to replay childhood insecurities. The therapist using TxP will help the couple shift into an intentional process leading toward a new dynamic that includes vulnerability, empathy, and compassion.

Vetere and Dallos (2008) highlight the clinical importance of family-focused attachment narratives being viewed through a systemic lens. The FCM[3] provides a mapping tool to depict the various family scripts that are based on the Circumplex Model of couple and family systems (Olson, 2011), which provides a method for assessing family dynamics and styles based on three dimensions: (1) flexibility, (2) connection, and (3) communication. Parents who are mutually dismissive within their couple relationship typically carry avoidant childhood attachment patterns into their relationships with their own children. Likewise, parents who are mutually preoccupied typically carry ambivalent childhood attachment patterns. Parents with mixed attachment styles can also intensify power struggles between the partners. Thus, parenting styles, based on childhood attachment experiences, will then influence the contemporary family type. With reflection many people become aware of the similarities between themselves and their own parents, (which we suggest is an intergenerational process of transmission between and among the generations, as depicted in Figure 1.1).

When partners are mutually dismissive (revealing avoidant IWMs) in their parenting, they tend to create a more distant and disconnected family script. Similarly, FOO loyalties are often played out in the parenting dimension of the intergenerational domain which continues an ongoing negative-feedback loop that reinforces the styles of the family attachment script. Ecomaps (Bronfenbrenner, 1977; Hartman, 1975; Hartman & Laird, 1983) provide a wider view of client-systems, including those who have experienced pervasive trauma and oppressive socioeconomic, political, educational, and other impediments. The Ecomap also focuses the therapist's attention on the various resources that may contribute to a client's resilience.

Exercise 1.2 Integrating the FG with Attachment Theory

Directions: In the space below, describe how using the IA, FG, mapping, and timelines with attachment theory might help you in your ability to conceptualize a case.

_____

_____

_____

_____

Summary

The amalgamation of the IA with the application of attachment-based FGs is a unique and powerful theoretical integration that provides methods for assessment and treatment. *Together with Focused Genograms,* 2nd Edition, the Attachment-Based FGW brings the IA and FG tools to practitioners in a user-friendly manner. Mapping and timeline tools, along with the attachment-based FGs, clearly reveal the guiding structure for FG assessment. The application of TxP as the bond within the therapeutic alliance has also been further developed in FGW.

The FGW Roadmap provides opportunities for a broader understanding of the attachment-focused tools as they are applied to each of the domains. Chapter 2 introduces the CMM to help with this integrational assessment. Chapters 3 and 4 discuss TxP and the self-of-the-therapist approach for better understanding of an attachment-focused therapeutic alliance. Chapters 5-8 address all the four domains using the accompanying tools. Finally, we include chapters on the CF, BG, and Addictions Genogram. Each of these chapters was specifically chosen and designed to guide clinicians on the application of these concepts to their assessments. Overall, the purpose of this FGW is to help clinicians learn to make comprehensive, systemic assessments about their client-systems, as they form an attuned TxP that fosters second-order change. Thus, in this FGW, we provide ample access to additional theory and exercises to hone these skills.

Notes

1 Goldstein (1983) was the first to use the term starting where the client is, a phrase that underscores collaboration and empowerment for clients in treatment.
2 See Weeks (1986) and Weeks' complete body of work on couples in therapy, sex therapy, and couple therapy techniques.
3 See Chapters 3 and 9 for further details and description.

References

Bernier, A., & Dozier, M. (2003). Bridging the attachment transmission gap: The role of maternal mind-mindedness. *International Journal of Behavioral Development, 27*(4), 355-365.

Bordin, E. S. (1980). Of human bonds that bind or free. Paper presented at the annual meeting of the Society for Psychotherapy Research, Pacific Grove, CA.

Bordin, E. S. (1994). Theory and research on the therapeutic working alliance: New directions. *The working alliance: Theory, Research, and Practice, 173,* 13-37.

Bowlby, J. (1969). *Attachment and loss. Vol. 1 attachment.* New York, NY: Basic Books.

Bronfenbrenner, U. (1977). Toward an experimental ecology of human development. *American Psychology, 32,* 515-531.

Byng-Hall, J. (1995). Creating a secure family base: Some implications of attachment theory for family therapy. *Family Process, 34,* 45-58.

Cowan, C. P., & Cowan, P. A. (2005). Two central roles for couple relationships: Breaking negative intergenerational patterns and enhancing children's adaptation. *Sexual and Relationship Therapy, 20*(3), 275-288.

Cowan, P. A., & Cowan, C. P. (2009). Couple relationships: A missing link between adult attachment and children's outcomes. *Attachment & Human Development, 11*(1), 1-4.

Cowan, C. P., Cowan, P. A., Pruett, M. K., & Pruett, K. (2007). An approach to preventing co-parenting conflict and divorce in low-income families: Strengthening couple relationships and fostering fathers' involvement. *Family Process, 46,* 109-121.

DeMaria, R., Weeks, G. R., & Hof, L. (1999). *Intergenerational assessment of individuals, couples, and families: Focused genograms.* Philadelphia, PA: Brunner/Mazel.

DeMaria, R., Weeks, G. R., & Twist, M. L. (2017). *Focused genograms: Intergenerational assessment of individuals, couples, and families.* New York, NY: Routledge.

Dinero, R. E., Conger, R. D., Shaver, P. R., Widaman, K. F., & Larsen-Rife, D. (2008). Influence of family of origin and adult romantic partners on romantic attachment security. *Journal of Family Psychology,22*(4), 622.

Fosha, D., Siegel, D. J., & Solomon, M. F. (Eds.) (2009). *The healing power of emotion: Affective neuroscience, development & clinical practice.* New York, NY: W. W. Norton & Company.

Goldstein, E. G. (1983). Issues in developing systemic research and theory. In A. Rosenblatt & D. Waldfogel (Eds.), *Handbook of clinical, social work* (pp. 5-25). San Francisco, CA: Jossey-Bass.

Hartman, C. W. (1975). *Housing and social policy.* Englewood Cliffs, NJ: Prentice Hall.

Hartman, A., & Laird, J. (1983). *Family-centered social work practice.* New York, NY: Free Press.

Hill, D. (2015). *Affect regulation theory: A clinical model.* New York, NY: W. W. Norton & Company.

Kallio, E. (2011). Integrative thinking is the key: An evaluation of current research into the development of thinking in adults. *Theory & Psychology, 21*(6), 785-801. doi:10.1177/0959354310388344

Karavasilis, L., Doyle, A. B., & Markiewicz, D. (2003). Associations between parenting style and attachment to mother in middle childhood and adolescence. *International Journal of Behavioral Development, 27*(2), 153-164.

Kietaibl, C. M. (2012). A review of attachment and its relationship to the working alliance. *Canadian Journal of Counselling and Psychotherapy/Revue canadienne de counseling et de psychothérapie, 46*(2), 122-140.

McGoldrick, M., Gerson, R., & Petry, S. S. (2008). *Genograms: Assessment and intervention.* New York, NY: W. W. Norton & Company.

Olson, D. (2011). FACES IV and the Circumplex Model: Validation study. *Journal of Marital and Family Therapy, 37*(1), 64-80.

Schneider, W. F., Gruman, A. J., & Coutts, M. L. (2005). Defining the field of applied social psychology. In F. W. Schneider, J. A. Gruman, L. M. Coutts (Eds.), *Applied social psychology. Understanding and addressing social and practical problems* (pp. 5-18). Thousand Oaks, London, New Delhi: SAGE Publications.

Siegel, D. J. (2004). *Parenting from the Inside Out.* Tarcher, reprint edition.

Vetere, A., & Dallos, R. (2008). Systemic therapy and attachment narratives. *Journal of Family Therapy, 30*(4), 374-385.

Weeks, G. R. (1986). *Treating couples: The intersystem model of the Marriage Council of Philadelphia.* New York, NY: Routledge.

2 The Clinical Mind Map
A Visual Perspective

Overview

The Focused Genogram (FG) attachment-focused tools help the practitioner conceptualize the client-system systemically. In this chapter, we introduce you to mind maps, specifically, the Clinical Mind Map (CMM). The CMM (Figure 2.1) is a visual tool that helps the reader comprehend the inclusiveness of the FG tools. The process of developing a unique CMM for each client strengthens and deepens the clinician's knowledge of the client-system. It is this depth of knowledge shared and therefore experienced between client and therapist that enables the formation of an attachment-focused therapeutic alliance and a thorough and well-integrated treatment plan. The Case Formulation (CF), described in Chapter 9, provides the structure for gathering pertinent and crucial information about the client-system. The CF in this workbook organizes information using the Intersystem Approach (IA) meta-framework with specific attention to using the attachment theory construct.

> ## Objectives
>
> 1 Describe how the CMM will help you begin to think systemically and dialectically (Exercise 2.1).
> 2 Explain how the therapeutic bond develops in the client-system when thinking systemically and dialectically using the CMM (Exercise 2.2).
> 3 Identify your learning styles as you begin to explore the IA, FG, and therapeutic posture (TxP) (Exercise 2.3).
> 4 Create a CMM and incorporate the FG mapping and timeline tools using a case example (Exercise 2.4).

The CMM: An Integrative Approach to Differentiating the Four Domains

The purpose of the CMM is to strengthen the therapist's bond with the client-system by engaging the more experiential and creative right hemisphere of the brain. The CMM is an innovative application that uses mind mapping, which helps you conceptualize the client-system treatment in a more deliberate and conscious manner. When applying the attachment construct within a clinician's clinical practice, the clinician begins to develop an empirical foundation that guides practice, but simultaneously, the clinician uses this information to develop the most effective TxP. Consequently, the process of developing a unique CMM for each client strengthens and deepens the clinician's knowledge of the client-system. The formation of an attachment-focused therapeutic alliance and an integrated treatment plan provides an individually tailored approach to treatment.

We developed the CMM to help students, clinicians, supervisors, and others to visualize how to think systemically and dialectically (meaning to be able to think holistically and logically, resulting in ideas and opinions). The greater the use of the FG mapping and timeline tools, the quicker one learns how to develop a systemic and dialectical assessment. For many practitioners who have adapted to using the IA, conceptualizing the client-system and the presenting problem is an implicit or unconscious process. The CMM in this workbook becomes a graphic representation of the clinician's knowledge, understanding, and application of how the FGs and the related FG tools come together to be used early on, shortening the time of conceptualizing the presenting problem, while enhancing the TxP. The CMM provides the skeletal structure for developing TxP,

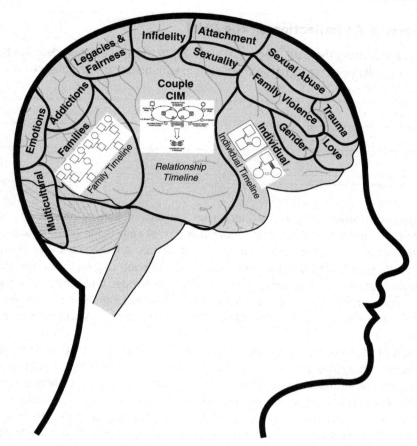

Figure 2.1 Example of a CMM.

which has been honed by the FG assessment process, and, therefore, strengthens the therapeutic relationship. Consequently, the CMM makes the FG assessment process come alive, leading the clinician to become more deliberate and conscious about a client-system.

Example of a Personal Reflection: (Veronica's Perspective)

Thinking systemically is what most of us normally do in our everyday lives when we think before we speak and respond to others. So, it is not a foreign concept to think of oneself in relationship to others. This is how the IA meta-framework begins to help the clinician use the attachment-based tools to help the client-system. It is the clinician who needs to learn the unique aspects of any given client-system to assess the difficulties people are struggling with. The CMM presented here is where we begin. We want to get to know them as an individual, a couple, a family, and a participant in the community. We ask ourselves, what tools do I need to begin to gather this information? I will plan to do Basic Genogram, individual timelines, get to know their early attachment patterns, and provide a safe environment, while I gather information for the Couples Interaction Map (CIM). What am I noticing that is different between them? And so the process begins. I start to form a therapeutic bond with my client that will further their growth and development and provide them success in achieving their goals.

The CMM helps me to identify what Focused Genogram I may need. Perhaps reviewing the couples' individual domains, I notice substance abuse in their intergenerational history; I might never have thought to ask more questions about the clients, about their own habits, and how those might be interfering with their relationship. So you can see how the CMM is key to the therapist's knowledge of the client-system.

Exercise 2.1 Reflection on the CMM

Directions: Using the CMM diagram (Figure 2.1) in the space below, describe how CMM can begin to help you to think of the client-system both holistically and dialectically.

_____

_____

_____

_____

Understanding a coordinated method for exploring, understanding, and learning how to apply the various attachment terms that can be found in the literature is a crucial knowledge base for systemically focused clinicians. Practitioners are sometimes confused by the differences in the terminology of attachment styles for children and adults (see Table 1.1). Many articles, books, and book chapters describe attachment styles and provide the history of how these terms or categories were developed, but they do not provide a practical way to apply this information in an integrative fashion. In subsequent chapters, specific mapping tools also provide guidance for developing your understanding of the terms and applications for the attachment-based assessments.

The four domains of the IA (individual, couple, intergenerational, and contextual) provide a method for a comprehensive vision of the client-system. The CMM illustrates the interconnections of the FG tools, which include various FGs and the associated mapping and timeline tools. Further, the CMM provides a picture of the overall perspective of the client-system that emerges in the therapist's mind. The clinician can conceptualize the complexity, apparent contradictions, and various distinctions that emerge during the early phases of therapy. As a result, the CMM diagram demonstrates a simplistic and flexible way for the therapist to differentiate various systems.

A systemic approach to treatment ensures that you will learn and understand how to work with individuals, couples, families, and community relationships. Conceptualizing each client-system is a unique and important skill. The CMM worksheet provides a guide for visually organizing information as the clinician gathers information about the client-system. As the FG tools are applied using the CMM worksheet, a CMM begins to emerge and helps the therapist develop a comprehensive understanding of a unique client-system using all of the FGs, maps, and timelines. The tools are particularly useful during the early phase of treatment.

Developing a BG at the outset of the treatment is an important first step for the therapist. This goal allows the counselor, therapist, or supervisor to create a foundation for getting to know the client-system's process. The initial interview is an important phase of being introduced to the client-system, obtaining information about the participant's life or lives, and gathering preliminary information about the network of couple and family relationships, as well as a preliminary assessment of the relationship attachment styles. For example, the BG encourages therapists to include the broad range of people who are significant as parents, couples, families, and various communities. These people can include fictive kin who are people that are part of the client-system, but who are not defined by a bloodline relationship.

Attachment Theory: The Keys to Building a Comprehensive Clinical Approach

Attachment theory is integrated throughout all the FGs and the accompanying mapping and timeline tools. It also provides a relational foundation for establishing a therapeutic relationship, goals for treatment, and specific interventions that aim to support successful counseling. More significantly, this attachment-based workbook will help you explore attachment theory from numerous perspectives. These perspectives include the various intergenerational attachment bonds through all four domains of the IA. Adult attachment styles are included in the adult and the couple domains. Childhood attachment patterns are key to individual assessment, focusing on internal working models of attachment. The FCM provides a method for identifying a collective attachment-based family style as well as differentiating the individual family members within the FCM. The Contextual domain is the fourth domain that pinpoints the various aspects in the sociocultural context of the client-system including historical, political, natural, racial, cultural, and socioeconomic factors.

With influences by the thought leaders of their time, such as Ashley Montague (1978), Donald Winnicott (1965, 1973), Harry Harlow (1958, 1962), Renee Spitz (1946, 1965), and Klaus and Kennel (1976), attachment theory became securely rooted in the first half of the 20th century. Bowlby's influence was the most notable, with his focus on the importance of early bonding and reciprocal relationship between childhood and adult attachment experiences. In contrast to Freud's psychodynamic approach, Bowlby's behavioral focus revealed the important qualities that fostered bonding between parents and children, between couples, and among families. Our overarching goal is to help clinicians establish more secure therapeutic relationships with clients and explore the multiple dimensions of relationship patterns.

Exercise 2.2 FG Tools Help to Build a Therapeutic Bond

Directions: Using the CMM diagram, (Figure 2.1) in the space below, explain how a therapeutic bond with the client-system is developed.

_____

_____

_____

_____

The Therapist and the Client-System: Mind Maps and Dialectics in Action

The key to integrative thinking is a highly developed cognitive ability to view issues simultaneously from multiple perspectives and to arrive at the quickest and most reasonable reconciliation of seemingly contradictory information (Riegel, 1976). Of the several major elements of dialectical thinking, the most applicable concept to the mind map is that of being able to comprehend the relationship between and among various aspects of a phenomenon that may on the surface appear to be disconnected but have deeply rooted reciprocal connections.

Mind maps are a useful method for therapists to use in order to strengthen their therapeutic relationships. The purpose of a mind map is to help organize a vast array of information that a therapist gathers in both the early interviews and updates throughout the early clinical process. Typically mind maps have both structural and process dimensions. For many practitioners, conceptualizing the client-system and the presenting problem is an implicit and/or unconscious process.

The mind map is a graphical and practical method for organizing multiple ideas and concepts that emerge from the ability to think dialectically. The mind map helps practitioners visualize and comprehend the relationships between and among various aspects of a phenomena that may appear to be disconnected on the surface, but have deeply rooted reciprocal connections. The CMM provides a visual diagram that illustrates how a therapist conceptualizes the various genograms, maps, and timelines for each unique clinical experience with a client-system. A primary aim of the CMM is to support and strengthen the clinician's therapeutic alliance. As the client provides information about the presenting problem, previous efforts to deal with the problem, and how the client thinks and feels about the problems, the therapist will be able to attend to the client's unique life experiences and challenges.

We introduce the CMM to illustrate the mentalizing capacity that students, clinicians, and clinical supervisors develop as they expand their ability to think dialectically and relationally. Fonagy and Bateman (2008) and Wallin (2007) suggest that mentalizing is a basic state of attention to the therapeutic relationship to physical, emotional, and cognitive states of being. Mentalizing is a term to describe a form of imaginative mental activity about others or oneself, namely, perceiving and interpreting human behavior in terms of intentional mental states (e.g., needs, desires, feelings, beliefs, goals, purposes, and reasons) (Fonagy & Bateman, 2008). Siegel (2010) developed a unique term "mindsight" to describe our human capacity to perceive the mind of the self and others. His conception of mindsight supports our development of "therapeutic posture." Mindsight can be applied to the therapist's ability to comprehend the complexity of the relationships between and among the domains of the IA, which are represented in the FG Roadmap.

The FG Roadmap is a graphic representation of the four domains of the client-system and their corresponding FG maps and timelines. Consequently, we propose that both mentalizing and mindsight are contemporary ways of viewing any system or domains of the IA from an integrative perspective. Basseches (2005), similar to Siegel's development of mindsight, emphasizes the adult cognitive capacity for dialectical thinking as "a form of organization of thought, various aspects of which can be identified in individual adults' approaches to conceptualizing a range of problems" (p. 47).

The influence of a comprehensive CMM is that the strategies and techniques the therapist then chooses to use are based on the IA with an emphasis on the attachment construct. The CMM allows practitioners to mindfully integrate the four domains while addressing the complexity and apparent contradictions that exist among the individuals within the various relational systems. The CMM represents a visual and conceptual schema that helps clinicians organize their clinical experience of a particular client-system into a complex model.

The CMM: Thinking Integratively

The CMM provides you a structured worksheet to organize your thoughts and identify additional ideas using the various FG tools. The primary goal is to help you strengthen your therapeutic relationship with the client-system and to begin to think integratively. For many practitioners, conceptualizing the client-system and the presenting problem is often an implicit or unconscious process. The CMM helps make that process more deliberate and conscious. The impact of a comprehensive CMM is that the strategies and techniques the therapist then chooses to use, are based on the IA with an emphasis on the attachment construct. For example, by applying the attachment construct within their clinical practice, clinicians then have an empirical foundation that guides practice using the four domains. The therapist can also use this information to develop the most effective TxP with the client-system.

Example of Using the Blank CMM

During the initial interview, the clinician enters the various FG tools. The client-system (couple) presented with wanting help with infidelity on behalf of the man and substance abuse on behalf of the female. The clinician is immediately addressing the crisis and simultaneously gathering information on the individuals using the Basic Genogram and then Couple Interaction Map to perhaps further understand the couple dynamics of behavior and emotions. As sessions progress, the clinician adds timelines and the couple's ecomap (Figure 2.2).

There are two challenges in couple and family training: learning to think systemically and learning to think dialectically. Couple and family therapy training strengthens one's ability to think systemically as well as explore the myriad of interpersonal and intrapersonal relationships in clinical practice. Students in Relational and Family programs must learn to think in terms of systems theory (Henry & Storm, 1984; Liddle & Saba, 1982). We have noted that this task is a challenge, especially difficult for clinicians who have developed specific attention to individual therapies, in particular when using targeting techniques. Their training tends to teach with a focus on individual behavior, pathology, and problem-solving with modest consideration of other relationship influences. We do not suggest that such techniques are not useful and helpful to many people, however, when techniques are applied without a full conceptual understanding of the person's relational network, likely the therapist will not be able to develop a comprehensive understanding of the client.

The second challenge is to think dialectically. We propose that using the FG tools (FGs, maps, and timelines) help the practitioner conceptualize the client-system dialectically. Dialectics is a method for exploring

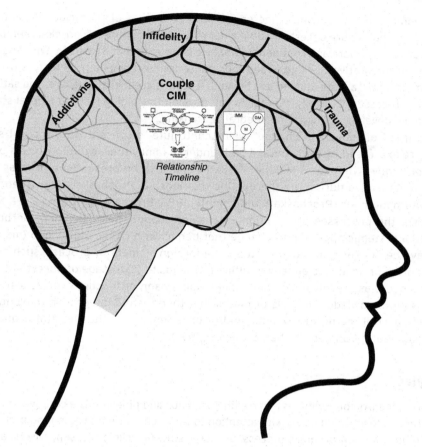

Figure 2.2 CMM Partially Filled.

and understanding various perspectives which are contradictory, for example, exploring internal emotional processes for individuals while simultaneously exploring family relationships. A dialectical framework helps a therapist to strengthen the attachment-focused bond between therapist and members of the client-system. In this workbook, you will have the opportunity to develop your own IMMs (individual domain) so that you can identify your strengths and challenges as a clinician.

Developing Clinical Competence: Stages of Professional Growth and Your Learning Styles

The IA provides a framework and secure foundation that will support both learning and professional development throughout your experiences as a clinician. The IA fosters change for individuals, couples, and families and allows therapists to expand the conceptual capacity to think systemically. Professional change and personal growth are interrelated for those who provide counseling, psychotherapy, family therapy, couple therapy, groups, and other forms of behavioral/cognitive/emotional approaches. Similarly, professional development has basic stages that contribute to each practitioner's development beginning with interest and curiosity that leads to motivation to engage with your career. The next few phases include learning about the profession including advanced education, specialized training experiences, supervision, and a sense of competence. Later, in the middle stages as well as the later stages, clinicians tend to develop more sophisticated and expanded approaches to clinical problems with clients. A unique aspect of practicing systematic and integrative professional work is a potential for a long-lasting career. In addition, there are a variety of paths to learning different treatment models and techniques throughout one's professional journey.

The "Conscious Competence Learning Model" may be one of the oldest approaches to change. The baseline change begins with "unconscious incompetence" in stage one – we are unaware and we go about being indifferent and unmindful. The second stage emphasizes awareness of "conscious incompetence: we are aware of not knowing, but we are uncertain about what to do. In stage three, "conscious competence" begins to emerge and we become aware and confident in what we know and what we can do. With ongoing awareness and the capacity for integrative thinking, stage four, "unconscious competence" fosters what Csikszentmihalyi (2008) termed "flow," a state of mind and being that fosters creativity, pleasure, and satisfaction during work and creative processes. Clinically, therapists can develop this highly focused mental state of flow that can also support and develop intuitions and integrative thinking.

There are a variety of "stages of change" which contribute to conceptualizing client-systems. Three considerations are expressed by Carl Whitaker, a founder in family therapy, who wrote a book called *The Roots of Psychotherapy* (Whitaker & Malone, 1953). In that text, he presented a process through which therapist and clients evolve during the therapeutic relationship. Prochaska's Transtheoretical Model is rooted in behavioral methods (Prochaska & DiClemente, 1983; Prochaska, DiClemente, & Norcross, 1992) that conceptualize the processes of intentional behavior change. Satir, Banmen, Gerber, and Gomori (1991) suggested a systemic approach to change that begins with (1) the status quo (maintaining things the way they have been). Then, in the next step, (2) a foreign element or process, such as engaging in a new training program or academic endeavor, ultimately leads to (3) a stage of uncertainty or chaos, during the change process as it evolves. As the student, supervisor, or teacher evolves, each one practices and develops (4) new knowledge or skills or habits that then fosters integrative thinking. When the old learnings become part of the new knowledge and/or experiences, (5) the new status quo becomes normalized once again (Satir, Banmen, Gerber, & Gomori, 1991).

Learning Styles

The art of exploring the IA's four domains along with FGs, maps and timelines is a creative, rewarding and clinically relevant process. Developing an FG with attention to the client-system's presenting problem is an important part of an initial interview or intake process. Similarly, students, clinicians, supervisors, and faculty bring unique abilities, interests, and backgrounds into academic and clinical experiences. Identifying learning styles can provide practitioners a better understanding of more comprehensive and integrative thinking patterns of the client-system. The most common styles include (1) visualizing, (2) auditory, (3) kinesthetic/physical, and (4) verbal reading/writing processing (Kolb, 2015; Kolb & Kolb, 2011).

The various ways of processing information about a client-system typically include moving from current experiences that lead to observations, which are affective, behavioral, or cognitive tendencies with any given client-system. These observations and reflections can be taken and then applied to the CMM. The learning process includes cycles of reflecting, thinking, listening, and attending to physical sensations that help experienced and inexperienced professionals incorporate a unique sense of self during the assessment process.

Identifying Your Learning Preferences

Clinicians who are **visual** will tend to prefer the CMM process. Charts, notes, and videos are key examples. Those who are visual also tend to lean towards concepts, words, and diagrams as well as the use of color and graphics.

Clinicians who are **auditory** and often musical tend to be listeners. They may prefer recording lectures, listening to audiobooks, and then summarizing using notes. These learners may also enjoy sharing and discussing new material, articles, and group activities such as clinical role-playing.

Clinicians who are more **physical** (**kinesthetic**) are more attuned to body language and nonverbal cues. Notes can be very important for these therapists – role-playing and gestalt exercises are often a preferred way of working. These techniques include taking on various physical postures as well.

Clinicians who are more **verbal** prefer words in any form. Writing, speaking, sharing, and asking questions are also likely to attend to what any given client or client-system might share or discuss. Structured questions are typically helpful to more verbal clinicians in contrast to those who are auditory and visual.

Exercise 2.3 Identifying Your Learning Style

Directions: For each of the learning style preferences above, place a number which correlates to the following styles: (1) visual, (2) auditory, (3) physical/kinesthetic, and (4) verbal. Then rank your results in order with the most like numbers, which would tend to be your most preferred learning style.

_____Watching videos	_____Presenting to others
_____Direct instruction	_____Taking online questionnaires
_____Reading articles	_____Role-playing
_____Writing class notes	_____Experiential exercises
_____Listening to lecture/presentations	_____Small group discussion
_____Group exercises	_____Other

My preferred learning styles: List your three favorite ways to learn, from the above list, on the lines below.

1 _____

2 _____

3 _____

Question:

What type of learning style comes up most often on this list? Do you agree or disagree with the results? Were you surprised?

_____

_____

_____

How to Develop the CMM

The CMM is formatted using an adaptation of "the triune brain," which was popularized by Paul MacLean's work, who was a behavioral and brain scientist in the early days of neuroscience.[1] In the upper portion around the top of the CMM are the FGs. A variety of FGs can be included. The Mapping and Timeline tools are in the middle part of the CMM. Identifying the various attachment patterns, styles, scripts/narratives, and social bonds is revealed through the initial interviews. Each of the domains reveal aspects of the individual, couples, and/or family relational dynamics within their cultural/ecological milieu based on their historical and geographic locations. Using the CMM as another aspect of developing a case formulation reveals a new visual perspective.

The CMM template can be used to organize the clinician's perspective and approach to identifying key aspects of the unique client-system. Each FG, map, or timeline fits in one of the empty spaces provided. These spaces are not random. The FGs around the top of the brain are located in the thinking or cognitive part of the brain. The maps and timelines can also be drawn as part of clinical notes for those who want to use their individualized process. The timelines are another part of the mapping tools that can be used to explore the early childhood attachment experiences from birth to age 3 and then from ages 4 to 10. The middle years of adolescence through ages 10–16 are also important to consider through the attachment lens.

Applying the FG tools, keeping in mind the IA meta-framework, becomes an asset to clinicians, as students or clinicians begin their assessment of the particular client-system. The focus can be both broad and specific, depending on the client-system's presentation in the initial interview. Covey's (1989/2004) "Begin with the end in mind" has been applied in both personal and professional areas. Consequently, paying immediate attention to the uniqueness and needs of the client-system will guide the therapist from the initial interview or even the initial contact. Having this knowledge, you will begin to focus on the therapist's TxP with the client-system. The therapeutic alliance being developed at the initial contact begins to develop goals and tasks that address the client-system's needs, hopes, and fears. Development of the various FG maps, as they emerge from the initial and ongoing interviews using the CF provides a comprehensive clinical assessment. This IA using the CMM process now becomes a constructive habit with a clear clinical focus.

Developing a CMM: Case Example of James and Celia

The case presented is of a cohabiting couple, struggling with communication issues, breakdowns in trust, and complex grief, resulting from a miscarriage. James is aged 32 and Celia 28. They have a history of three years of dating and one year of cohabitation. Both are Christians. The reason to seek therapy is that James believes Celia might be having an affair after her emotional distance from him and going out excessively with friends and texting a male coworker. Celia is resentful of James due to his seeming lack of extended compassion after her miscarriage nine months ago. Her anger has caused her to withdraw from him, physically and emotionally. Both clients are feeling isolated and are suspicious of one another. They defend themselves but feel abandoned by the other, leading to loneliness, which results in inadequate communication, hidden feelings, and then pursuing one another in maladaptive ways.

Exercise 2.4 Creating the CMM

Directions: Using the CMM diagram (Figure 2.1) and the case example of James and Celia, create a CMM that incorporates the FG tools, maps, and timelines.

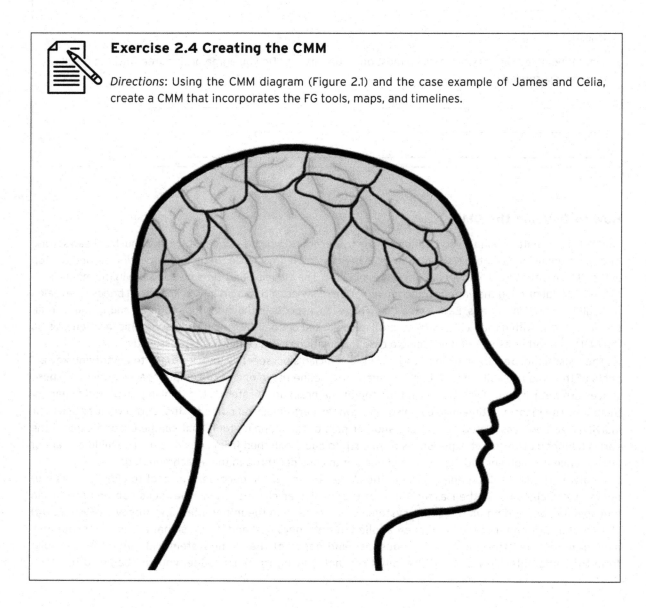

Summary

We introduced the CMM early in this workbook to illustrate the mental processes that students and clinicians develop as they expand their ability to think integratively. The process of developing a unique CMM strengthens and deepens the clinician's knowledge and understanding of each client-system, thus enabling the formation of an attachment-focused therapeutic alliance and a thorough and well-integrated assessment and treatment plan. In contrast to the CMM, the CF provides a more traditional and structured approach to identifying the causes and conditions that influence a client-system's emotional, relational, and behavioral problems and concerns.

The CMM graphically illustrates the systemic interconnections of the four domains (individual, couple, intergenerational family system, and the contextual) while addressing the complexity and apparent contradictions that exist among the individuals within the various relational systems. Clinicians experience, learn, and develop a far more emotionally attuned understanding of each of their unique client-systems using the CMM.

Note

1 See Pearce (2008).

References

Basseches, M. (2005). The development of dialectical thinking as an approach to integration. *Integral Review, 1*(1), 47–63.

Covey, S. (1989/2004). *The 7 habits of highly effective people.* New York, NY: Free Press.

Csikszentmihalyi, M. (2008). *Flow: The psychology of optimal experience.* New York, NY: Harper Perennial Modern Classics.

Fonagy, P., & Bateman, A. (2008). The development of borderline personality disorder – A mentalizing model. *Journal of Personality Disorders, 22*(1), 4–21.

Harlow, H. F. (1958). The nature of love. *American Psychologist, 13*(12), 673–685. doi:10.1037/h0047884

Harlow, H. F. (1962). Development of affection in primates. In E. L. Bliss (Ed.), *Roots of behavior* (pp. 157–166). New York, NY: Harper.

Henry, P. W., & Storm, C. L. (1984). The training metamorphosis: Teaching systemic thinking in family therapy programs. *Journal of Strategic and Systemic Therapies, 3*(2), 41–49.

Klaus, M. H., & Kennell, J. H. (1976). *Maternal-infant bonding: The impact of early separation or loss on family development* (257 p). St Louis, MO: C.V. Mosby.

Kolb, D. A. (2015). *Experiential learning: Experience as the source of learning and development* (2nd ed.). Upper Saddle River, NJ: Pearson Education.

Kolb, A. Y., & Kolb, D. A. (2011). *Kolb learning style inventory 4.0.* Boston, MA: Hay Group.

Liddle, H. A., & Saba, G. W. (1982). Teaching family therapy at the introductory level: A conceptual model emphasizing a pattern which connects training and therapy. *Journal of Marital and Family Therapy, 8*(1), 63–72.

Montague, A. (1978). *Psychology.* New York, NY: Harper & Row.

Pearce, J. (2008, January 10). Paul MacLean, 94, neuroscientist who devised 'Triune Brain' theory, dies. *The New York Times.* Retrieved June 2, 2018. https://www.nytimes.com/2008/01/10/science/10maclean.html

Prochaska, J. O., & DiClemente, C. C. (1986). Toward a comprehensive model of change. In W. R. Miller and N. Heather (Eds.), *Treating addictive behaviors* (pp. 3–27). Boston, MA: Springer.

Prochaska, J. O., DiClemente, C. C., & Norcross, J. C. (1992). In search of how people change: Applications to addictive behaviors. *American Psychologist, 47*(9), 1102–1114.

Riegel, K. F. (1976). The dialectics of human development. *American Psychologist, 31*(10), 689.

Satir, V., Banmen, J., Gerber, J., & Gomori, M. (1991, January 6). *The Satir model: Family therapy and beyond.* Palo Alto, CA: Science & Behavior Books (Reprinted: October 31, 2006).

Siegel, D. J. (2010). *Mindsight: The new science of personal transformation.* New York, NY: Bantam.

Spitz, R. A. (1946). Hospitalism: A follow-up report on investigation described in volume I, 1945. *The Psychoanalytic Study of the Child, 2,* 113–117.

Spitz, R. A. (1965). *The first year of life. A psychoanalytic study of normal and deviant development of object relations.* New York, NY: International Universities Press, Inc.

Wallin, D. J. (2007). *Attachment in psychotherapy.* New York, NY: Guilford Press.

Whitaker, C., & Malone, T. P. (1953). *Roots of psychotherapy.* New York, NY: Blakiston/Routledge.

Winnicott, D. W. (1965). Ego distortion in terms of true and false self. In D. W. Winnicott (Ed.), *The maturational process and the facilitating environment: Studies in the theory of emotional development* (pp. 140–152). New York, NY: International UP Inc.

Winnicott, D. W. (1973). *The child, the family, and the outside world.* Middlesex: Penguin Books.

Part II

Foundations of Therapeutic Posture

3 Therapeutic Posture
Developing the Collaborative Therapeutic Alliance

Overview

Therapeutic posture (TxP) is a unique contribution to the therapeutic alliance, which is the therapist's adaptation to a client's internal working models of attachment. This chapter outlines and describes the process of forming TxP, with a discussion on the four styles of relating to clients and when to use them. Research shows the significant role of the bond, within the therapeutic alliance, that facilitates the successful collaboration about tasks and goals, and potentiates the impact of interventions. Applying attachment theory to a description of TxP within a systemic framework, empowers the therapist to use various therapeutic styles to establish an attuned bond with clients, which helps maximize therapeutic impact. TxP is a differentiated approach to individuals, couples, and families, whereby the therapist attunes to each individual's attachment style within a systemic framework for enhanced treatment outcomes.

The evolution of TxP draws from existing models for developing safe and secure therapeutic alliances. In addition, practitioners can use stages of treatment to guide the clinical formulation and phases of development for movement from insecure to secure attachment bonds within the therapeutic alliance. Attachment theory provides the foundation for the application of TxP and is not only a major part of the theoretical foundation of *Focused Genograms: Intergenerational Assessment of Individuals, Couples, and Families*, 2nd edition (FG2) (2017) but also a key integrational concept in the Intersystem Approach (IA). A number of theoreticians and researchers noted similarities between systems thinking and attachment theory. For example, Kozlowska and Hanney (2002) asserted that dyadic, triadic, and extended family relationships represent different structures within the system. Other writers expressed an interest in combining the two theories because of their compatibility and the fact that they would mutually enhance each other (Akister, 1998; Byng-Hall, 1995; Dallos, 2006; Erdman & Caffery, 2003; Johnson, 2004; Strahan, 1991).

TxP was introduced in the first edition of *Focused Genograms* (DeMaria, Weeks, & Hof, 1999) and comprehensively expanded in FG2 (2017). The primary goal of TxP is to deliver interventions in a way that is sensitive to the special needs of the clients (e.g., attachment histories, gender, age, socioeconomic status, culture/race/ethnicity, sexual orientation, disability, personal history, larger systems issues of the client) and utilize the therapist's unique personhood and attachment strengths in attuning to the client. The Internal Models Map (IMM) and Family Connections Map (FCM) specifically provide the students and practitioners guidance on how to develop varying therapeutic styles based on the assessment of a client's childhood attachment styles.

Objectives

1. Identify the four TxP styles and use the styles to begin the formation of a relational bond attuned to specific childhood attachment patterns (Exercise 3.1).
2. Recognize the four IA domains and describe the four attachment-based terms (Exercise 3.2).
3. Identify childhood attachment patterns, adult attachment styles, family attachment scripts, and attachment-focused social bonds, and provide examples for the four domains of the IA (Exercise 3.3).
4. Enter the key words or phrases you might use when enacting each of the therapeutic styles in a client interaction (Exercise 3.4).
5. Describe how the four phases of the TxP helps to establish a therapeutic bond with the client-system (Exercise 3.5a–d).

Developing TxP: Foundations for Establishing a Therapeutic Bond

We have defined and clarified the definition of the therapeutic bond by using the term TxP, for which we have provided specific directions and instructions. We also include tools to help guide the therapist in conducting an FG through all the domains. The current literature available for the common factors recognizes the importance of the therapeutic alliance, but has not moved to the next step of TxP discussed in the FG (DeMaria, Weeks, & Twist, 2017). Common factors are those aspects of treatment which transcend any particular therapeutic model and are believed to have curative influences in the outcome of therapy (Davis, Lebow, & Sprenkle, 2012; Sprenkle & Blow, 2004). Meta-analytic and quantitative studies of outcome literature have shown that techniques account for anything between 5% and 15% of change, while the therapeutic alliance accounts for about 30% of the change (Lambert & Barley, 2001; Wampold, 2001). Moreover, the therapist relationship with the client (Luborsky et al., 1999) is the most important condition for the client's outcomes in individual therapy (Safran & Muran, 2000).

Fife, Whiting, Bradford, and Davis (2014) developed a pyramid model of treatment which first involves the therapist's way of being toward the client, followed by the therapeutic alliance, and later covers skills and techniques. Fife et al. (2014) also reviewed a number of studies showing that common factors (particularly alliance) and technique are essential elements of therapy. If the alliance is not strong, the technique is likely to fail, and if the client does not believe the techniques are relevant or pertinent to their problem, the alliance is weakened. While this model is an advance in the conceptualization of treatment, no effort was made to further refine the concept of the therapeutic alliance (see Weeks & Fife, 2014). Interestingly, two clinical papers on attachment theory and culture showed that an understanding of attachment styles within different cultures should be taken into account when building the therapeutic alliance (Keitaibl, 2012; Rothbaum, Rosen, Ujiie, & Uchida, 2002).

Establishing the Collaborative Client-Therapist Alliance

The FG2 outlined a newly detailed conceptualization defining the bond within the therapeutic alliance as TxP. Adult attachment styles are typically evident in the first few interviews with a client-system and help form an appropriate TxP from the initial contact. Although this approach has not been researched, there are others who have conducted research on a similar concept of tailoring the therapeutic alliance (Mallinckrodt, 2010; Obegi, 2008). In the FGW, we describe both TxP and parenting to have similar goals to nurture, support, direct, and guide client-systems. There are many clinical approaches to therapeutic techniques. There are four TxP styles available that can be used as part of the therapeutic alliance. The Working Alliance Inventory (WAI) (Horvath & Greenberg, 1989) reflects the clients' perspective about the therapist–client interactions. Parenting styles provide a structure that can be adapted to meet underlying childhood attachment needs. The context for TxP rests on a collaborative helping relationship.

Introducing TxP: Comparison of WAI, Parenting Styles, and TxP Styles

TxP provides four styles that a clinician can use in therapy to begin with during the first few meetings. The choice of TxP styles will depend on the client's self-presentation as more or less secure, more or less dismissive, more or less preoccupied, or more or less disorganized. The first column depicts the WAI, a commonly used measure for identifying four types of statements that clients might make about their therapy. The second column depicts parenting styles that have four types of parenting responses. The third column addresses attachment-focused responses based on the therapeutic styles that attune to the client's self-presentation during the initial interviews. The clinician's role is to provide a welcoming and responsive professional relationship.

Table 3.1 Identifying the Ways of Being from Three Perspectives: WAI, Parenting Styles, and TxP

Working Alliance Inventory *Client statements*	Parenting Styles *Parental Types*	Therapeutic Posture Styles *Used by Therapist*
Positive statements "Genuine concern"	**Nurturing/Permissive** "I will help"	**Reassurance** "Ability to help"
Negative statements "Time together inefficient"	**Uninvolved/Neglectful** "Other things to do"	**Validation** "Accepting the client's perspective"

Working Alliance Inventory *Client statements*	Parenting Styles *Parental Types*	Therapeutic Posture Styles *Used by Therapist*
Challenging "Disagreement on needs"	**Authoritarian** "My way is best"	**Challenging** "Encourage direct request(s)"
Advice giving "Agreement on issues"	**Authoritative** "Let's set up a way to share our views"	**Guidance** "Trust in suggestions/options"

Exercise 3.1 Therapeutic Styles and Parenting Styles

Directions: Using Table 3.1 draw a line to match up each parenting style with the appropriate therapeutic style.

Therapeutic Posture	Parenting Styles
Challenging	Nurturing/Permissive
Guidance	Uninvolved/Neglectful
Reassurance	Authoritarian
Validation	Authoritative

Introducing the Domains and the Attachment Exercises

The IA, introduced in FG2, is a meta-theory which describes the relationship between four domains: individual, couple, family, and contextual. For each of these domains, there is an attachment term: pattern, style, script, and social bond, respectively. We include the table below to help readers learn to differentiate the terms of each domain.

Childhood and adult attachment bonds are core to understanding the application of attachment within all four domains. Differentiating these attachment bonds guides TxP as you respond to the attachment patterns and styles. Within the Family Domain, the overall Attachment term is a Family Attachment Script (drawn from Byng-Hall (1995), Olson (2011) and Vetere and Dallos (2008)). Use Adult Attachment Styles for reference specifically to parents and Childhood Attachment Patterns for children.

Table 3.2 provides an overview of how attachment terms are linked to each IA domain and can be applied to the next exercise.

Table 3.2 The Four Domains and Attachment Terms

The Intersystem Approach: Domains	Individual	Couple	Family	Cultural/ Contextual
Attachment term for each domain	Childhood attachment patterns	Adult attachment styles	Family attachment scripts	Community Social bonds

Exercise 3.2 The IA Domains and Attachment Terms

Directions: In the space below, match by drawing a line from the attachment patterns and styles on the left to the childhood and adult domains on the right.

Preoccupied Attachment Style	Child: Individual Domain
Anxious-Avoidant Attachment Pattern	Adult: Couple Domain
Dismissive Attachment Style	Child: Individual Domain
Disoriented Attachment Style	Child: Individual Domain
Disorganized Attachment Pattern	Adult: Couple Domain
Anxious-Ambivalent Attachment Pattern	Adult: Couple Domain
Dismissive Attachment Script	Family Script: Family Domain

(Continued)

Bonus: Describe a social bond from the contextual domain. You can use your own life or a client's story to consider the quality of social bonds in your community and multicultural environment.

_____

_____

_____

_____

The IA, Differentiated Attachment Terms, and FG Mapping Tools

Table 3.3 identifies the terms for differential FG mapping tools for each domain. The IMM depicts childhood attachment patterns. The CIM depicts the adult interaction styles. The FCM uses terms for children and for parental figures within the FCM. The Social Bonds Ecomap (SBE) describes the social bonds in the client-system with its community.

Table 3.3 Attachment and the Focused Genogram Tools

Focused Genogram tools	Internal Models Map	Couple Interaction Map	Family Connections Map	Social Bonds Ecomap
Mapping Attachment in each Domain	Childhood attachment patterns	Adult attachment styles	Family attachment scripts _____ Adult for parents, childhood fo children	Social bonds

Exercise 3.3 Identifying Attachment Patterns, Styles, Scripts, and Social Bonds

Directions: Using the Attachment Terms given in Table 3.3, circle in the space below, the correct attachment terminology to describe the connections in your life in each of the domains. You could also use a client's life for this activity.

Examples are as follows:

Childhood Attachment Patterns

Terms: Secure, Anxious-Ambivalent Pattern, Anxious-Avoidant Pattern, Disorganized Pattern

For example: I was ambivalent with my mother and father as a child. I never wanted to leave their side and was always worried that they would never come back when they went to work.

Adult Attachment Styles

Terms: Secure, Preoccupied, Dismissive, Disorganized

For example: I feel that I now have a preoccupied attachment style because I am constantly worried about what others think of me, if I am doing enough, and whether people I love will leave me.

Family Attachment Scripts

Terms: Secure, Preoccupied, Dismissive, Disorganized

Terms: Referring to the family, use Family Attachment Scripts. Referring specifically to the children, use Childhood Attachment Patterns; for the adults, use Adult Attachment Styles.

(Continued)

For example: My family attachment script is Dismissive (disengaged-structured). In my family, my siblings and I all had ambivalent attachment patterns because we were trying to impress our parents and prove ourselves. We never believed we were good enough. My parents seemed to have dismissive attachment styles because they did not show affection to each other or to my siblings and me.

SBE

Terms: Secure, Preoccupied, Dismissive, Disorganized

Describe the social bonds within your community.

For example: I feel a secure attachment to my church because my faith in God is unwavering and I feel that my church community is there for me and my family when I need them.

Describe the connections in your life:

- Individual

  _____

- Couple/Family

  _____

- Intergenerational

  _____

- Contextual

  _____

The Therapeutic Bond: Focus on Empathic Attunement

TxP ultimately aims to work with any given client's internal working models of attachment. However, upon initially meeting a client, adult attachment styles start to become more evident in the first two clinical interviews. In order to identify childhood attachment patterns, listen closely as the client describes their current and/or historical family relationships. The therapist's observations of behavioral and emotional patterns with these key figures determines an initial hypothesis for how to enact the TxP.

Table 3.4 presents the therapeutic styles that are key to establishing TxP. Across the top of the table are the four bonding styles within TxP and the strategies associated with each. The left-hand vertical side shows attachment patterns. Inside the table, we have matched the type of strategy that is more likely to work best for a client with each attachment pattern.

Table 3.4 Therapeutic Styles

Therapeutic Posture		Therapeutic Styles within Therapeutic Posture			
		Validation	**Guidance**	**Reassuring**	**Challenging**
Childhood attachment patterns – foundations for TxP	**Secure**	X	X	X	X
	Ambivalent		X	X	
	Avoidant	X			X
	Disorganized	X	X	X	X

Examples are as follows:
Describe Validation as a Clinical Skill
For example: I understand how you feel.
Describe Guidance as a Clinical Skill
For example: Have you thought of saying it to your partner this way?

Describe Reassuring as a Clinical Skill
For example: You will feel better soon.
Describe Challenging as a Clinical Skill
For example: How do you think you would feel hearing what you just said to your partner?

 Exercise 3.4 Responding to Childhood Attachment Patterns

Directions: Using Tables 3.3 and 3.4 and the above examples, enter the key words or phrases you might use when enacting each of the therapeutic styles in a client interaction.

- Validation

  _____

- Guidance

  _____

- Reassuring

  _____

- Challenging

  _____

The Progression of TxP over Time

FG2 primarily emphasized assessment by using the IA and the FG Tools. In the FGW, we propose that TxP promotes the development of a secure attachment between clinician and client-system in a stepwise process that begins with specific attuning to the client's childhood attachment pattern from the outset of treatment. From our perspective, corrective emotional experiences are titrated in phases from the beginning to the end of treatment dependent on a client-system's unique combinations of attachment patterns within the Internal Working Models (IWMs) of attachment. In this approach, we propose that TxP is a catalyst for change by beginning with the client's presenting adult attachment style. Consequently, the practitioner must be intentionally reformulating TxP throughout the phases of treatment so that the clinical setting and experience provides a comfortable and optimally responsive therapeutic milieu. The use of FGs and the attachment theory construct will help the therapist identify childhood, adult, and intergenerational attachment needs.

As the client-system changes, so must the TxP to ensure that the clinician is consistently meeting the emotional needs of the client-system toward the goals established at the outset of treatment. Freeman's (1992) Multigenerational Family Therapy model describes three phases for the therapeutic alliance that also mirror the goals of treatment: (1) the beginning phase is problem-solving and developing positive connections with the therapist; (2) the middle phase is identifying additional relational problems that undermine cognitive, emotional, and behavioral change; and (3) the ending phase is focused on empowerment for the client as well as strategies for maintaining a secure base for the individual couple and/or family system.

Developing TxP and Facilitating Secure Connections in Treatment

Using Freeman's (1992) model of phases of treatment, we redefined the phases of TxP that take place during treatment as follows:

- Phase 1: Establishing a collaborative therapeutic alliance
- Phase 2: Resolution of presenting problem and reduction of relationship conflict
- Phase 3: Promoting behavior change, vulnerability, and empathy; identifying individual, relationship, intergenerational, and contextual and challenges[1]
- Phase 4: Consolidating and strengthening relational changes, reevaluation goals, and updating treatment tasks and strategies; collaborative decision-making between therapist and client-system.

Phase 1: Establishing a Collaborative Therapeutic Alliance

Each phase of treatment has complex issues based on the client-system's constellation of attachment styles. In the first phase of treatment, the clinician must engage emotionally, cognitively, and behaviorally with the client's IWMs of attachment in order to join, engage, and bond with the client, establishing an environment of safety, respect, compassion, and attunement. Attunement is a term that describes the clinician's development of a focused and harmonious, even sympathetic, relationship with each person in the treatment system. Attunement is both nonverbal and verbal. It fosters the clinician's ability to empathize with the client's current life situation as well as the historical family patterns. Both past and present are crucial for the clinician to understand in order to effectively attune to the client's relational needs based on the IMM, CIM, and FCM developed during this phase of treatment. However, even before the assessment is complete, TxP has been implemented. The therapist attends to the attachment styles of the client-system with a focused TxP as quickly as possible, using the information gathered from all interactions with the client-system from the very beginning when he/she/they contact the therapist and when therapy begins in the first session.

As we have described previously, Phase 1 of the treatment begins with the assessment of the IWMs within the first two sessions that will help guide the practitioner toward developing the IMM and, thus, a more secure therapeutic bond.[2] Clues to the individual attachment styles often reveal themselves in the most basic interactions, including arranging the first appointment or how the first interview transpires. When clients enter treatment in crisis, or with recent trauma, their IWMs are revealed most readily because stress intensifies or amplifies their attachment style. Those who have secure IWMs of attachment are typically more resilient. However, a person with a secure attachment style could present as preoccupied or may be in shock and seem avoidant. Infidelity is one of those crises that challenge even the most secure individuals.

Under continual stresses over a longer period of time, clients can even appear to be disoriented. Consequently, a flexible TxP responsive to the client's is indicated in many initial interviews. The practitioner may respond in various ways such as using guidance, validation, reassurance, or even challenging. The choice of challenging styles depends primarily on the immediacy of the crisis and the danger involved. Use of the reassurance and validation styles also depends on the presenting problem, as well as the client's attachment and relationship experiences, as assessed by the IMM.

As the clinician begins to establish an attuned TxP, the client's sense of safety is likely to improve. Establishing TxP is a potent way of creating a strong therapeutic alliance. The earlier the TxP is established, the more likely it is to yield therapeutic change. If a positive bond does not occur early on in treatment (by the sixth to eighth session) change is not likely to occur within that particular therapeutic relationship (Lebow, 2006).

Exercise 3.5a Phase I: Establishing a Collaborative Therapeutic Alliance

Directions: Describe in the space below how your understanding of Phase I will help you begin to develop TxP with a client.

_____

_____

_____

_____

Mid-Phase: Resolving the Problem and Promoting Change

The mid-phase of treatment is twofold. Phase 2 involves a focus on resolution of the presenting problem and reducing relationship conflicts. Phase 3 is (1) promoting behavior change, vulnerability, and empathy as well as (2) identifying individual, relationship, intergenerational, and contextual challenges. These distinctions are important to clarify.

It is commonly understood among clinicians that the presenting problem is not always the only problem in the system, and sometimes the problem cannot be solved until other relational dynamics are dealt with (i.e. in a couple with a sexual complaint). Yet in order for the client-system to feel heard and taken seriously, the therapist must attend to the presenting problem before moving on to addressing the underlying dynamics within the relationship. Therefore, the treatment focus in Phase 2 is on the presenting problem and, typically, behavioral change, in addition to the shifting of dynamics, development of empathy, and identification of challenges. In Phase 3 of the treatment, various techniques can be used to strengthen the client-system's awareness, knowledge, and insight into their own individual, interpersonal, and intergenerational patterns of relationships based on their attachment styles.

Typically, the TxP shifts from beginning to middle phase toward a more consistent, secure base for personal and relational exploration and change. The client's confidence in the therapist usually increases as the client-system accomplishes goals and tasks identified at the outset of treatment. In this mid-phase of treatment, the therapist can begin to flexibly move toward a secure TxP by employing the therapeutic styles mentioned above: validation, guidance, reassurance, and challenging. Sometimes, clients will challenge the therapist's availability to test the security of the attachment bond. The therapist should remember that this expression of attachment insecurity is clinically significant and act according to the appropriate therapeutic styles that correspond to the activating or deactivating behavior and the client's IMM. Often at this stage in treatment, clients will begin to feel safe and reveal long-held secrets, which can be both quite surprising and a relief for the client with either avoidant or ambivalent internal models.

Exercise 3.5b Phase 2: Resolution of Presenting Problem and Reduction of Relationship Conflict

Directions: What impact are you aware of for yourself as the clinician and for the client-system when you are able to reduce the difficulties of the "presenting problem"?

_____

_____

_____

_____

What impact are you aware of for yourself as the clinician and for the client-system when you are able to guide the client-system to resolve a relationship conflict?

_____

_____

_____

_____

Exercise 3.5c Phase 3: Promoting Behavior Change, Vulnerability, and Empathy; Identifying Individual, Relationship, Intergenerational, and Contextual and Cultural Challenges

Second-order change goes beyond the immediate problem for the client-system and focuses on using common factors that are (1) keys to successful treatment and (2) include the therapeutic alliance, with these three goals for the client: hope, identify client needs and goals, and treatment models and/or techniques.

An example:

For me, I sometimes find it difficult to build a hopeful therapeutic alliance when I myself have not experienced the presenting problem. I feel unfamiliar and confused and I think my clients can sense

(Continued)

that. However, I can lean on my technique of reflective listening and emotion-focused therapy to listen for the client's experience of the problem and find a core emotion that I can empathize with. This is a good start.

Directions: Describe your perspective about forming an attuned TxP as well as selecting various treatment models to meet the needs of specific client-systems.

_____

_____

_____

_____

_____

Late Phase: Consolidating and Strengthening Therapeutic Change

In the late phase, Phase 4, empowerment and strategies for continued personal growth is a priority as well as consolidating and strengthening relational changes, reevaluating goals, and updating treatment tasks and strategies. The clinician moves from a reparental role into one of a "mentor" who provides encouragement, connection, and empowerment. The late phase goal aims to support the client into the world as a securely attached person based on the treatment experience.

In this phase, there are four specific processes to achieve successful treatment:

- Consolidating and strengthening relational changes
- Reevaluating goals
- Updating treatment tasks and strategies
- Collaborative decision-making between therapist and client-system

Carl Whitaker's Contribution to an Evolutionary Perspective of TxP

Another way to think about the evolution of TxP over the course of treatment is through our adaptation of Whitaker and Malone's model of the therapist-client relationship, shown in Table 3.5. Whitaker and Malone (1953)[3] were pioneers who understood the importance of a developmental perspective for the therapist-client relationship, which they termed a "symbolic representation" with a focus on encouraging family members to become more emotionally and physically open and aware. Their approach was both experiential and existential. TxP supports clients in their efforts to become more vulnerable, empathetic, and compassionate with themselves and their family members.

As a family therapist, Whitaker articulated the role of the therapeutic alliance (Whitaker & Malone, 1953). The influence of psychoanalysis is illustrated in his "vector" model, which the senior author has adapted to include attachment theory using both adult attachment styles and childhood attachment experiences. Table 3.5 depicts the evolution of the therapist-client relationship, which is now grounded in attachment theory and the larger meta-theoretical model of the IA.

As Table 3.5 illustrates, the therapist becomes a surrogate attachment figure who adopts a TxP that is compatible with the client's current attachment needs.

The goal is to provide the client with an attachment-based experience with the clinician that leads to a secure therapeutic attachment bond. In order to achieve this goal, the therapist must be prepared to move flexibly between the therapeutic styles discussed in this chapter. Further, this table shows the evolution of TxP. Column 1 describes the stepwise progress of TxP. Columns 2-5 illustrate Whitaker and Malone's model. Column 6 describes the client's experience, moving from a sense of disempowerment and insecurity to more secure attachment based on TxP and focus on the client's emotional needs.

Table 3.5 Models of Therapeutic Posture in Phases of Treatment

Evolution of the Therapeutic Posture	Therapist			Client			Evolution of the Client
	Sees Himself/ Herself As	Sees Client As		Sees Therapist As	Sees Himself/ Herself As		
Therapist attunes to client's childhood attachment patterns	A therapist	Adult		A doctor	Adult		Disempowered
Therapist assumes a corrective therapeutic posture	"Good enough parental figure"	Child		Parental figure	Adolescent		Regression
Therapeutic posture fosters building of trust between client and therapist	"Good enough parent"	Child-self		Basic parent	Child-self		
	Parent	Adolescent		Parent	Adolescent		Progression
Secure attachment is formed between client and therapist	Therapist	Adult		Adult	Adult		Empowered

Summary

Therapists themselves have secure, insecure, and/or disorganized attachment styles of their own. In this chapter, we propose that a clinician's use of TxP, widely known as a "bond," provides a perspective that supports the therapist's innate ability to become a reparental figure for the client. By virtue of attending to the client's attachment style, the therapist can put his/her own needs aside because the process of forming a good enough reparental relationship with the client will help the therapist be his or her own best self. We will address the therapist's own attachment and history in Chapter 4.

As the therapist responds to the client's unique IMM, the client begins to experience the therapist as a prospective secure parental figure. Given the client's likely experience of attachment anxiety within the therapeutic relationship (regardless of whether they are otherwise securely attached in the outside world), it is critical for the therapist to have a "felt" sense of the client's underlying emotional needs that were unmet and thus led to the formation of insecure attachment. As the therapeutic relationship between therapist and client evolves, the therapist takes on a "good enough" parent role and slowly begins to provide appropriate and directed corrective emotional experiences based on the client's attachment style.

TxP is a collaborative process during which clients move emotionally through feelings of being disempowered toward empowerment. Mediating stages include regression in the service of emotional repair/corrective emotional experiences moving toward progression in the form of new thoughts, behaviors, and feelings. This results in a sense of empowerment and an ability to maintain an internalized sense of secure attachment from an "adult" position in contrast to the sense of disempowerment that comes from insecure attachment styles rooted in childhood experiences. Attuning to the insecure attachment style and then using the corrective TxP is necessary for the therapist to facilitate this change in the client.

Notes

1 Phases 2 and 3 can be circular depending on the focus of treatment and complexity of presenting problems.
2 Often, the client's IWMs are identifiable from the first contact.
3 *The Roots of Psychotherapy*, 1953. Whitaker's development of symbolic representation for the evolution of the therapeutic relationship was an important contribution to the development of the concept of an attachment-focused TxP.

References

Akister, J. (1998). Attachment theory and systemic practice: Research update. *Journal of Family Therapy, 20*(4), 353–366.
Byng-Hall, J. (1995). Creating a secure family base: Some implications of attachment theory for family therapy. *Family Process, 34*, 45–58.
Dallos, R. (2006). *Attachment narrative therapy*. Maidenhead: McGraw-Hill Education.

Davis, S. D., Lebow, J. L., & Sprenkle, D. H. (2012). Common factors of change in couple therapy. *Behavior Therapy, 43*(1), 36–48.

DeMaria, R., Weeks, G. R., & Hof, L. (1999). *Intergenerational assessment of individuals, couples, and families: Focused genograms*. Philadelphia, PA: Brunner/Mazel.

DeMaria, R., Weeks, G. R., & Twist, M. L. (2017). *Focused genograms: Intergenerational assessment of individuals, couples, and families*. New York, NY: Routledge.

Erdman, P., & Caffery, T. (2003). *Attachment and family systems*. New York and Hove: Brunner-Routledge.

Fife, S. T., Whiting, J. B., Bradford, K., & Davis, S. (2014). The therapeutic pyramid: A common factors synthesis of techniques, alliance, and way of being. *Journal of Marital and Family Therapy, 40*(1), 20–33.

Freeman, D. S. (1992). *Multigenerational family therapy*. New York, NY: Haworth Press (Original work published 1979).

Horvath, A. O., & Greenberg, L. S. (1989). Development and validation of the working alliance inventory. *Journal of Counseling Psychology, 36*(2), 223–233.

Johnson, S. (2004). *The practice of emotionally focused couple therapy: Creating connection. Basic Principles into Practice Series*. New York, NY: Brunner/Mazel.

Kietaibl, C. M. (2012). A review of attachment and its relationship to the working alliance. *Canadian Journal of Counselling and Psychotherapy/Revue canadienne de counseling et de psychothérapie, 46*(2), 122–140.

Kozlowska, K., & Hanney, L. (2002). The network perspective: An integration of attachment and family systems theories. *Family Process, 41*(3), 285–312.

Lambert, M. J., & Barley, D. E. (2001). Research summary on the therapeutic relationship and psychotherapy outcome. *Psychotherapy: Theory, Research, Practice, Training, 38*(4), 357–361.

Lebow, J. (2006). *Research for the psychotherapist: From science to practice*. New York, NY: Routledge.

Luborsky, L., Diguer, L., Seligman, D. A., Rosenthal, R., Krause, E. D., Johnson, S., … & Schweizer, E. (1999). The researcher's own therapy allegiances: A "wild card" in comparisons of treatment efficacy. *Clinical Psychology: Science and Practice, 6*(1), 95–106.

Mallinckrodt, B. (2010). The psychotherapy relationship as attachment: Evidence and implications. *Journal of Social and Personal Relationships, 27*(2), 262–270.

Obegi, J. H. (2008). The development of the client-therapist bond through the lens of attachment theory. *Psychotherapy: Theory, Research, Practice, Training, 45*(4), 431–446.

Olson, D. (2011). FACES IV and the circumplex model: Validation study. *Journal of Marital and Family Therapy, 37*(1), 64–80.

Rothbaum, F., Rosen, K., Ujiie, T., & Uchida, N. (2002). Family systems theory, attachment theory, and culture. *Family Process, 41*(3), 328–350.

Safran, J. D., & Muran, J. C. (2000). Resolving therapeutic alliance ruptures: Diversity and integration. *Journal of Clinical Psychology, 56*(2), 233–243.

Sprenkle, D. H., & Blow, A. J. (2004). Common factors and our sacred models. *Journal of Marital and Family Therapy, 30*(2), 113–129.

Strahan, B. J. (1991). Attachment theory and family functioning: Expectations and congruencies. *Australian Journal of Marriage and Family, 12*(1), 12–26.

Vetere, A., & Dallos, R. (2008). Systemic therapy and attachment narratives. *Journal of Family Therapy, 30*(4), 374–385.

Wampold, B. E. (2001). *The great psychotherapy debate: Models, methods, and findings*. Mahwah, NJ: Lawrence Erlbaum Associates Publishers.

Weeks, G. & Fife, S. (2014). *Couples in treatment: Techniques and approaches for effective practice* (3rd ed.). New York: Brunner-Routledge.

Whitaker, C., & Malone, T. P. (1953). *Roots of psychotherapy*. New York, NY: Blakiston/Routledge.

4 My Mothers, My Fathers, My Self
Self-of-the-Therapist Project

Overview

This chapter introduces the Self-of-the-Therapist (SoT) project, which has been developed and used for many years to help therapists increase their multidimensional awareness of themselves. This personal study uses the Gender-Focused Genogram (GFG) as the foundation for the *My Mothers, My Fathers, My Self* (MFS) genogram. The SoT project will help you explore your internal working models of attachment related to both your same and opposite gender parents (and grandparents, other caregivers, or fictive kin, as indicated by your childhood experiences) and will also include a comprehensive and integrative attachment-focused exploration based on mapping and timeline tools. In order for students, postgraduates, early/mid-career clinicians, as well as others to develop effective therapeutic posture (TxP) with a range of client-systems, this SoT project provides students and practitioners a unique window into childhood history and gendered attachment experiences. Satir was an advocate for self-study to strengthen the therapeutic relationship. There is a considerable amount of literature on the role of the SoT in the common factors literature (Nero, 2016; Weeks & Fife, 2014).

Objectives

1   Draw a diagram of an intergenerational family genogram through the lens of gendered life experiences, including pivotal childhood experiences.
2   Identify key intrapersonal and interpersonal topics which influence your contemporary life experiences.
3   Expand your interpersonal flexibility during treatment using TxP.
4   Explore your childhood attachment experiences to help identify your personal awareness of your relational strengths as you attune yourself to your client-system using TxP.

Historical Background: Developing a SoT Project

Sluzki (1978) and Pistole (1995) pointed out that having clinicians in training do their own genogram helped them to begin to think systemically. Their findings suggested that all the Marriage Family Therapy (MFT) students should be required to construct their own genogram in order to better understand themselves, their own families, and consequent reactive thoughts and feelings about their clients.

The experience of constructing one's own genogram does more than giving the student clinician a greater understanding of their own family and themselves, even though they might struggle with the concepts inherent in an intergenerational or systemic view of themselves. For example, Keiley et al. (2002) found that students who constructed their own personal cultural genogram reported it as having been a transformative experience. They reported that the genogram experience helped them to grow personally and professionally and that it facilitated change in their family of origin (FOO). An earlier study also showed that when students did their own genograms it helped them identify a number of patterns within their own families which allowed them to recognize how they tended to repeat with their clients what they had learned in their families.

The most common patterns the MFT students noted in their own families were over and under-functioning, triangulation, and pursuing-distancing (Getz & Protinsky, 1994). The use of the cultural genogram in training has also enhanced students' awareness and sensitivity to issues of diversity (Halevy, 1998; Hardy & Laszloffy, 1995; Kelly, 1990; Keiley et al., 2002). Thus, the genogram created a contextual understanding consistent with systems theory. The value of this experiential learning experience cannot be overstated.

A professional genogram was also developed and used to help students develop a clearer sense of their own professional identity and theoretical influences (Magnuson, 2000). In contrast, Aponte et al. (2009) suggested three reasons why the person of the therapist is so important in the therapeutic process: (1) the therapists' culture, values, and spirituality; (2) the clinician's ability to observe oneself and "exercise judgment" over their emotions, memories, and behaviors; and (3) be able to manage themselves, including emotional, cultural, and spiritual aspects. All these appear to be important themes for the therapist to regulate. Balaguer, Mary, and Levitt (2000) and Beck (1987) viewed the genogram not just as a diagnostic device but also as a process of mutual collaboration. Most of the literature examines the structural elements of the genogram and the content that is learned about the client-system from the genogram. These writers were concerned with the process of creating the genogram and whether it was done in a way that involved mutual collaboration. This emphasis on process encourages therapists to examine how the therapeutic alliance was created through the process of collecting the genogram information.

Another genogram with a similar purpose was developed by Aten, Madson, and Kruse (2008). This genogram involves drawing a timeline on their supervisors. Symbols are then used to indicate the following information: gender of supervisor, nature of supervisory alliance (normal, close, conflictual, distant, terminated prematurely), the context in which the supervision took place (e.g., academic program, school system, private practice), and the mode of supervision (individual, group, etc.). Besides serving as a history of their supervisory experiences, the supervisee may note some patterns such as the gender of the supervisor and the alliance with the supervisor, whether there was conflict or distance, and any other pattern that might be replicated.

Although beyond the scope of this workbook, collaboration among proponents of these professional development experiences is an important contribution to the MFT field. This simple genogram involves the student tracing back their most significant academic and supervisory training. They identify the instructors who had the greatest influence on them; they then identify the supervisors who had the greatest influence on their work and investigate who influenced all these professors and supervisors as far back in history as possible. Ideally, they will be able to identify a number of early pioneers in the MFT field who had an influence on their training. Seeing all these professors/supervisors on paper gives the student a sense of who developed some of the ideas that they have internalized and how these ideas have been passed down through generations of professors/supervisors.

Creating Your Attachment-Focused SoT Project

This chapter will help you explore your own intrapersonal and interpersonal attachment experiences so that you will be better equipped to establish a therapeutic attachment-focused bond with your clients. Exploring your own life history helps you develop personal narratives that contribute to your narrative identity, sense of well-being, and personal meaning. Affective (or emotional) themes are particularly important because emotions are factors associated with mental and emotional health (Adler et al., 2017). Consequently, the SoT study will guide your development of a comprehensive personal narrative that pinpoints relational strengths and challenges.

The SoT project can also be presented as a paper to share with teachers, faculty, supervisors, colleagues, and others. To do the SoT project as a paper, students or clinicians should follow the comprehensive list of SoT project components in the book and use the workbook pages to inform what they write in the paper. Finally, whether a written or a visual project, the process of developing the SoT project is the most important. In addition, reviewing the project or paper with a supervisor or mentor can elicit feedback and healing for the clinician. While supervising or mentoring someone who is sharing a SoT with you, it is important to look for clinical or supervisory issues and advise the student appropriately.

Simultaneously, the SoT project exercise fosters the development of dialectical thinking by learning to use the Clinical Mind Map to organize the vast array of information that a therapist gathers using the IA and focused genograms (FGs), in both the early interviews and updates throughout the clinical process. Mind mapping is also a method that is used to visualize and organize information and concepts. Typically mind maps have both structural and process dimensions. Integrative and systemically focused clinicians must develop both concrete and intuitive ways for conceptualizing each unique client-system dialectically.

The SoT project is foundational for professional development as well as supervision of the student in both individual and group supervision. Overall, the GFG is the broad umbrella that includes themes such as self-identity, gender roles, and the dynamic interplay of those roles, along with attachment-focused partnered and parental gender considerations. Several different perspectives provide a guide for developing a SoT exploration from an attachment-focused and gendered perspective. In order for students to develop effective TxP with clients, the SoT project provides the student, clinicians, and supervisors a unique window into the student's personal history and how it may affect the formation of TxP. Knowledge of one's own gendered parenting experiences in the FOO is essential to understanding TxP. For example, a client who enters therapy with a dismissive attachment to his mother may expect the female therapist to ultimately dismiss him. The therapist may sense something is wrong but if the therapist does not understand her own gender experience she may react poorly. The therapist who is secure with their gender and attachment will recognize the projection of the client and be able to process it accurately.

The SoT Project

This personal study includes a revision of the GFG called "My Mothers, My Fathers, My Self" as well as a comprehensive and integrative attachment-focused exploration of one's FOO. We call this study a "project" because it has been developed to provide a guide for understanding yourself as a person who provides psychotherapy, couple therapy, family therapy, and other clinical variations. The purpose of the SoT project is to help practitioners clarify the influences of childhood attachment experiences, in particular, for establishing TxP with client-systems. A primary goal is to become aware of our childhood gendered attachment experiences that influence therapeutic relationships based on the IA and the FG mapping and timeline tools.

The SoT project begins with a GFG. The GFG attends to the unique combinations of the gendered therapist/client-system and has a title named "My Mothers, My Fathers, My Self (MFS)." The MFS provides a variation of the GFG with specific topics to consider. Gendered attachment experiences are important considerations with client-systems who often present with preferences for female- or male-identified therapists; research also supports the idea that gender is important in this area (Karaırmak & Oguz-Duran, 2008). We note gender orientation is a complex relationship with oneself. After reviewing many variations of symbolic representations of gender, we developed the Gender Diversity Symbol (Figure 4.1). It represents a variety of gender orientations that can be used when creating the MFS FG.

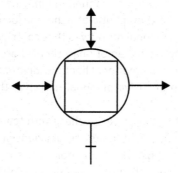

Figure 4.1 Gender Diversity Symbol.

This project will help you explore your internal working models of attachment related to both your same and/or opposite gender parents (and grandparents or fictive kin, as indicated by your childhood experiences). Polkinghorne (1996) suggests that a negative or victim role disempowers a person's sense of agency in life and that a positive or assertive role empowers a person's sense of agency in life. Consequently, knowledge and acceptance of one's own gendered parenting experiences in the FOO are essential to understanding TxP. Clients often present with preferences for female- or male-identified therapists. The importance of the therapist's understanding of their own attachment bonds will strengthen engagement with new clients. The goal of the SoT exercise project is learning how to be more effective in developing an attachment-focused therapeutic alliance and, in particular, how to develop the therapeutic bond.

Introducing MFS: A GFG

The first step in developing the SoT study is constructing the MFS and then highlighting the topics that emerge. The MFS explores the gender identification experiences in childhood with the parent(s) we most identify with, typically the parent of the same gender. The MFS template provides guiding questions to explore this topic, which was first published in *Focused Genograms*, 2nd edition (FG2; DeMaria, Weeks, & Twist, 2017) within the GFG. Sharing the MFS in a group setting with others who are developing their own genograms, if this opportunity exists, is also an important step in the SoT experience because it provides the clinician with witnesses to their emotional experience of telling the stories of their gendered attachment (Figure 4.2).

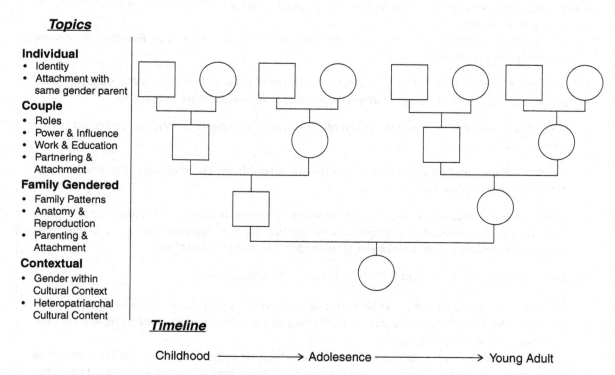

Topics

Individual
- Identity
- Attachment with same gender parent

Couple
- Roles
- Power & Influence
- Work & Education
- Partnering & Attachment

Family Gendered
- Family Patterns
- Anatomy & Reproduction
- Parenting & Attachment

Contextual
- Gender within Cultural Context
- Heteropatriarchal Cultural Content

Timeline

Childhood ⟶ Adolesence ⟶ Young Adult

Figure 4.2 My Mothers, My Fathers, My Self FG.

Format for the SoT Project: 11 Steps for the SoT Project

The SoT Project

Directions: Below is a list of the 11 steps for the SoT project. Each component has an accompanying FG Workbook page after the comprehensive list below.

Review Chapters 5–8 to provide you the specific details for developing your Internal Models Map, your Couple Interaction Map, your Family Connections Map (FCM), and your Social Bonds Ecomap. Family stories and life experiences contribute to your own family attachment narrative. Timelines are especially useful for your family attachment narrative. A Self Compassion quiz is also important, given the role of providing a variety of treatment goals and tasks, which are integral to the therapeutic bond.

1   Prepare the MFS FG using the template and questions (provided in the MFS FG section). This includes the four-generation FG and a written summary of the topics addressed.

2   Identify and describe a Pivotal Story, which is an important and memorable childhood experience that underscores the quality of your relationship with your same gender parent, typically between the ages of 3 and 10. Family scripts reveal repeated negative interaction patterns that result in repetitive attachment experiences, which help explore family narratives as part of the Pivotal Story.

3   Identify relational strengths based on the identification with, and experience of, your childhood attachment patterns. We recommend use of Fraley's online instruments for assessments of adult attachment styles.

Information about the use of Fraley's questionnaires can be accessed through the links identified here:
Fraley, C. R. (2014). Your Personality. Retrieved from https://yourpersonality.net/attachment/
Fraley, C. R. (2014). Attachment styles and close relationships. Retrieved from www.web-research-design. net/cgi-bin/crq/crq.pl
Fraley, C. R. (2014). Relationship structures: Attachment styles across relationships. Retrieved from www. yourpersonality.net/relstructures/

4   Develop an Internal Models Map and describe each set of relationships – same and opposite/other gender parents, other significant caregivers, and marital/parental couple interaction.

5   Develop a Couple Interaction Map, if currently involved in a romantic/committed partnered couple relationship.

6   Develop a Basic Family Map as part of the GFG to establish the contemporary attachment styles among current family members.

7   Develop an FCM to identify family attachment styles as secure, dismissive, preoccupied or one of the four types or disorganized family connections. The four types of disorganized Family Connections include (a) overinvolved, (b) uninvolved, (c) unpredictable, and (d) controlling.

8   Construct a Family Attachment Narrative (pulled from Dallos, 2004).

   a)   Describe your relationships within your family, using terms other than attachment terms.
   b)   Write about the following in your family: feeling and anxieties; parental caregiving and comfort; physical affection; punishment.
   c)   Think about how your parents might have been thinking and feeling in some specific memories evoked by a and b; ask them if you want/can. Think about how this may have affected your relationships with others.

9   Develop a Social Bonds Ecomap. Use the template provided, with concentric circles for Family and Community Networks, Institutional Networks, Cultural Conditions, and World Changes

(Continued)

Over Time. Place each resource, like a religious community or therapist, in the appropriate concentric circle.

10 Timelines: Identify events that changed the course of how you viewed yourself or your family.

11 A Self Compassion Quiz by Dr. Kristin Neff[1] that can be accessed at http://self-compassion.org/test-how-self-compassionate-you-are/.

Developing Your SoT Project

Exercise 4.1 MFS GFG

My Mothers, My Fathers, My Self

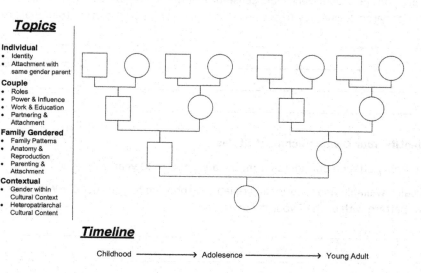

Topics

Individual
- Identity
- Attachment with same gender parent

Couple
- Roles
- Power & Influence
- Work & Education
- Partnering & Attachment

Family Gendered
- Family Patterns
- Anatomy & Reproduction
- Parenting & Attachment

Contextual
- Gender within Cultural Context
- Heteropatriarchal Cultural Content

Timeline

Childhood ⟶ Adolesence ⟶ Young Adult

Questions about MFS come from the GFG, published in FG2 (DeMaria, Weeks, & Twist, 2017).

1 In childhood, how would you describe the relationship with your parent(s)? Did your gender or their gender influence this relationship?

2 In childhood, were there any adults with whom you had a close relationship – people who were like parents or fictive parents maybe? Did your gender or their gender influence this relationship?

3 How would you describe the relationship with your parent(s) and/or with your fictive parent(s) at present? Does your gender or their gender influence those relationships?

4 In childhood, which of your parents did you feel closest to and why? At present, which of your parents do you feel closest to and why?

5 When emotionally upset as a child, what would you do? What would your parent(s) do?

6 When was the first time you recollect being apart from your parent(s)? How was this experience for you? How was this experience for your parent(s)?

7 Are there any parts of your growing up experiences that you believe set you back in your individual development? Are there any parts of your growing up experiences that you believe significantly positively influenced your individual development? How have these experiences influenced who you are in the present?

(Continued)

8   In childhood, did you experience the death or loss of a parent or another person with whom you were close? How did you manage this experience? How did your parent(s) manage this experience? What about other people with whom you were close?

Exercise 4.2 The Pivotal Childhood Story

The next step is identifying a pivotal story. Exploring the impact of a pivotal story in childhood with one parent, either same or opposite/other gender, will help the student/clinician develop greater awareness of an individual's relational style. The pivotal story is a memory of an experience with a parent that has emotional meaning and is representative of one's relationship with that parent. This story is important to understanding the quality of the parent-child relationship, the influences on the relational aspects that contributed to one's attachment experience with parents which holds the roots of one's attachment experience in adulthood. The pivotal story is often repeated throughout one's childhood with the parent and has a lasting impact on the student/clinician' sense of identity as well as attachment styles with same- and opposite-gender parents. One way to access the pivotal story is to construct the timelines (Item 9).

_____

_____

_____

_____

Exercise 4.3 Identify Your Own Attachment Styles

Who were your primary attachment figures from the ages of 0 to 10 years?

Were they physically available and emotionally reliably responsive to your needs? What was your childhood attachment pattern with each of your caregivers?

Caregiver 1_____

Caregiver 2_____

If applicable, other caregiver(s):_____

_____

Using Fraley's attachment scales, discover your adult attachment styles and list them below. The attachment figures from this stage of life can start in early adolescence and continue onward to the present day.

Adult Attachment Styles:_____

General _____

Partner _____

Mother _____

Father _____

Exercise 4.4 Internal Models Map

Identify your childhood attachment figures. Describe each set of relationships – same and opposite/other gender parents, other significant caregivers, and marital/parental couple interaction. Use the space below to describe and create an Internal Models Map.

_____

_____

(Continued)

_____

_____

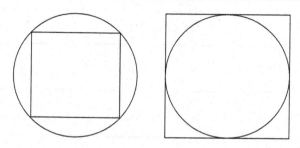

Exercise 4.5 Couple Interaction Map

Using the blank Couple Interaction Map below, complete the ten steps if currently involved in a romantic/committed partnered couple relationship. Refer to Chapters 6 and 9 for complete examples.

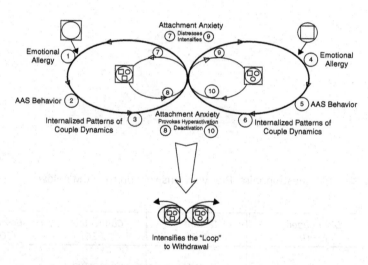

The Couple Interaction Map

"The Loop"

10 Steps to Emotional Disconnection and Insecure Attachment

Step 1:

_____

Step 2:

_____

Step 3:

_____

Step 4:

_____

Step 5:

_____

(Continued)

Step 6: _____

Step 7: _____

Step 8: _____

Step 9: _____

Step 10: _____

Exercise 4.6 Basic Family Map

Using the space below, develop your Basic Family Map.
Refer to Chapter 7 for examples.

Exercise 4.7 FCM

Refer to Chapter 7 for the FCM questionnaire. Plot your answers on the FCM below.

F L E X I B I L I T Y		Disengaged (5-10)	Distant (11-15)	Connected (15-20)	Enmeshed (20-25)
	Chaotic (5-10)	UNPREDICTABLE **Disorganized**	Distant Chaotic **Dismissive**	Connected Chaotic **Preoccupied**	OVERINVOLVED **Disorganized**
	Flexible (11-15)	Disengaged Flexible **Dismissive**	**Secure**	**Secure**	Enmeshed Flexible **Preoccupied**
	Structured (16-20)	Disengaged Structured **Dismissive**	**Secure**	**Secure**	Enmeshed Structured **Preoccupied**
	Rigid (20-25)	UNINVOLVED **Disorganized**	Distant Rigid **Dismissive**	Connected Rigid **Preoccupied**	CONTROLLING **Disorganized**
		C O N N E C T I O N			

(Continued)

Exercise 4.8 Family Attachment Narratives

a   Describe your relationships within your family, using terms other than attachment terms.
b   Write about the following in your family: feeling and anxieties; parental caregiving and comfort; physical affection; punishment.
c   Think about how your parents might have been thinking and feeling in some specific memories evoked by a and b; ask them if you want/can. Think about how this may have affected your relationships with others.

_____

_____

_____

_____

Exercise 4.9 Social Bonds Ecomap

Using the Ecomap graphic, fill in your social bonds in the community.

_____

_____

_____

_____

Exercise 4.10 Timelines: Your Life, Your Parents' Lives, and Others

Timeline of important events in your life that you feel shaped you as a person and clinician.

_____

_____

_____

_____

(Continued)

Timeline of important events in your parents' lives. If you are able, it may be a good idea to talk with them about their lives to gain their perspective on important pieces of the timeline.

_____

_____

_____

_____

Timeline of important others in your life – significant grandparents and extended family, fictive kin, mentors, and friends. How has their interaction in your life shaped you as a person?

_____

_____

_____

_____

Exercise 4.11 Your Self-Compassion Perspective

Take the quiz on Dr. Kristin Neff's website (Neff, 2019).[2] It includes scoring. https://self-compassion.org/test-how-self-compassionate-you-are/

What are your observations of the Self-Compassion test results?

_____

_____

_____

_____

What surprised you?

_____

_____

_____

What can you do differently, going forward, to be more compassionate toward yourself?

_____

_____

_____

_____

Dr. Neff's website also includes Self-Compassion meditation to use if you would like to cultivate self-compassion and loving kindness toward yourself as part of this exercise.

** End of the exercise. Congratulations! **

Using Genograms to Facilitate Self-Awareness

Virtually all the authors who write about the use of the genograms in training mention how the genogram facilitates greater self-awareness and self-understanding (Halevy, 1998). Most of the articles reviewed earlier in the chapter are clinical or theoretical in nature. Lim (2008) has been one of the few researchers to conduct a study using phenomenological and survey questions in order to gain an understanding of the benefits of using the genogram in training. In spite of the fact that the number of subjects was small (only 8, but with great diversity) Lim's study revealed several findings and supported a number of clinical reports. The results suggested seven insights:

1   Trainees believed they had experienced personal growth through the process and developed a greater sense of self.
2   Trainees stated they had developed a healthier sense of self in relation to their FOO.
3   Trainees experienced a feeling of greater emotional connection with their family.
4   Trainees said they found new ways of relating to their FOO.
5   Trainees felt they had become more differentiated.
6   Trainees believed overwhelmingly that doing the genogram enhanced their ability to understand how their dynamics would impact their clients.
7   Trainees reported a greater sense of confidence in using the genogram with their clients.

Numerous reports on the use of the genogram in training seem to reveal that it is an effective form of experiential learning that facilitates a therapist's competence and personal growth. The SoT project, when completed, increases the student's ability to think systemically and contextually. There are various studies available that are all based on either the traditional genogram as developed by McGoldrick, Gerson, and Petry (2008) or more specific genograms such as the cultural genogram (Hardy & Laszloffy, 1995). Within the Post Graduate Program in Couple and Family Therapy at Council for Relationships in Philadelphia (originally The Marriage Council, founded by Emily Mudd in 1932), all postgraduates in training will participate in developing their individual SoT project. They are introduced to several FGs, which form an important part of developing their skill set with their client-systems within the postgraduate training program.

The FG and SoT project provides a much richer experience for students and trainees. The FG examines various other aspects of functioning based on an integrative theoretical approach. Hopefully, similar studies will be performed on the FG demonstrating that students who have applied various FGs to themselves will develop a broader theoretical perspective and a more in-depth understanding of themselves, their clients, and the interface between the two. Metaphorically, the traditional genogram is like watching a 1950s black-and-white television, while the FG is like watching high-definition Virtual Reality. We propose that the GFG, as part of the SoT project, is the first step for helping students and trainees begin to explore their own attachment history.

Summary

Through the lenses of the GFG, the experience of sharing a pivotal story, and the identification of one's attachment style in each domain, students and other clinicians can relate to and help a wide range of people with clinical issues. As therapists begin to develop an attachment-focused TxP with individuals, couples, and families, they begin to gain insight and understanding of their strengths and vulnerabilities. The process of identifying patterns of intergenerational transmission of attachment will now no longer be a mystery to therapists or others using the tools provided in this FGW. Finally, we recommend that a SoT project be shared in classroom discussions or with a supervisor, peer group, personal therapist, or classroom discussion for further reflection.

Notes

1   Included with permission, granted 12/2/2018.
2   Included with permission, granted 12/2/2018.

References

Adler, J. M., Dunlop, W. L., Fivush, R., Lilgendahl, J. P., Lodi-Smith, J., McAdams, D. P., ... Syed M. (2017). Research methods for studying narrative identity. *Social Psychological and Personality Science, 8*(5), 519-527.

Aponte, H. J., Powell, F. D., Brooks, S., Watson, M. F., Litzke, C., Lawless, J., & Johnson, E. (2009). Training the person of the therapist in an academic setting. *Journal of Marital and Family Therapy, 35*(4), 381-394.

Aten, J. D., Madson, M. B., & Kruse, S. J. (2008). The supervision genogram: A tool for preparing supervisors-in-training. *Psychotherapy: Theory, Research, Practice, Training, 45*(1), 111-116.

Balaguer, A., Mary, D., & Levitt, M. (2000). The genogram: From diagnostics to mutual collaboration. *The Family Journal, 8*(3), 236-244.

Beck, A. T. (1987). Cognitive models of depression. *Journal of Cognitive Psychotherapy, 1*(1), 5-37.

Dallos, R. (2004). Attachment narrative therapy: Integrating ideas from narrative and attachment theory in systemic family therapy with eating disorders. *Journal of Family Therapy, 26*(1), 40-65. doi:10.1111/j.1467-6427.2004.00266.x

DeMaria, R., Weeks, G. R., & Twist, M. L. (2017). *Focused genograms: Intergenerational assessment of individuals, couples, and families.* New York, NY: Routledge.

Fraley, C. R. (2014). Relationship structures: Attachment styles across relationships. Retrieved from www.yourpersonality.net/relstructures/

Fraley, C. R. (2014). Attachment styles and close relationships. Retrieved from www.web-research-design.net/cgi-bin/crq/crq.pl

Fraley, C. R. (2014).Your Personality. Retrieved from https://yourpersonality.net/attachment/

Getz, H. G., & Protinsky, H. O. (1994). Training marriage and family counselors: A family-of-origin approach. *Counselor Education and Supervision, 33*(3), 183-190.

Halevy, J. (1998). A genogram with an attitude. *Journal of Marital and Family Therapy, 24*(2), 233-242.

Hardy, K. V., & Laszloffy, T. A. (1995). The cultural genogram: Key to training culturally competent family therapists. *Journal of Marital and Family Therapy, 21*(3), 227-237.

Karaırmak, Ö., & Duran, N. O. (2008). Gender differences in attachment styles regarding conflict handling behaviors among Turkish late adolescents. *International Journal for the Advancement of Counselling, 30*(4), 220-234.

Keiley, M. K., Dolbin, M., Hill, J., Karuppaswamy, N., Liu, T., Natrajan, R., ... & Robinson, P. (2002). The cultural genogram: Experiences from within a marriage and family therapy training program. *Journal of Marital and Family Therapy, 28*(2), 165-178.

Kelly, G. D. (1990). The cultural family of origin: A description of a training strategy. *Counselor Education and Supervision, 30*(1), 77-84.

Lim, S. L. (2008). Transformative aspects of genogram work: Perceptions and experiences of graduate students in a counseling training program. *Family Journal: Counseling and Therapy for Couples and Families, 16*(1), 35-42.

Magnuson, S. (2000). The professional genogram: Enhancing professional identity and clarity. *The Family Journal, 8*(4), 399-401.

McGoldrick, M., Gerson, R., & Petry, S. S. (2008). *Genograms: Assessment and intervention.* New York, NY: W. W. Norton & Company.

Neff, K. (2019). Self-compassion: Test how self compassionate you are. Retrieved from http://self-compassion.org/test-how-self-compassionate-you-are/

Nero, M. M. (2016). Toward a secure base: The relationship between adult attachment pattern and theoretical orientation among clinical social workers (Unpublished doctoral dissertation). University of Pennsylvania, Philadelphia, PA.

Pistole, M. C. (1995). College students' ended love relationships: Attachment style and emotion. *Journal of College Student Development, 36*, 53-60.

Polkinghorne, D. E. (1996). Transformative narratives: From victimic to agentic life plots. *American Journal of Occupational Therapy, 50*(4), 299-305.

Sluzki, C. (1978). Marital therapy from a systems theory perspective. In T. Paolino and B. McCrady (eds.), *Marriage and marital therapy.* New York: Brunner/Mazel.

Weeks, G. & Fife, S. (2014). *Couples in treatment: Techniques and approaches for effective practice* (3rd ed.). New York, NY: Brunner-Routledge.

Part III

Applications in the Four Intersystem Approach Domains

5 The Individual Domain

Childhood Attachment Patterns, Internal Models Map, and Identification of Disorganized Attachment Bonds

Overview

This chapter will guide the development of an Internal Models Map (IMM). The IMM is pivotal in the formation of therapeutic posture. The IMM is a clinical tool for obtaining a comprehensive understanding of any given client's internal working models (IWM) of attachment. Gendered considerations are also important as infant and child bonds are formed with the parental attachment figures. The child internalizes attachment patterns with the key parental figures. As a result, childhood attachment patterns become the focus, based on information about childhood experiences of secure, insecure, or disorganized patterns. The individual timeline is an important aspect of a child's early experiences, from birth to age 10 that lay the foundation for secure bonds for their future mate, which will result in the intergenerational family process.

The first goal of the therapist is to provide a bond between the clinician and the client-system within the therapeutic alliance, which has been named therapeutic posture (TxP). The second goal is to begin by exploring the reason for therapy. The third goal is to learn about the client's intergenerational family system, which is based on a preliminary basic genogram.

Objectives

1   Identify your childhood attachment patterns, drawing the appropriate symbol(s) for your attachment relationship for each parental figure (Exercise 5.1).
2   Describe four adults who have different types of childhood attachment patterns with either a mother or a father figure (Exercise 5.2).
3   Apply the childhood attachment pattern symbols to the clinical example given and create an IMM from this example (Exercise 5.3).
4   Create your own timeline to show how an individual's history influences their attachment patterns, and their presentation in therapy (Exercise 5.4).
5   Create the IMM and the timeline for the individual domain (Exercise 5.5).

Introducing the Individual Domain of the Intersystem Approach and the Attachment Map

Using the IMM for the individual domain provides a unique method for gathering information that guides practitioners in understanding and applying attachment theory throughout the four domains - individual, couple, intergenerational, and contextual. Bowlby (1973) foreshadowed a systemic perspective that provided a clear reference to the importance of the IWMs of attachment as a behavioral system that young children internalize as they are parented by significant others in their early years. Bowlby further identified that children will carry their own experience to the next generation, which Bowlby described as intergenerational transmission of attachment. When children become secure adults, assuming they have had responsive and available primary caregivers, they will have opportunities to further strengthen family bonds through effective connection and communication. The Adult Attachment Interview was a link that provides an opportunity for an adult to reflect on childhood and adult intergenerational transmission process (Steele, Steele, & Croft, 2008), and identified ten clinical applications.[1]

Intergenerational transmission across and among filial relationships within the family system will move toward health or toward disease. This intergenerational dynamic is a complex and relational multi-generational context. Bowlby was not alone in his conceptualization of intergenerational family process. Boszormenyi-Nagy and Spark (1973), in particular, developed a contextual approach to family systems that focused on loyalty, trust, and relational ethics between and among family members. Parents who provide secure attachment with their children by being emotionally reliable and physically available set in motion secure intergenerational bonds. However, when traumatic experiences take place for individuals within the client-system, there can be disruptions in those secure bonds that may then lead to insecure and disorganized relational bonds.

For a clinician, therapist, student or others who work with individual client-systems, developing the IMM for all members of the client-system provides a crucial guide for discovering any disruptions of these secure bonds. The therapeutic alliance will be established by attuned responsiveness based on the individual client(s) needs. The goal is to begin with attunement to the attachment styles noted during the initial interviews. An early therapeutic relationship must be collaborative so that the client-system experiences the therapist as safe, structured, trustworthy, and comfortable. Early signals of the client's preoccupation, dismissiveness, disoriented/disorganized, or fear and discomfort must be recognized. With focus, the clinician will adapt the TxP that meets the observable emotional needs of the client-system, using the therapeutic styles. When applying the focused genograms (FGs), mapping tools and timelines, the clinician will also begin to highlight unique aspects of childhood attachment patterns that are based on childhood and adolescent emotional experiences.

The IMM - Application of Attachment Theory

The IMM reveals the unique attachment patterns of each individual with their significant childhood attachment figure. Attachment figures in childhood typically include mother, father, other significant family members such as grandparents, aunts, uncles, and caregivers. The individual's childhood attachment patterns will often be different with each parent or other (surrogate) parental figures. The configuration of attachment patterns with parental figures can be both complex and unique for each individual.

Gendered Considerations for the IMM

As the therapist assesses adult attachment styles within the initial interviews, there is a window of time in the early sessions for exploring relationships with the parental attachment figures. Typically, clients experience early bonding experiences with the same and opposite-gendered attachment figures. Consequently, gender is a significant aspect of assessment for the IMM. Attachment studies suggest that a same-gender, parent–child attachment bond influences parental attachments and family dynamics (Mikulincer & Shaver, 2005). The internal model of attachment with both same and different-gender parental figures influences childhood attachment styles in gendered ways, which paves the way for the development of gender roles.[2]

Childhood Attachment Patterns in the IMM

Childhood attachment patterns reflect the nature of relationships with primary caregivers. Starting in infancy, babies are completely dependent on caregivers for survival. With growth and development, this relationship becomes more complex, as children begin to seek proximity to caregivers when they are distressed (Bowlby, 1969). The basic foundation of attachment is physical and emotional availability. Securely attached children have secure attachments with caregivers who are reliably available when they are in distress. Insecurely attached children can have two variations on their attachment patterns. Ambivalently attached children have caregivers who are physically available but emotionally unreliable. This leads to proximity seeking but inconsistent satisfaction. Avoidantly attached children have caregivers who are not physically or emotionally available. These children do not seek proximity because they learn to rely on themselves for comfort. In both ambivalent and avoidant attachment patterns, children may feel considerable anxiety, but the distinguishing factor is whether or not they seek proximity of caregivers for comfort. Main and Solomon (1986) were the first to describe disorganized/disoriented attachment during which children (and adults) generally experience both high anxiety and high avoidance in varying emotional and physical responses to their primary attachment figures. The identification of a fourth attachment pattern was termed disorganized attachment.

Figure 5.1 shows symbols for each of these childhood attachment patterns, to be used in creating the IMM.

For example, Sherrod enters therapy for anxiety. He states that he lived with his grandparents until he went to college in another state. His parents, he says, were never around much when he was growing up. Sherrod's dad left when he was 5 and barely visited, and his mother, whose parents he and his mother lived with, was always working to try and get them their own house. Sherrod says he appreciates what his mother did for him but really felt like his grandparents were his true caregivers. Now, they are both aging and their health is deteriorating, and this makes him anxious (Figure 5.2).

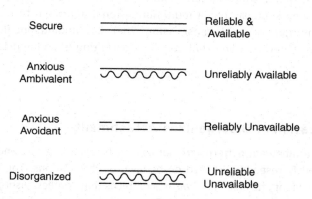

Figure 5.1 Attachment Mapping Symbols: Childhood Attachment Patterns.

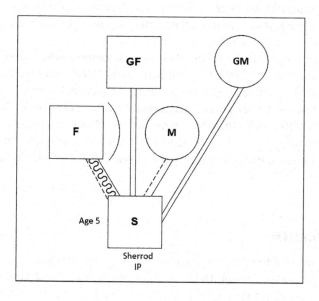

Figure 5.2 Sherrod's IMM.

Sherrod's Key: IMM

Sherrod: Ambivalent with Mother; Secure with Grandfather and Grandmother; Disorganized with Father.

Intergenerational Transmission of Attachment

Another function of the IMM is that it reveals the internalized couple/marital relationship attachment patterns, which also highlights the parental role that the couple/marital partners must negotiate as well. In addition to the childhood attachment patterns with each parent, children similarly develop IWMs about the nature of intimate relationships. Learned parental behaviors from childhood interact within the couple relationship as parents, which either mediate secure patterns of attachment or contribute to insecure or disorganized attachments for each parent and child. This intergenerational transmission process impacts each generation as the client-system progresses forward over the cycles. It is becoming more common for four-generation client-systems. Van IJzendoorn and Bakermans-Kranenburg (2019) are exploring the mechanisms for intergenerational transmission, in particular, the roles of sensitive parenting and parental mentalization. However, they suggest that a multi-dimensional approach to parenting is needed to understand the "how" of intergenerational transmission. Their key findings include that adult attachment is transmitted to the next generation and that sensitive parenting is an important link leading from one generation to the next.

Exploring the Application of Disorganized Attachment

Disorganized/Disoriented attachment patterns are not as easy to assess. Secure and insecure attachment patterns have been meticulously researched based on behavioral observations. The Disorganized patterns are more confusing in that the infant and child have various patterns that conflict. Disorganized attachment results from trauma and significant loss in early childhood. The early patterns can be complicated due to a variety of attentional and behavioral options that a child in an emotional crisis without a secure base may appear to collapse, either actively or passively. The importance of differentiating childhood attachment patterns from adult attachment styles and, similarly, from family attachment scripts and narratives is significant because it provides a way to explore important areas of a client-system's life that sometimes might be overlooked. Often, a specific inquiry into the nature of attachment relationships in childhood leads to key information and has a bonding effect with clients.

Disorganized attachment was identified by Main and Solomon (1990), and Main and Hesse (1990) went on to propose a taxonomy of child and adult attachment. Main and Hesse (1990) identified seven types of attachment pattern types as they developed their theoretical construct : (1) sequential display of contradictory behavior patterns; (2) simultaneous display of contradictory behavior patterns; (3) undirected, misdirected, incomplete, and interrupted movements; (4) stereotypes, asymmetrical movements, mistimed movements, and anomalous posture; (5) freezing, stilling, and slowed movements and expressions; (6) direct indices of apprehension regarding the parent; and (7) direct indices of disorganization or disorientation.

Learning to Create an IMM

To begin the clinical application of the IMM, the clinician uses the symbols to denote childhood attachment patterns with each parent or primary caregiver. There are four sets of attachment mapping symbols within the FG mapping methods. The first set of symbols address childhood attachment patterns. The other sets are included in the next three chapters.

Exercise 5.1 Creating Your IMM

Directions: Using Figure 5.1, apply one of the Childhood Attachment Pattern symbols to each caregiver (mother, father, grandparents, etc.) during your childhood.

Note that there are four childhood attachment symbols that you can apply to each caregiver. Your attachment pattern with each caregiver can be different. After you have drawn the IMM with the attachment symbol(s), write a brief description of that person you knew growing up which depicts the chosen attachment pattern in your IMM.

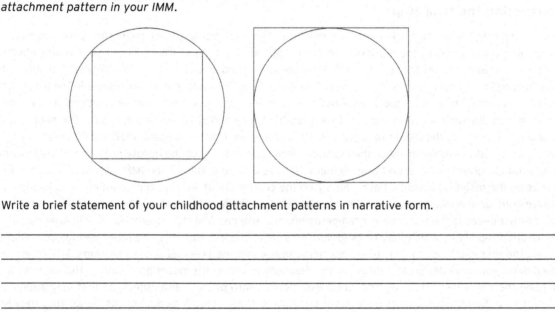

Write a brief statement of your childhood attachment patterns in narrative form.

_____

_____

_____

_____

Exercise 5.2 Composing Words to Match Childhood Attachment Patterns

Directions: Describe four adults who have different types of attachment with either a mother or a father figure and fill in each one of the four examples.

Example: Ambivalent Attachment Pattern – Travis really wants to lean on his dad when he is sad, but sometimes his dad gets upset that Travis is upset. Travis gets the impression that his dad is inconsistently emotionally available, so Travis sometimes has to pretend he is ok when he is not, or demand attention when he needs support. This maneuvering behavior for attachment makes Travis feel unsure of whether he can count on his dad to be there for him.

Secure Attachment Pattern:

_____

_____

Ambivalent Attachment Pattern:

_____

_____

Avoidant Attachment Pattern:

_____

_____

(Continued)

Disorganized Attachment Pattern:

_____

_____

Constructing the IMM Map

To develop the IMM, the clinician asks questions about the client's relationships with his/her/their parents and other primary caregivers. Generally, the questions (found in Appendix) focus on early childhood (0–3 years), childhood (4–10 years), and early adolescence (11–14 years). The clinician also inquires about the availability and reliability of affection, holding, emotional openness, and physical closeness by various attachment figures within the family. Other important considerations include questions about how attention was shared with siblings or others in a household, how intense parental work schedules or travel impacted the family, and other contextual factors that might provide clues about the quality of the client's relationships with parents and other significant attachment figures.

As the therapist learns more about the client, focused questions about the quality of the relationships with a mother, a father, grandmothers, and grandfathers will reveal more detail for the IMM. Typically, most clinicians will focus on the maternal parental figure, but given the complexity of a child's temperament, it is important to recognize both (or even multiple) parental IWMs. For example, the female client may have identified more closely with her father because she had a similar temperament and also physical characteristics as well. Attending to the family relationship styles which may be reserved, energetic, chaotic, isolating and other various combinations will guide the therapist's ability to join and accommodate within the first and second sessions. The Attachment Focused Genogram provides greater detail for this assessment with concomitant questions on the various topics.

Helping the client describe their childhood experiences with parents and others, as that may apply, is an important step. Sometimes, clients have never considered these factors as part of the issues that they have been struggling with. The contemporary memories that are revealed by the client reflect his/her/their current attachment narrative. When clients indicate that there were changes in one parent or another over time, the attachment narrative will reveal childhood strengths or vulnerabilities. Our thesis is that adults can simultaneously act out childhood attachment patterns in their current or potential couple relationship, as well as replaying the family attachment scripts and narratives in their couple relationship as they parent.

Clinical Application of an IMM: Janelle

Scenario: Janelle's Story

Janelle arrived in treatment reluctantly because her husband gave her the ultimatum that if she did not come with him he would leave her. Her husband described Janelle as shutdown and unwilling to take responsibility for her part in their conflict.

Janelle shared with the therapist that she did not have a bad childhood growing up, that everything was fine in her household. She reported that her parents divorced when she was six. At that time, she and her mother went to live with her mother's sister, and she saw her father intermittently on weekends. With gentle pressing, the therapist ascertained that Janelle did not feel very connected with her parents because she did not feel like they cared about her thoughts and feelings growing up. As an only child, she was left to her own devices while her parents fought, divorced, dated, and remarried. Janelle was closer with her aunt, she said, but she still did not keep in touch much after she left for college.

Janelle's IMM indicates avoidant attachments with her mother, father, and aunt. She may have had a more secure attachment with her aunt at some point, but it seems that she was globally avoidant and thus did not know how to or feel it was a priority to stay connected once she left for college. Janelle's thinking that "everything was fine" despite a divorce also indicates some degree of avoidance, especially given the level of conflict in her marriage at this time. Another clue is that her husband reports that she is shutdown, which is a classic tactic for stress management for avoidant attachment styles.

Exercise 5.3 Constructing Janelle's IMM

Directions: Using the Attachment Mapping Symbols in Figure 5.1 for the IMM, create a unique IMM based on the clinical example of Janelle given.

Identifying Disorganized Childhood Attachment Patterns Using a New Application

The FCM, explained in detail in Chapter 7, provides a unique structure for exploring internal childhood attachment patterns for disorganized attachments. A unique facet of this FCM is that it is applied to all four domains of the IA, which allows for a more comprehensive and holistic assessment and therapeutic bond. The FCM can be used for individuals, couples, families, and communities. The FCM was developed in *Focused Genograms*, 2nd edition and we hypothesized that disorganized attachment could identify variations for individuals using applicable terms. In clinical practice this model provides four discriminate dimensions that can be applied. Parental figures can also be identified individually.

Individual applications using childhood attachment patterns are a reflection of basic adult recollections about their current or childhood experiences with their parental figures. Couple applications using adult attachment styles are assessed based on categorical descriptions of secure, dismissive, preoccupied, and fearful within the FCM.

Exploring Disorganized Attachment for the Individual using the attachment-based FCM[3]:

There are four secure attachment styles in the center and four disorganized attachment styles in the corners. There are four variations of dismissive attachment styles that reflect avoidant childhood attachment patterns, typified by a parental team that predictably deny, minimize, and/or exhibit miscues of emotional expression and physical affection on a regular basis. Conversely, there are four variations of preoccupied attachment styles that reflect ambivalent childhood attachment patterns, developed through unpredictable patterns of emotional attention while parental figure(s) are typically physically available (Table 5.1).

Table 5.1 Family Connections Map

FLEXIBILITY		Disengaged	Distant	Connected	Enmeshed
	Chaotic	Unpredictable	Dismissive	Preoccupied	Overinvolved
	Flexible	Dismissive	Secure	Secure	Preoccupied
	Structured	Dismissive	Secure	Secure	Preoccupied
	Rigid	Uninvolved	Dismissive	Preoccupied	Controlling
CONNECTION					

Creating the Individual Timeline

Weeks and Wright (1979) explored the dialectics of the family life cycle and emphasized the importance of the individual-biological and the individual-psychological dimensions of human development. The IMM helps identify the individual's childhood attachment patterns that influence emotional foundations within the family system as well as physical, sexual, and other developmental aspects for childhood and adolescence experiences. Parallel to the FG maps, the FG timelines correspond and can be added to each of the four domains. Expanding this tool for relational mapping, the timeline captures developmental information and life events on a continuum. Their subjects include the following:

- Exploring childhood attachment experiences and development struggles, abuse, or trauma.
- Intergenerational patterns of fairness and entitlement that impact secure/insecure attachment for individuals, couples, and families.
- Intimate relationship experiences through adolescence, young adulthood, and adulthood.
- Family life traumas and tragedies, along with patterns of intimate family violence during the client/couple/family life cycle.
- Multigenerational contextual and community impacts for contemporary individuals and families. (Questions for these can be found in Appendix.)

Learning about Your Individual Timeline

Timelines provide an important tool to assist the student and practitioner to integrate client feedback, clarification of life experiences, relationship, and contextual information that help develop diagnoses and treatment plans. Individual development cannot be overlooked in systemic practice just as couple and family relationships cannot be overlooked in individual treatment. Timelines can be flexibly applied throughout the use of the various FGs as treatment progresses.

Questions for Your Consideration

1   When and where were you born?
2   Was corporal or physical punishment part of your childhood experience?
3   What are your memories of grade school (K-8)?
4   Important memories of high school – good and/or bad?
5   Were you ever bullied? When?
6   When did you begin to date?
7   When were you sexually active?
8   When did you leave home to be on your own?
9   Did you attend college, trade school, or other educational experiences?
10   Any significant dates/events you can recall?

Clinical Application of Individual Timeline

To make a timeline, the clinician draws a horizontal line, setting an arbitrary beginning point, and notes the pivotal events and dates related to the particular presenting problem.

(Timeline: _____)

Exercise 5.4 Create Your Own Timeline

Directions: Draw a horizontal line, setting an arbitrary beginning point, and note the pivotal events and dates related to each of the events.

Describe your observations on this timeline:

_____

_____

Putting the IMM and the Individual Timeline Together

Exercise 5.5 Combining the IMM with the Individual Timeline

Directions: In the spaces below, draw your own IMM and timeline for an individual client, yourself, or a friend.

After drawing, describe your IMM and your timeline below:

_____

_____

_____

_____

What have you learned?

_____

_____

_____

_____

TxP Considerations

An important and primary function of TxP is the therapist's orientation toward each member of the client-system based on the attachment bonds with each client's IWM. Stages of treatment, as described in Chapter 3, enable the therapist to continually shift TxP toward a secure attachment bond between the therapist and the client-system. The therapist can identify the stages of treatment based on how they are relating to the client through the use of shifting TxP toward a more secure bond. In other words, if the client is stuck in a developmental phase or exhibiting insecure behavior you can provide a variety of approaches using the TxP styles that facilitate their growth and development along with advancing the treatment process. In a situation with an adult who has never resolved Erikson's stages, the TxP allows you to join with the client who are in those stages and use reparental moments to bring them forward into the present.

Summary

The value of the IMM tool is that it reveals the childhood attachment patterns with parental attachment figure(s). Children similarly develop IWMs about the nature of intimate relationships. The internalized couple/marital relationship attachment styles are learned based on parental attitudes, behaviors, and their emotional experience from childhood that simultaneously influence the child/adolescent's experience of their parental figures as a couple and incorporates this as part of their emotional development.

The combination of early emotional, cognitive, and behavioral experiences with parental attachment figures creates a unique IWM for attachment bonds as children, adolescents, and young adults. Consequently, the young adult will initially bring his/her/their combined attachment bonds into his/her/their romantic and intimate relationships.

Attachment bonds and experiences can promote the development of secure patterns of attachment or contribute to insecure or disorganized attachments in adult life. The FCM tool is foundational to the identification of childhood attachment patterns, couple interaction styles, family attachment scripts, and social bonds within a broad community. The focus for the individual is determining how they developed his/her/their particular disorganized childhood attachment patterns within the family attachment scripts.

Notes

1 The Adult Attachment Interview requires an intensive training process (Steele, Steele, & Croft, 2008).
2 The GFG and the Attachments Focused Genogram are included in *Focused Genograms, 2nd edition*.
3 The FCM can be applied differentially for individuals, couples, families, and communities using the specific attachment mapping symbols.

References

Boszormenyi-Nagy, I., & Spark, G. M. (1973). Invisible loyalties: reciprocity in intergenerational family therapy. Hagerstown, MD: Harper & Row.

Bowlby, J. (1969). *Attachment and loss: Volume 1. Attachment*. New York, NY: Basic Books.

Bowlby, J. (1973). *Attachment and loss: Volume 2. Separation: Anxiety and anger*. New York, NY: Basic Books.

Main, M., & Hesse, E. (1990). Parents' unresolved traumatic experiences are related to infant disorganized attachment status: Is frightened and/or frightening parental behavior the linking mechanism? In M. T. Greenberg, D. Cicchetti, & E. M. Cummings (Eds.), *Attachment in the preschool years: Theory, research and intervention* (pp. 161-182). Chicago, IL: University of Chicago Press.

Main, M., & Solomon, J. (1986). Discovery of an insecure-disorganized/disoriented attachment pattern. In T. B. Brazelton & M. W. Yogman (Eds.), *Affective development in infancy* (pp. 95-124). Westport, CT: Ablex Publishing.

Main, M., & Solomon, J. (1990). Procedures for identifying infants as disorganized/disoriented during the Ainsworth strange situation. *Attachment in the Preschool Years: Theory, Research and Intervention, 1*, 121-160.

Mikulincer, M., & Shaver, P. R. (2005). Attachment theory and emotions in close relationships: Exploring the attachment related dynamics of emotional reactions to relational events. *Personal Relationships, 12*(2), 149-168.

Steele, H., Steele, M., & Croft, C. (2008). Early attachment predicts emotion recognition at 6 and 11 years old. *Attachment and Human Development, 10*, 379-393.

van IJzendoorn, M. H., & Bakermans-Kranenburg, M. J. (2019). Bridges across the Intergenerational Transmission of Attachment Gap. *Current opinion in psychology, 25*, 31-36.

Weeks, G. R., & Wright, L. (1979). Dialectics of the family life cycle. *The American Journal of Family Therapy, 7*(1), 85-91.

Answer Key

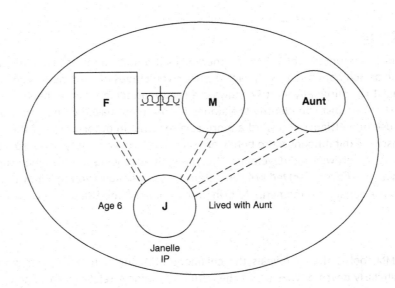

Janelle's Key:

Janelle: Avoidant – Parents remarry when Janelle is 16; When she is 17, she leaves home
Mother: Avoidant
Father: Disorganized/Unpredictable (Divorces Janelle's Mother – divorce indicated by line)
Aunt: Avoidant

6 The Couple Domain
The Couple Interaction Map, the Couple Flow, and the Interplay of Attachment Bonds

Overview

The Couple Interaction Map (CIM) was first developed by DeMaria (DeMaria & Hannah, 2004) and then was further developed in *Focused Genograms*, 2nd edition (DeMaria, Weeks, & Twist, 2017). This chapter focuses on the CIM and the Relationships Timeline. The CIM provides a method to identify both the underlying childhood attachment patterns for each partner along with their individual adult attachment styles. Relational challenges are a reality of committed couples that emerge from their unique relationships as well as their family-of-origin (FOO) influences. The CIM illustrates the progression of the Couple Interaction Infinity Loop (the Loop) within which each partner's IWM is illustrated by the IMMs. We explain steps 1–10 of the Loop moving from the observed adult attachment styles to the childhood attachment patterns as emotional distress intensifies the actions of the Loop.

The goal of the CIM is to help the clinician identify and explore the defensive interaction patterns observed in the Loop, which are driven by each partner's attachment insecurities. The CIM is also a guide to developing a comprehensive systemic view of intergenerational factors, which are part of the contemporary family system. We begin with a description of how intergenerational transmission of attachment influences each couple's adult attachment styles. In particular, the CIM shows the interplay of adult attachment styles that evolve into the adult attachment interaction patterns in the primary couple relationship.

Objectives

1   Discuss the adult attachment interaction styles within the couple dynamic in the Loop and imagine how the couple could attain Couple Flow (Exercise 6.1).
2   Describe the influence that family attachment scripts have on a couple's relationship using the CIM (Exercise 6.2).

The CIM: The Heart of the Family

The Loop highlights how the adult attachment interaction patterns emerge within the couple dynamic. The CIM provides practitioners a method for understanding the couple's relational dynamics, which will help reveal cognitive, emotional, and behavioral patterns of their interpersonal functioning. The value of the CIM in couples therapy is that it not only describes the interacting adult attachment styles, but that it simultaneously helps the therapist determine which childhood attachment patterns are more primary in the couple relationship (i.e., mother, father, or other). Identifying and responding to the IMMs are key in untangling the Loop in order to facilitate more effective bonding and strengthening secure attachment.

Figure 6.1 illustrates the Loop that is the negative interaction pattern between the couple in therapy. The ten steps of the Loop are introduced in more detail in the next section.

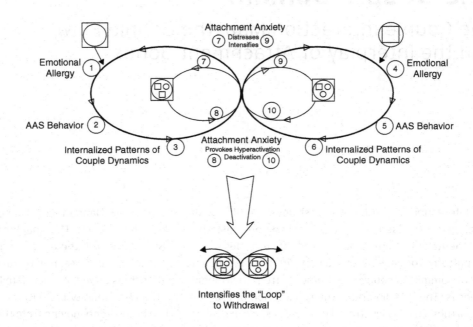

10 Steps to Emotional Disconnection and Insecure Attachment

Figure 6.1 Couple Interaction Map.

The CIM is a method that guides the therapist's attention to the process by which the couple interaction patterns emerge. As the patterns become evident, the therapist will be able to assess secure, dismissive, preoccupied, or disoriented (adult) attachment styles. Assuming that the therapist obtained preliminary information about the family background and childhood relationships with parental attachment figures for each partner, the clinician will slowly begin to recognize the childhood attachment patterns in action within the negative interaction infinity loop. To review, ambivalent attachment is marked by high anxiety and low avoidance, pursuit, and insecurity in the relationship. These individuals are afraid of rejection and become dependent and often clingy but do not allow vulnerability in the relationship – proximity is desired but emotional openness is unreliable and consequently unsatisfying. Those with avoidant attachment usually show low anxiety and high avoidance, and move away from their primary attachment figure, rather than move toward that person for connection, closeness, reassurance, and encouragement.

Disorganized childhood attachment patterns are more complex, and, in particular, with disorganized family styles, there are four variable types of disorganized patterns. Disorganized attachment often escalates very quickly within the negative couple interaction patterns. While there are various forms, histories of abuse, violence and/or trauma are challenging for many clinicians as they are typically complicated and difficult to connect with the therapist. Often, a partner in need who has a form of disoriented attachment initiates a request for connection and reassurance using demanding and simultaneously dismissing behavior. The other partner's response is often unlikely to soothe the disoriented partner. These couples can be distinguished by high levels of conflict that is chronic and difficult to resolve.

Introducing the Ten Steps to Emotional Disconnection and Couple Distress

The purpose of the CIM is not only to track couple process, which would be useful in and of itself. It is also an attachment-based tool for understanding how emotional allergies trigger conflict and/or abandonment for each partner. Understanding the CIM allows the clinician to follow the steps that are linked to the intergenerational transmission of attachment from an individual's childhood into their couple relationship(s) as an adult. A consequence is that children observe and experience how the parental figures interacted with one other in secure or insecure ways. Therefore, the new couple with children is likely then, to transmit such attachment patterns to their future children. Isolating the steps in this abstract conceptual process aids in the clinician's case conceptualization and targeted interventions.

The CIM explains how adult attachment styles lead to the formation of the Loop. Though this process is complex and unique for each couple, the CIM provides a specific sequence to follow using the ten steps. These steps have been tested in clinical practice so as to understand the emotional disconnection driven by attachment insecurity. The CIM (Figure 6.1) is presented in practical detail to assist the therapist in describing each client-system's unique relationship.

Identify and follow the CIM through ten steps:

1 Identify initial emotional allergy that activates the Loop for Partner 1.
2 Identify adult attachment style behavioral response to emotional allergy (Partner 1).
3 Identify internalized adult styles of couple dynamics held by Partner 1.
4 Identify emotional allergy that activates the Loop for Partner 2.
5 Identify adult attachment behavioral response to emotional allergy (Partner 2).
6 Identify internalized adult (dismissive or preoccupied) styles of couple dynamics held by Partner 2.

DEEPENING AND TIGHTENING OF THE LOOP THEN...
SWITCHES TO COUPLE'S CHILDHOOD ATTACHMENT

7 Identify Partner 1's deepening experience of emotional vulnerability and fear.
8 Identify Partner 1's childhood IWM to alleviate potential emotional vulnerability.
9 Identify Partner 2's deepening experience of emotional vulnerability and fear.
10 Identify Partner 2's childhood IWM to alleviate potential emotional vulnerability.

THE LOOP WILL CONTINUE TO TIGHTEN...
ENDING IN HOSTILITY AND/OR DETACHMENT
(if Loop is Uninterrupted)

The CIM helps the clinician identify each partner's steps in the Loop, which allows therapeutic opportunities to intervene and disrupt the negative behavioral sequence of the couple by supporting each partner's willingness to be open and vulnerable. This process allows the clinician to assist each partner's expression of unmet emotional needs as well as difficult and sensitive emotional needs. If either partner experiences hyperactivation or deactivation, an opportunity may become available to the therapist to help guide the partners to connect with their unmet childhood needs for emotional connection and physical affection, and be of help to the couple in their efforts for reconnection.

Couple Flow: Affect Regulation, Emotional Openness, and Physical Affection

What happens when the Loop is dismantled? The therapist has an opportunity to create an experience of Couple Flow for the partners (Figure 6.2).

Emotional responsiveness is the key to reinforcing the development of secure couple bonds. Couple Flow is a term we use to describe positive couple interactions that undo the Loop and lead to a Flow, that represents

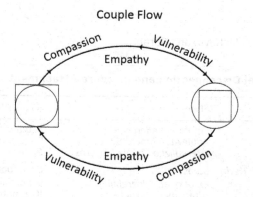

Figure 6.2 Couple Flow.

a positive state of emotion. Flow is a term developed by Csikszentmihalyi (2008) and is considered a mental state that occurs when one is engaged, immersed, and absorbed in an activity, like an intimate relationship. The application of the experience of flow for couples provides a progressive and positive development model for secure and more pleasureable couple relationships. Cultivating a positive intimate couple bond provides an expansive variety of benefits from stress reduction to increased optimism (Kumashiro & Sedikides, 2005). In order for couples to maintain confidence in their abilities to handle and address vulnerability within their relationship, each partner must feel confident in his/her/their ability to convey empathy. In addition, the couple must believe that the various challenges in the relationship are surmountable.

Sheets (2014) explored passionate love and self-expansion over the life cycle and found that some couples were motivated to seek personal growth experience. The findings suggested that couples who sought self-expansion reported more desire, attraction, and sensuality than those couples who were less inclined toward self-expansion for themselves or their partners. The development of Couple Flow as a therapeutic goal is an important consideration for many clinicians. While resolving relationship dysfunction is the first step in treatment, promoting relationship fulfillment that leads to personal satisfaction and self-expansion is also a growing consideration for many. Lastly, Couple Flow provides a model that is congruent with trends in positive psychology, wellness, and mindfulness.

Example of a Clinical Vignette of a CIM: Kevin and Sarah

Kevin and Sarah are a couple who have been married for 10 years and have no children. They presented for therapy because Kevin was threatening to leave Sarah, stating that he "could not figure out how to please her in any part of their relationship and was tired of feeling like a failure".

Their couple interaction can be observed using the ten steps, without intervention from the therapist, as an exercise in understanding their attachment patterns, conflict style, and communication, as well as myriad other emotional, behavioral, and psychological pieces of them as individuals and as a couple (Figure 6.3).

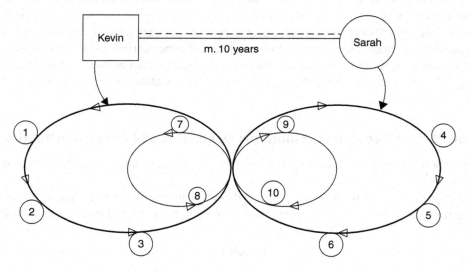

Figure 6.3 Clinical Example of a CIM: Kevin and Sarah.

Key: Ten Steps to Emotional Disconnection and Insecure Attachment		
Adult Attachment Style – Kevin	*Steps*	*Adult Attachment Style – Sarah*
1. Lonely and Hurt	*Emotional Allergy*	4. Blamed and Angry
2. Pursues – Preoccupied	*Adult Attachment Style*	5. Rejecting – Dismissive
3. Attempts Connection	*Internalized Couple Patterns*	6. Disappointed and Isolates
Childhood Attachment Patterns – Kevin	*Steps*	*Childhood Attachment Patterns – Sarah*
7. Sad and Fear	*Emotional Vulnerability*	9. Loneliness and Fear
8. Emotional Hyperactivity	*Attachment Anxiety*	10. Emotional Deactivation

Description of the Ten Steps

Step 1: Identify initial emotional allergy (Partner 1)
Kevin says to Sarah, "You make me feel like there's nothing you want from me and I can't do anything right."

Step 2: Identify adult attachment behavioral response to emotional allergy (Partner 1)
Kevin's adult attachment style is preoccupied (anxious, ambivalent). He is pursuing a connection with Sarah by telling her what he feels is wrong, and probably wishes for comfort and reassurance that he is worthy in the relationship.

Step 3: Identify internalized patterns of couple dynamics held by Partner 1
Kevin's internalized pattern of the couple dynamic is such that he reaches out and gets shut down. He will make these statements about his dissatisfaction, and remain dissatisfied because of Sarah's response. His presentation to therapy gives a clue that he has had these interactions many times and is unsure of how to change the pattern on his own.
We do not yet know whether Sarah will deny, deflect, reject, or shut down, which is her part of the Loop at this time.

Step 4: Identify emotional allergy triggered for Partner 2
When Kevin says, "You make me feel…" Sarah immediately gets angry and defensive. She responds with "I don't MAKE you feel anything! You do this to yourself. You're impossible to be married to." She feels attacked and blamed.

Step 5: Identify adult attachment behavioral response to emotional allergy (Partner 2)
Sarah's adult attachment style is dismissive. She deflects participation in Kevin's bid for connection by dismissing his feelings, instead of validating them.

Step 6: Identify internalized patterns of couple dynamics held by Partner 2
Sarah has internalized the couple pattern as dissatisfying, too. She dismisses or rejects Kevin because she does not understand that he is looking for a connection and does not believe that they can connect if she makes herself vulnerable to him. She feels isolated in this relationship.

DEEPENING AND TIGHTENING OF THE LOOP: THE SWITCH TO CHILDHOOD ATTACHMENT

Step 7: Identify Partner 1's deepening experience of emotional vulnerability and fear.
Sarah's response to Kevin initiates his deepening experience of emotional vulnerability because he did not get connected to her. He is fearful that he is a failure, that the relationship will end, and that he will be alone and not loved.

Step 8: Identify Partner 1's childhood IWM to alleviate potential emotional vulnerability.
Kevin's IMM shows that his IWM with his mother was anxious. Kevin initially had reported that he felt quite close with his mother, but further exploration of his IWM indicated that he felt he constantly had to earn her affection growing up and that she would criticize him when he failed at anything, large or small.

Step 9: Identify Partner 2's deepening experience of emotional vulnerability and fear.
Sarah's experience of emotional vulnerability and fear arise from her fear of being abandoned. She is afraid to become vulnerable and connected because she fears that she will be hurt by Kevin when he does not meet her needs, especially now that he is threatening to leave the marriage.

Step 10: Identify Partner 2's childhood IWM to alleviate potential emotional vulnerability.
Sarah's IMM reveals that her IWM with her father and stepfather were both avoidant. Further investigation during the initial session had revealed that her father was emotionally detached and largely absent after the divorce when she was 8. Following that relationship, Sarah was unable to trust her stepfather, and they settled into an emotionally distant relationship as well.

THE LOOP CONTINUES TO TIGHTEN,
ENDING IN HOSTILITY AND/OR DETACHMENT

This example illustrates how the CIM is informed by both childhood attachment patterns (illustrated by the IMM) and the adult attachment styles (that depict the insecure attachment driven interaction patterns in couple relationships). Consequently, the CIM provides a practical method for conceptualizing how relational partners interact with each other and how, based on their IMM, these insecure attachment styles foster the development and maintenance of the Loop.

Exercise 6.1 The CIM and the "Ten Steps to Emotional Disconnection and Insecure Attachment"

Directions: In the space below, please describe how you would apply the CIM tool to a clinical case of your own. Begin by predicting each partner's adult attachment styles with each other and then each partner's childhood attachment patterns. As the Loop tightens describe how these dynamics have impacted the adult couple relationship. Finally, imagine how the couple instead arrives at Couple Flow.

Partner 1:

_____

_____

Partner 2:

_____

_____

Describe the couples' Loop as you understand it:

_____

_____

_____

Imagine how they get to Couple Flow:

_____

_____

_____

The Relationship Experiences Timeline

Couple and marital relationships have a developmental progression that is unique to their relationship. Several authors have attended to this developmental relational experience (Campbell, 1990; Monte, 1989; Scarf, 1980; Harrar & DeMaria, 2007; Kovacs, 2007). The timeline is very important for helping couples identify where, when, and how their relationships faced intense conflict, trauma, loss, and a range of other life issues.

Clinical Application of the Relationships Experiences Timeline

The clinician begins by drawing a horizontal line at the base of the CIM (or another genogram) genogram to note the developmental milestones and deviations from what is typically normative. Be sure to include attachment abuse, trauma, or breaches in past relationships as these are essential for weighing the impact of adolescent relationship experiences. Life traumas and losses during adult development also have an impact on destabilizing internalized childhood attachment experiences.

Exploring the Relationship Experiences Timeline

The Relationship Experiences Timeline is often overlooked in clinical practice, but is important to the understanding of the developmental phases of the relationship, as well as any crises that may have occurred. Contextual information about the relationship that is provided during the timeline construction may not otherwise be revealed. The timeline can contribute to key details in the case conceptualization.

Relationship Experiences Timeline Questions:

- Adolescent relationship experiences?
- Previous partners – committed, uncommitted, marriage(s)?
- Early sexual experience(s)?
- With current partner: First kiss? First fight? First sleepover? First weekend together?
- First meet his/her parents?
- Meet friends? Breakup? Engagement?

Example of Integrating the CIM and Relationship Experiences

John and Maria have come in for couple's therapy because of chronically unresolved conflicts and emotional disconnection.

The following questions will guide you to understand the process of developing a CIM and timeline:

1 What relationships are you primarily interested when considering their IMMs?
    Answer: Each of them with their parental figures or other significant caregivers.
2 What are some significant events you may screen for when making their timeline?
    Answer:
    Examples:
    - *Milestones in parental relationship (new siblings, divorce, remarriage)*
    - *Dating relationships and breakups*
    - *Marriages and divorces*
    - *Unwanted sexual experiences*
    - *When they met, became intimate (their definition), and became engaged/married if applicable*
    - *Any children they may have*
3 What attachment dynamics will you focus on when making their CIM?
    Answer:
    Describe *the dynamics they witnessed between their parents.*
    - *The nature of their relationship with their "primary caregiver" with whom they identify most closely (we argue that this will be the same-gender parent in MOST cases with two heterosexual parents)*
    - *The nature of their relationship with their "supporting caregiver" (we argue that this will be the opposite-gender parent in MOST cases with two heterosexual parents)*
4 *What sets off the CIM for a couple? How will you find that out?*
    Answers:
    Emotional allergies for both partners
    - *How their reactions feed into one another's emotional allergies*
    - *Maladaptive behaviors for seeking safety and/or connection energize FOO experiences with their parental-couple attachment dance*

Analysis of the CIM

This section presents another clinical example, of John and Maria, to illustrate how the CIM is constructed using the information presented by both partners and interpreted by the therapist.

Case Presentation of John and Maria

John describes his feelings towards Maria as love and lust, while she describes her feelings towards John as strained. John cheated on Maria because he felt rejected by her, and then he asked for forgiveness. Maria admits that there were times in the relationship when she felt cold towards him because she felt he was not supportive.

(Note: family background will be provided in the analysis).

Situational Event described by client-system:

- *John makes an advance towards Maria, but she is not in the mood or not feeling supported at the time, so she refuses in what she thinks is a neutral way.*
- *John feels triggered by this rejection and asks how long she expects to shut him out for.*
- *Maria responds by saying that she can't just let him back in when he's betrayed her so obviously. She says she needs support.*
- *John says that he can't support her if she won't let him near her.*
- *She says that all he wants is sex and there's no way he's getting that from her.*
- *He says that's not true.*
- *She says, "Yes it is or you wouldn't have slept with someone else. What am I not good enough?"*
- *John says, "Of course you are."*
- *Maria, crying, says, "Don't come near me."*
- *Their Loop has tightened.*
- *Maria gets up and goes to the bathroom.*

Next, we modify the scenario above by including John and Maria's FOO as seen below:

John's FOO	Maria's FOO
John identified with his dad. Growing up, they were buddies, and as John got older, he was allowed to accompany his father to outings. John says he can remember times when there were other women around, but never saw his dad do anything suspicious. He never suspected that his dad might cheat, but inexplicably, his parents got divorced when he turned 18 and left the house. They had never fought in front of him, but were also not very affectionate toward one another. John loved his mother and knew his mother loved him, but they never had what he would call a "close-knit bond".	Maria's father and mother divorced when she was 5. She remained in contact with her father, but describes that relationship as disconnected. She was close with her mother until she remarried her stepfather when Maria was 12. At that time, Maria was going through puberty and wished her mom would have been there for her instead of focusing on having another baby with her new stepdad. Maria does not remember her parents fighting before they got divorced, and said that her mother and stepfather are affectionate.
Note: Secure with dad, ambivalent with Mom. Mom and dad were dismissive and preoccupied as adults, respectively.	*Note: Secure with mom and avoidant with both dads. There was an attachment rupture at age 12 which may have added an avoidant element to the relationship with Mom.*

Exercise 6.2 Case Presentation of John and Maria including FOO and CIM

Directions: Using the added background from John and Maria's FOO, describe below, the influence family attachment scripts have on a couple's relationship using the CIM and the Loop.

_____

_____

_____

_____

Returning to the case presentation above, and perhaps you have already noted, John and Maria's emotional allergies are more evident in their negative emotional interaction patterns. The interplay of each partner's relational and behavioral patterns indicate that their relationship disconnections led them to this particular place in their marriage. Next, we will explore the Loop above, to see how our understanding is enhanced.

The scenario continues: *John makes an advance towards Maria, but she is not "in the mood" or not feeling supported at the time, so she refuses in what she thinks is a neutral way. - (We know that not being supported is an emotional allergy for Maria, especially when she feels vulnerable and alone.)*

John feels triggered by this rejection and asks how long she expects to shut him out. - (We knew that John was triggered by rejection, but the added dimension of wanting to be closer with his mother may add to the strength of this emotional allergy.)

Maria responds by saying that she can't just let him back in when he's betrayed her so obviously. She says she needs support. - (Asking for what she needs may be a sign of Maria's secure relationship with her mother, however, her mother's emotional abandonment during puberty may be triggered here. Also, her relationship with her father may have influenced her to not trust that John will be there for her.)

John says that he can't support her if she won't let him near her - (John is unsure how to act due to his parents' abrupt dissolution of their marriage. In his ambivalent bond with his mother, he also didn't know how to act to get the love he wanted. He is hyperactivating here with Maria.

She says that all he wants is sex and there's no way he's getting that from her. - Maria is in full avoidant mode now, shutting down, feeling isolated, and self-protective.)

John says, "That's not true." - (This is both hyperactivating and retreating, ambivalent.)

Maria says, "Yes it is or you wouldn't have slept with someone else. What am I, not good enough?" - (Still Maria is engaged, but barely.)

John says, "Of course you are," moving toward her again. - (Moving towards.)
Maria, crying, says, "Don't come near me." - (Avoidant, and over.)

Their Loop has tightened. Maria gets up and goes to the bathroom.

Exploring the Interplay of Childhood Attachment Patterns and Adult Attachment Styles

Attachment theory suggests that insecure attachment patterns developed in childhood are malleable in adult love relationships and the couple relationship can establish a milieu for emotional healing and growth (Cowan & Cowan, 2005). Mikulincer and Shaver (2005, 2012), among others, have emphasized the role of adult relationships in mediating and enhancing secure attachment in couple relationships. Unfortunately, significant trauma in life without sufficient emotional support in adulthood can have a negative impact on secure attachment or reinforce insecure attachment, leading to repeating intergenerational transmission of insecure attachments.

The foundation of secure attachment is based on both partners looking toward each other when in distress. Attachment security rests on connection, or what is referred to as proximity seeking. In addition, the attachment behavioral system is distinct from the caregiving behavioral system (Mikulincer & Shaver, 2012). The need for proximity under stress is a feature of attachment while the need for empathy and support when a partner is vulnerable is a feature of caregiving. Caregiving is a different dimension of the couple bond which can be defined as a nurturing physical and emotional bond. When a couple begins an intimate relationship, the quality of both the attachment experience and the emotional and physical nurturing responsiveness creates a powerful pair-bond. The experience of a healthy romantic love relationship helps couples strengthen their attachment bond and move toward a more secure attachment style. Sexuality, when the chemistry of romantic love is developing, fosters a unique sexual bond.

Our hypothesis is that there are primary and secondary defensive interaction patterns within the Loop. The primary defensive interaction pattern is typically a reflection of a partner's overall adult attachment style, typically related to a parental adult attachment style. The secondary defensive interaction pattern taps into a childhood longing for safety, comfort, and availability. The Loop is often initiated when one partner has an emotional or physical need, which establishes a level of vulnerability for that partner. As the vulnerable partner seeks the other partner for comfort, the other partner may or may not provide comfort, the vulnerable partner will either become physiologically activated or deactivated as the vulnerable partners seeks comfort from the other partner. If emotionally and physically willing to reach out to the other partner, the vulnerable partner is likely to request comfort. In this scenario, the vulnerable partner will attempt to express feelings of sadness and even fear. If the other partner is open and willing to respond to the vulnerable partner, then comfort may be established. If comfort is not established, then attachment anxiety increases for the anxious-ambivalent partner, who is likely to be insistent or even demanding about the need for comfort. In contrast, if the anxious-avoidant partner is less likely to request comfort, then the vulnerable partner may even withdraw emotionally and physically. In either situation, the Loop prevails and begins to tighten until one or both partners abandon the other emotionally.

Typically secure couples are able to maintain a level of emotional flow for vulnerability, compassion and problem-solving. In contrast, insecure couples with high anxiety are likely to engage in negative communication patterns that may escalate. Insecure couples with high avoidance minimize communication and connection. Then there are the mixed secure-insecure couples, which experience other variations of the Loop. Insecure attachment styles of each partner intensify with experiences of empathic failures, misunderstandings, and conflicts over differences. When insecure IWM prevails, the partners typically do not have the physical, emotional, and verbal skills to establish an emotionally and physically safe relationship with each other. Each partner's insecure IWM influences the other's attitudes, feelings, and behaviors. Even if both partners have more secure attachment styles, as conflict escalates, most couples become engaged in the "negative emotional infinity loop" (DeMaria & Hannah, 2003; Gordon, 1994). The Loop undermines both attachment and caregiving bonds. Assessing the patterns of interaction within the Loop is the foundation for developing what we term the Couple Interaction Infinity Loop (the Loop), which is used in the CIM. Repetitive experiences of the Loop of defensive interaction patterns in the couple relationship interfere with attachment and caregiving behaviors.

We propose that defensive interaction patterns are fueled by one or more "emotional allergies." Emotional allergies can be referred to as "triggers" that cause "emotional flooding." However, the use of the term emotional allergies is more descriptive than that of a "trigger." Emotional allergies activate emotional reactivity. Emotional allergies are hypersensitive reactions to physical stimuli with specific antibodies. Within the limbic system is a complex part of the brain where instincts are directed toward physical safety and protection. Painful and other traumatic emotional memories, conscious or unconscious, stimulate the development of emotional allergies. These emotional allergies, much like physical allergies, are physiologically motivated and thus are the stimulus for the Loop (reminder - negative *emotional* infinity loop).

As mentioned, the primary defensive interaction pattern presented by a partner is likely to be representative of that partner's primary childhood attachment patterns, which is typically with the same-gender parent for insecure partners (Mikulincer & Florian, 1998). If the partner in need, who has a secure IWM then initiates contact, as the other partner responds with compassion then this couple will likely experience Couple Flow, defined as a continuous loop of caring, support, affection, and responsiveness. On the other hand, an insecure partner in need will stimulate the beginning of the Loop in either typical ambivalent attachment style or typical avoidant style. The other partner's response may be compassionate (caregiving), an expression of physical comfort (physical presence in proximity), dismissing (avoidant response - "you'll be fine in the morning") or preoccupied (ambivalent response - I will "fix" this for you let's do x, y, z). The response by the other partner determines the escalation or de-escalation of the Loop.

The insecure partner in need may yet be met with compassion and affection, however, if stress increases and/or conflict intensifies, then the secondary defensive interaction patterns will begin to be enacted. These secondary defensive interaction patterns are defined as hyperactivating and deactivating attachment strategies and result from failure to respond to the need for connection (Mikulincer & Shaver, 2005). Hyperactivating strategies are common for people who tend to score high on attachment anxiety who then seek connection, closeness, affirmation, and support from their current primary attachment figure. In contrast, deactivating strategies are common for people who tend to score high on avoidance.

Summary

This chapter introduced and detailed the steps for the CIM, illustrating the interplay of childhood and adult attachment experiences in the couple relationship. The Loop is an interaction pattern that can be identified in the couples' relationship during any given therapy session. Using the ten steps, therapists can diagram the Loop as couples engage in preoccupied or dismissive ways, or even disorganized patterns. The goal of the CIM is to delineate the emotional, behavioral, and psychological makeup of this negative interaction pattern and its derivatives from attachment experiences. An example was provided, as in the case of John and Maria above, as well as some background on the terms of attachment, emotional allergies, and the Loop.

Using the CIM has two important functions for the practitioners. First, it depicts the couples' relationship dynamics as influenced by the IWM of each partner's parental attachment figures, which focuses on defensive interaction patterns that inhibit empathy, compassion, and support that fosters more secure connection. Second, the IWM of each partner influences, and is influenced by, each partners' past and present relationship experiences.

The focus of this chapter is on operationalizing the CIM and Relationship Experiences Timeline during the early phases of treatment through collaboration with the couple as treatment begins. After the CIM has been addressed the practitioner can then move into each partner's Relationships Timeline experiences. Through clinical application, exercises, and a theoretical analysis and explanation, this workbook we have provided has ample practice and background for clinicians at any level to integrate this groundbreaking tool into their practice.

References

Campbell, J. D. (1990). Self-esteem and clarity of the self-concept. *Journal of Personality and Social Psychology, 59*(3), 538-549.

Cowan, C. P., & Cowan, P. A. (2005). Two central roles for couple relationships: Breaking negative intergenerational patterns and enhancing children's adaptation. *Sexual and Relationship Therapy, 20*(3), 275-288.

Csikszentmihalyi, M. (2008). *Flow: The psychology of optimal experience.* New York, NY: Harper Perennial Modern Classics.

DeMaria, R., & Hannah, M. T. (2003). *Building intimate relationships: Bridging treatment, education, and enrichment.* New York, NY: Brunner/Mazel.

DeMaria, R., Weeks, G. R., & Twist, M. L., (2017). *Focused genograms: Intergenerational assessment of individuals, couples, and families.* New York, NY: Routledge.

Gordon, L. H. (1994). *PAIRS curriculum guide and training manual.* Falls Church, VA: PAIRS Foundation. Retrieved February 9, 2005, from http://pairs.com/ln/downloads/pairstrainingbookonline.pdf

Harrar, S., & DeMaria, R. (2007). *The 7 stages of marriage: Laughter, intimacy and passion today, tomorrow and forever.* Pleasantville, NY: Reader's Digest Association.

Kovacs, L. (2007). *Building a reality-based relationship: The six stages of modern marriage.* Lincoln, NE: iUniverse.

Kumashiro, M., & Sedikides, C. (2005). Taking on board liability-focused information: Close positive relationships as a self-bolstering resource. *Psychological Science, 16*(9), 732-739.

Monte, E. P. (1989). The relationship life cycle. In G. R. Weeks (Ed.), *Treating couples* (pp. 287-316). New York, NY: Brunner/Mazel.

Mikulincer, M., & Florian, V. (1998). The relationship between adult attachment styles and emotional and cognitive reactions to stressful events. In J. A. Simpson & W. S. Rholes (Eds.), *Attachment theory and close relationships* (pp. 143-165). New York: Guilford Press.

Mikulincer, M., & Shaver, P. R. (2005). Attachment theory and emotions in close relationships: Exploring the attachment-related dynamics of emotional reactions to relational events. *Personal Relationships, 12*(2), 149-168.

Mikulincer, M., & Shaver, P. R. (2012). An attachment perspective on psychopathology. *World Psychiatry, 11*(1), 11-15.

Scarf, M. (1980). *Unfinished business: Pressure points in the lives of women.* Garden City, NY: Doubleday.

Sheets, V. L. (2014). Passion for life: Self-expansion and passionate love across the life span. *Journal of Social and Personal Relationships, 31*(7), 958-974.

7 The Intergenerational Domain
The Family Connections Map

Overview

The intergenerational domain is the bedrock for systemic assessment. Using the meta-framework of the Intersystem Approach (IA) provides a path for creating an integrative attachment-based framework for developing a comprehensive approach that encourages exploration of the intergenerational transmission of attachment. The Family Connections Map (FCM) allows for the identification of differentiated disorganized childhood patterns and adult styles. The intergenerational domain provides two maps: (1) a traditional Family Map (notably used in Structural Family Therapy) and (2) the FCM. Family timelines allow for a family life chronology that identifies important considerations for understanding the impact of family life events. Exploring family events focuses on childhood attachment wounds, adult relationship injuries, and intergenerational traumas. A unique feature of the FCM, which is based on Olson's (2011) Circumplex Model – FACES IV, resulted in a new clinical focus for disorganized attachment that identifies four types of disorganized attachment styles. With these tools, clinicians can assess the contemporary family system and the family of origin at any point in its history, as well as recognizing their effects on the patterns and processes during attachment-focused treatment. The goal for the intergenerational domain focuses on the application and use of the tools in the assessment process, with the aim of revealing intergenerational attachment scripts as they exist in the presenting client-system.

Objectives

- Illustrate the use of a Basic Family Map and the companion FCM for determining an individual client's attachment style (Exercise 7.1).
- Apply the FCM to a client-system or use your family to answer the ten questions on flexibility and connection for the FCM (Exercise 7.2).
- Draw a timeline identifying key attachment experiences for the client-system from early development through age 14 based on the Attachments FG.

The Basic Family Map

The Basic Family Map provides a traditional family assessment that uses symbols based on a variety of terms developed by family therapy pioneers. The Bowen Multigenerational Family Systems model (Bowen, 1978) is well known for its application of a traditional pedigree format for genograms, which also uses symbols to depict relational patterns between and among the members of an intergenerational client-system. Other models, which apply similar formats for developing genograms, abound. For example, Satir's transformational systemic therapy (Banmen, 2002) used a genogram format as a process for beginning work with family members, and Minuchin's (1974) approach to genograms used a structural format for mapping dynamics with a family system. *Focused Genograms* (FG1) (1999) was the first organized approach to developing and using FGs, family maps, and family timelines that also included attention to attachment theory. Developing a family map begins in a simple manner and reveals important clinical information. The clinician has a variety of options, which include paper and pencil, software, and use of charts and graphs; squares are used to denote males and circles are used to denote females; however, more fluid gender identities can be expressed using other shapes, that is, squares inside circles, or the new gender diversity symbol included in *Focused Genograms, 2nd Edition* (FG2).

FG2 (DeMaria, Weeks, & Twist, 2017) provides a new symbol that denotes a person with a gender diverse identity. This symbol includes all of the following: cisgender female symbol, cisgender male symbol, "transgender" double-sided arrow in the upper left corner symbol, and genderqueer or "gender nonconforming" double-sided arrow with a horizontal bar in the midpoint of the middle symbol (Figure 7.1).

To draw familial relationships on the family map, keep in mind the client-system's attachment information ascertained from the construction of the Internal Models Map (IMM) (see Chapter 5 for details on the IMM). For some clients, fictive kin will be important family members; for others, parents and children will be the members included within the IMM. The IMM shows an individual client's relationships with his/her/their primary attachment figures. Typically, this is a mother and father figure, but often could be a stepparent, grandparent, godparent, or any other caregiving figure.

The identification of the client's attachment relationships with each family member is important to understand his/her/their adult attachment styles and their influence on the presenting problem. This information will also help you connect with them, using the appropriate Therapeutic Posture (TxP). Each attachment relationship can be noted using the appropriate attachment symbols (figures below). If you are drawing a Family Map snapshot of a time in the adult client's childhood, use the childhood attachment pattern symbols. If you are drawing a contemporary Family Map of a client's current family relationships, use the adult attachment style symbols. We provide questions to begin to assess these relational dynamics (Figures 7.2-7.3).

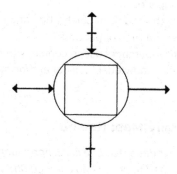

Figure 7.1 Gender Diversity Symbol.

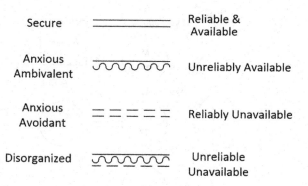

Figure 7.2 Mapping Symbols: Childhood Attachment Patterns.

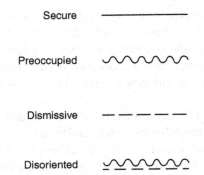

Secure   ——————

Preoccupied   ∿∿∿∿∿

Dismissive   — — — —

Disoriented   ∿∿∿∿∿

Figure 7.3 Mapping Symbols: Adult Attachment Styles.

Exploring Family Functioning: Family Dynamics and Family Connections

Whom would you list as the most important people in your family system? This can include very close family friends who might also be considered family.

1   What are the ways in which people express both positive and negative emotions?
2   How do family members provide support, security, and encouragement to one another?
3   What are the patterns of time spent together?
4   What kinds of established alliances, coalitions, and cutoffs exist between and among family members?
5   Do people in your family respond quickly to help one another? How? Who reaches out? Does anyone hold back?
6   Describe family beliefs, feelings, and actions with regard to individual uniqueness, needs, motives, and group identity for members of the family.
7   How does the family system celebrate rituals of connection: family meals, rising and retiring, coming and going, going out and going away, couple rituals?
8   How does the family system observe the rituals of celebration and community, such as special person rituals, community and religious rituals, and rites of passage?
9   What abilities and resources do family members use in coping with crises?
10 What are the client-system's (i.e., each individual, marital and/or partnered relationship, family as a unit) links to the wider community?

Clinical Example of a Basic Family Map: Keisha

Keisha lives with her mother, sister, and her daughter. She is 23, her daughter is 3, her sister is 18, and her mother is 54. Keisha's father left when she was 6 and they have no contact. She was also raised by her grandmother, but her grandmother passed away last year at 77, which is what brought Keisha to therapy (grief). Keisha's Family Map is below (Figure 7.4).

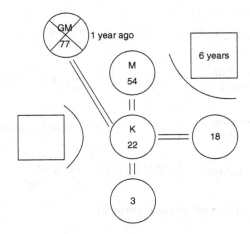

Figure 7.4 Clinical Example: Keisha's Basic Family Map.

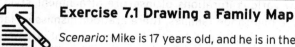

Exercise 7.1 Drawing a Family Map

Scenario: Mike is 17 years old, and he is in therapy because he has been having trouble getting ready to go to college. He seems anxious and depressed and cites fear as his reason for refusing to take the SAT or apply for college, despite good grades. He has an older sister (21 years old), who went to college. He lives with his mother, father, and paternal grandfather who he is especially close with. His mother and father are successful physicians, but they work long and irregular hours. Mike also has a younger brother who is 13 years old, whom he says really looks up to him.

Directions: In blank space below draw Mike's Family Map using the childhood attachment symbols.

The FCM: Exploring Family Attachment Scripts

We developed a specific attachment focused FCM as a new addition to the FG Tool Box, based on the Circumplex Model. The Circumplex Model was first introduced in 1979 by Olson and his associates (1979, 1983) and updated in 2011 (Olson, 2011). Olson's model provides a useful approach to exploring the family/intergenerational domain of the IA because of its emphasis on "relational diagnosis" for couples and families. The Circumplex model is a fluid model that uniquely identifies how family members view their relationships within the family, based on their sense of connection and flexibility within the system at any given point in time (Olson, 2011). There have been over 1,200 studies of this model and its applications in the past 30 years (Olson, 2011). There are two dimensions to the Circumplex Model: Cohesion (originally termed Connection) and Flexibility (originally termed Adaptability), which are comparative with other family assessment models. Olson suggested that Cohesion corresponds to terms such as validation, affection, affective involvement, and affiliation. Flexibility, on the other hand, corresponds to terms such as adaptability, interdependence, capacity to change, dominance/submission, and problem-solving.

The FCM (Table 7.1) reformulated the terms of the Circumplex Model into attachment terms. Attachment styles describe parent-child relationships, and they also explain how intergenerational patterns of attachment are passed on from one generation to the next through the couple relationship (Cowan & Cowan, 2005). Byng-Hall (1995) was among the first to apply Bowlby's attachment theory to intergenerational family patterns, which he termed "scripts." He emphasized the importance of a secure family base and described characteristics of secure and insecure families based on attachment style, calling these patterns attachment scripts. Attachment scripts are the intergenerational patterns that emerge over time and influence the family significantly over time, often without knowledge or understanding from contemporary family members. The intergenerational transmission of attachment styles is a consistent finding in developmental psychology (Bernier & Dozer, 2003).

The FCM identifies 16 family attachment scripts, which highlight the client-system's overarching family/intergenerational attachment narrative. Based on the Circumplex Model of family functioning, the FCM is a guide to identifying relationship resources and needs that may exist within the extended family system. More specifically, the FCM identifies 16 family types ranging from secure to insecure to disorganized attachment scripts, which are identified through specific questions. The FCM provides a method for identifying family styles that influence the client-system.

Incorporating terms from the Circumplex Model and attachment theory, the FCM proposes 16 types of family attachment scripts. Central to the table are four balanced family styles that we identify as secure. Radiating outward from secure, there are eight mid-range family attachment scripts. These will lean toward either preoccupied attachment family scripts or dismissive attachment family scripts as described in Table 7.1, but not least, there are four disorganized scripts in the four corners, reflecting the different combinations of extremes. Next, we explain each type in more detail to allow the clinician to begin to recognize them quickly.

There are four secure family attachment scripts. Secure families are balanced in their connection and flexibility, with some potential variation in one or both dimensions under duress/developmental stress. Most individuals in a secure family will have secure IWMs as well.

In contrast, the eight mid-range families show various iterations of insecure attachment styles as the predominant family attachment script. In these mid-range families, there are four dismissive family attachment scripts that reflect avoidant childhood attachment styles, typified by a parental team that predictably deny, minimize, and/or exhibit miscues of emotional expression and physical affection on a regular basis. There are four preoccupied family attachment scripts that reflect ambivalent childhood attachment patterns, developed through unpredictable patterns of emotional attention but physical availability.

There are four disorganized family attachment scripts that we term as Overinvolved, Unpredictable, Uninvolved, and Controlling. Enmeshed and Disengaged family type descriptors are commonly used in family therapy. We identify enmeshed family members as Overinvolved and disengaged family members as Unpredictable. In contrast, there are rigidly disengaged and rigidly enmeshed families that do not have common terms within the field. We call rigidly disengaged families Uninvolved and rigidly enmeshed families Controlling. Based on our adaptation of the Circumplex Model, these four disorganized attachment scripts are described:

- *Unpredictable*: *Disengaged-chaotic* families are extremely disconnected and extremely flexible, leaving family members to fend for themselves due to unclear rules and roles.
- *Uninvolved*: *Disengaged-rigid* families are extremely disconnected and extremely rigid, leaving family members continually isolated and excessively independent.
- *Overinvolved*: *Enmeshed-chaotic* families are extremely connected and extremely flexible, leaving members feeling suffocated by one another, again because of unclear rules and roles.
- *Controlling*: *Enmeshed-rigid* families are extremely connected and extremely inflexible, such that family members have difficulty with autonomy and self-reliance.

The FCM is particularly useful in understanding the historical family system to discern the origins and presentation of the secure, preoccupied, dismissive, and disorganized attachment scripts for the family system. Determination of the type of disorganized family style is an important aspect of developing TxP because these families present with complex and divergent attachment styles.

Table 7.1 shows the FCM with words in each square explaining the dynamics of each typology. For example, in the first square, the dominant family attachment script is disorganized, that is, the disengaged and chaotic type. We call this Unpredictable.

Cowan and Cowan (2005) highlighted that the couple/parenting relationship is the moderating relationship between the generations. The method that was developed in FG2 for mapping the family system identifies four disorganized family types as part of the FCM, based on their levels of connection and flexibility. Disorganized attachment styles become evident in individual, couple, and family therapy as the

Table 7.1 Family Connections Map with Typology Dynamics

High F L E X I B I L I T Y Low	Disengaged Chaotic **Unpredictable**	Distant Chaotic **Dismissive**	Connected Chaotic **Preoccupied**	Enmeshed Chaotic **Overinvolved**
	Disengaged Flexible **Dismissive**	**Secure**	**Secure**	Enmeshed Flexible **Preoccupied**
	Disengaged Structured **Dismissive**	**Secure**	**Secure**	Enmeshed Structured **Preoccupied**
	Disengaged Rigid **Uninvolved**	Distant Rigid **Dismissive**	Connected Rigid **Preoccupied**	Enmeshed Rigid **Controlling**
	Low	CONNECTION		High

clinician begins to utilize the IMM. If one or both partners have a predominantly disorganized attachment, the family attachment script is likely to reflect one of the four types of disorganized families identified by the FCM.

For example, in a couple's therapy case, one partner exhibited a disorganized attachment style. She was fearful in the presence of people she did not know as well as with her friends. She did not trust anyone because she had been physically and emotionally abused by her parents throughout her entire childhood and adolescence. However, the abuse was not chaotic and unpredictable. Her parents' religious orientation was a justification for the abuse and fostered a more rigid structure. If religious teachings were not followed, the client was punished with shaming and corporal punishment. In this type of rigidly enmeshed family, which we call Controlling, the client both feared and desired connection with her parents. In the couple relationship, she both fears and desires connection with her partner. Simultaneously, the client is rigid in her own lifestyle, with rules about when to wake up, how the house should be, and what she is allowed to do. Consequently, she is terrified of breaking rules and of physical intimacy.

This brief vignette illustrates how the family-of-origin experiences directly affect and promote an intergenerational process for developing a Controlling family attachment script. The vignette also illustrates the interactions between the IMM and the FCM that leads to intergenerational transmission of further disorganized attachment experiences.

FCM Questionnaire and Scoring

To implement the FCM, the clinician will work from the perspective of the clients in the presenting system, keeping in mind that each client may have a distinct way of describing the family dynamics. The goal of the FCM is to understand the family attachment script. In the most basic sense, the clinician can gather information about what it was like growing up in the family to begin to get a feel for the family climate. The clinician can then ask more targeted questions to discover specific attachment dynamics using the two concepts of flexibility and cohesion. Based on these two continua, the clinician can fill in the square which best fits the family attachment script based on the client's reports.

FCM Questionnaire Directions

The therapist can provide a copy of the questions or can simply interview the client(s). State the following:

These questions are to help you think about how close you felt to your mother, father, step parents, grandparents, or other adults in your life when you were growing up. Also think about if all family members felt close to each other or maybe some did and some didn't. It can help to think about what happened if you moved or changed schools or had troubles in your life. Sometimes emotional problems for adults can interfere with them being connected to a child.

For example, in Mel's family, her parents did not get along, and she felt she had to step up and be there for her younger sister when her mom had a breakdown and her dad left. Mel was 13 at the time, and her sister was 10. As a client now, at age 24, Mel recounted this dynamic when asked about her family because she felt that this was a pivotal moment where her family life changed from generally hectic to downright difficult. In gathering more specific information, the therapist discovered high levels of loyalty and dependency between the women in the family, and that the father had been cut off from everyone. Despite the high level of cohesion, the rules and roles in the family were overly flexible to the point where they seemed chaotic. Mel described being unsure of who was really in charge of the family, as she felt burdened to be the parent at times. Because of the lack of supervision due to the trauma her parents suffered as a result of their failing relationship, Mel could do whatever she wanted and often stayed out late in high school. According to all this information, the practitioner could map Mel's family in the Overinvolved corner (enmeshed-chaotic) or one of the preoccupied squares (enmeshed-flexible or connected-chaotic) depending on the specific answers to the questions provided above. This process of assessment may illuminate attachment dimensions that may have otherwise gone unnoticed and can aid in the clinician's understanding of current attachment-based relational behavior.

Flexibility:	Closeness:
Was there someone in charge of the family or were responsibilities shared?	How close do/did you feel to other family members?
1. Leadership is unclear 2. Usually shared 3. Generally shared 4. Sometimes shared 5. One person	1. Not very close 2. Generally close 3. Close 4. Very close 5. Extremely close
How often do/did family members do the same things (roles) around the house?	How often does/did your family spend free time together?
1. Never 2. Sometimes 3. Often 4. Usually 5. Almost always	1. Rarely or never 2. Seldom 3. Sometimes 4. Often 5. Very often
What are/were the rules like in your family?	How does your family balance separateness and togetherness?
1. Unclear and changing 2. Clear and flexible 3. Clear and structured 4. Clear and stable 5. Rules very clear and very stable	1. Mainly separately 2. More separateness than togetherness 3. Equal separateness and togetherness 4. More togetherness than separateness 5. Mainly togetherness
How is/was the discipline of children handled?	How independent of or dependent on the family are/were family members?
1. Very lenient 2. Lenient 3. Democratic 4. Somewhat strict 5. Very strict	1. Very independent 2. More independent than dependent 3. Equally independent and dependent 4. More dependent than independent 5. Very dependent
How open is/was your family to making changes when they are necessary?	How loyal or trustworthy are/were family members to the family?
1. Very open 2. Generally open 3. Somewhat open 4. Seldom open 5. Not open	1. Not very loyal 2. Somewhat loyal 3. Generally loyal 4. Very loyal 5. Extremely loyal

FCM Scoring

Directions: Add the participant's answers in each category (Flexibility and Connection) to arrive at two separate totals between 5 and 25. Next, plot the scores on Table 7.2 FCM Questionnaire Scoring Table. Match the number for Connection with the column in which it is encompassed. Then match the number for Flexibility with the

Table 7.2 FCM Questionnaire Scoring Table

F L E X I B I L I T Y		Disengaged (5-10)	Distant (11-15)	Connected (15-20)	Enmeshed (20-25)
	Chaotic (5-10)	UNPREDICTABLE **Disorganized**	Distant Chaotic **Dismissive**	Connected Chaotic **Preoccupied**	OVERINVOLVED **Disorganized**
	Flexible (11-15)	Disengaged Flexible **Dismissive**	**Secure**	**Secure**	Enmeshed Flexible **Preoccupied**
	Structured (16-20)	Disengaged Structured **Dismissive**	**Secure**	**Secure**	Enmeshed Structured **Preoccupied**
	Rigid (20-25)	UNINVOLVED **Disorganized**	Distant Rigid **Dismissive**	Connected Rigid **Preoccupied**	CONTROLLING **Disorganized**
		C O N N E C T I O N			

Exercise 7.2 Using the FCM

Directions: Provide each client with the ten-question assessment (provided at the end of this chapter). Five questions for flexibility and five for connection allow the client/clinician to obtain a score which he/she or the clinician can plot on the FCM table. The scores from each family member will cluster in one area of the table, showing the family's predominant relational dynamics.

For example, if three family members land in enmeshed-flexible category, one lands in balanced, and one lands in connected-chaotic, the family dynamic is considered primarily enmeshed-flexible, suggesting a predominantly Preoccupied family attachment script.

Where would you place the members of the family you're practicing with? What would be their predominant family attachment script? Circle or shade in that square.

F L E X I B I L I T Y		Disengaged (5-10)	Distant (11-15)	Connected (15-20)	Enmeshed (20-25)
	Chaotic (5-10)	UNPREDICTABLE **Disorganized**	Distant Chaotic **Dismissive**	Connected Chaotic **Preoccupied**	OVERINVOLVED **Disorganized**
	Flexible (11-15)	Disengaged Flexible **Dismissive**	**Secure**	**Secure**	Enmeshed Flexible **Preoccupied**
	Structured (16-20)	Disengaged Structured **Dismissive**	**Secure**	**Secure**	Enmeshed Structured **Preoccupied**
	Rigid (20-25)	UNINVOLVED **Disorganized**	Distant Rigid **Dismissive**	Connected Rigid **Preoccupied**	CONTROLLING **Disorganized**
		C O N N E C T I O N			

row in which it is encompassed. Follow the column down and the row across until they meet – this is the client-system's predominant attachment script.

The FCM Questionnaire provides a method for exploring family dynamics that result in a suggested intergenerational attachment script. Byng-Hall (1995) attempted this type of categorization of family attachment scripts, however, the FG maps provide a structured method based on substantive research on couple and family typologies (Table 7.1).

While the FCM describes the family attachment script, the individual attachment styles may differ from the family attachment script. If one person's score on the FCM is different from the others on the FCM, they will tend to experience the family through a different attachment lens than most other members of the family. For example, there might be a preoccupied member within a primarily dismissive family, which often results due to unique childhood experiences. For example, a child who is ill for an extended period of time may develop a more connected but unreliable attachment bond with the caregiver. If a complete IA assessment takes place (see Chapter 9 for an example), it may be possible to see how individuals in a family with one particular set of dynamics on the FCM style will have different IMMs depending on their experiences with their parents and others.

In understanding the FCM and what it means for any presenting family, the element of time is important. Children can be exposed to one or more family systems depending on life experiences such as single-parent families, extended family, and alternate kinship experiences. For many children/adolescents family life can be variable over time and place. The FCM helps identify the attachment scripts at play within the family system based on parenting patterns that reveal transmission of attachment styles from generation to generation. The Circumplex model also highlights the value of role flexibility through time in family systems, which is important when developing couple and family timelines. Couple and family timelines will illuminate events and/or transitions that might have caused issues in flexibility for families. Finally, with communication as a moderating variable, we suggest that the various TxPs can adapt to these family styles.

Summary

Creating Family Maps, both the Basic Family Map and the FCM, gives the clinician tools to examine relational patterns to establish goals, tasks, and bonds as part of the treatment plan. The FCM is an essential part of the Case Formulation (described in Chapter 9), which includes a complete assessment, including the FCM. Each type of map reveals the impact of (intergenerational) attachment scripts, (couple) interaction patterns, and (individual) childhood attachment styles throughout the client-system. As the practitioner begins to work with the client-system, attention to assessing family relationships, for both the contemporary family of origin[1] and the intergenerational family system, is a way for practitioners to understand the emotional and behavioral strengths and deficits a client-system brings into the treatment setting. As clients bring their personal, relationship, and family stories into treatment the therapist becomes an active participant with the client-system as they identify and explore the family themes.

Note

1 We recommend that clinicians develop a four-generation genogram to highlight multiple generational themes for those whose family roots are more recent or more distant. Socio-geopolitical context is a crucial part of intergenerational exploration.

References

Banmen, J. (2002). *Satir transformational systemic therapy*. Taipei: Zhuan ji gong zuo shi.

Bernier, A., & Dozier, M. (2003). Bridging the attachment transmission gap: The role of maternal mind-mindedness. *International Journal of Behavioral Development, 27*(4), 355-365.

Bowen, M. (1978). *Family therapy in clinical practice*. New York, NY: Jason Aronson, Inc.

Byng-Hall, J. (1995). Creating a secure family base: Some implications of attachment theory for family therapy. *Family Process, 34*, 45-58.

Cowan, C. P., & Cowan, P. A. (2005). Two central roles for couple relationships: Breaking negative intergenerational patterns and enhancing children's adaptation. *Sexual and Relationship Therapy, 20*(3), 275-288.

DeMaria, R., Weeks, G., & Hof, L. (1999). *Focused genograms: Intergenerational assessment of individuals, couples, and families*. New York, NY: Brunner-Routledge.

DeMaria, R., Weeks, G. R., Twist, M. L. C. (2017). *Focused genograms: Intergenerational Assessment or individuals, couples, and families* (2nd ed.). New York, NY: Brunner-Routledge.

Minuchin, S. (1974). *Families and family therapy*. Cambridge, MA: Harvard University Press.

Olson, D. H. (2011). FACES IV and the Circumplex model: Validation study. *Journal of Marital and Family Therapy, 37*(1), 64-80.

Olson, D. H., Russell, C. S., & Sprenkle, D. H. (1979). Circumplex model of marital and family systems cohesion and adaptability dimensions, family types, and clinical applications. *Family Process, 18*, 3-28.

Olson, D. H., Russell, C. S., & Sprenkle, D. H. (1983). Circumplex model of marital and family systems: VI. Theoretical update. *Family Process, 22*(1), 69-83.

Answer Key

Here is how we might have constructed Mike's family map.

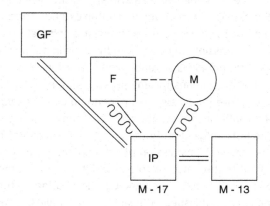

8 The Contextual Domain
The Social Bonds Ecomap

Overview

The Social Bonds Ecomap (SBE) depicts the family's relationships and connections with the larger social and community networks. We have focused on developing an SBE that is influenced by the various relationship encounters in our lives that provide a common experience within your community. Attachment scripts for families using attachment narratives can be an important part of connections with others. The SBE is a method to represent information about the family system and its relationship to outside resources, organizations, and agencies. The objective of the SBE is to guide students and practitioners to incorporate community members and institutions as part of their assessments and interventions.

Objective

1 Construct your personal SBE from your life or from a clinical case. A case example is provided as a reference (Exercise 8.1).

The Importance of SBEs

SBEs are a popular tool in human service programs as well as other settings that work with complex families. SBEs are useful in identifying the "village" around any given client-system. The quote "it takes a village to raise a child" is often spoken, and the most likely source came from Toni Morrison in *Essence*, July 1981: "I don't think one parent can raise a child. I don't think two parents can raise a child. You really need the whole village."[1] The SBE format is at the end of this chapter and is included in Chapter 9, the Attachment-Based Case Formulation, which uses all the FG tools.

The contextual domain for FGs, represented in the SBE (Figure 8.1), has been expanded in this text because of the increasing diversity of life and challenges that environmental and resource limitations place on family systems. Attention to the styles of social bonds within a community, geographical movements, and other institutional structures are a very important reflection for a practitioner. For example, one's culture puts boundaries around their interpersonal behavior and sense of identity. The ways in which an individual, couple, or family system engages within the community is an important systemic assessment. Significant challenges can be identified by using a series of questions that guide the clinician's attention to intergenerational historical legacies that may be relevant for their life experiences.

An Example: Information below has been taken from the case that is used in the Case Formulation in Chapter 9. Celia and James are in couples therapy because James thinks Celia is cheating on him with a coworker, and Celia feels distant from James after her miscarriage nine months ago (Figure 8.2).

Points on Celia's SBE:

- Siblings
- Work friends (controversial if these are helpful because James thinks there is an affair)
- Parents

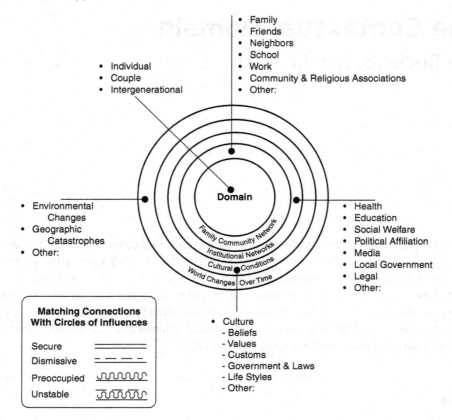

Figure 8.1 The Attachment Focused Ecomap.

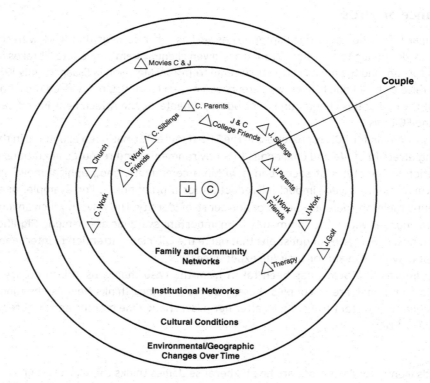

Figure 8.2 James and Celia's SBE.

- Church/spirituality
- Therapy
- Yoga
- The Movies – their first date and a mutual hobby
- Mutual college friends

Points on James' SBE:

- Siblings
- Work friends
- Parents
- Therapy
- Golf
- The Movies – their first date and a mutual hobby
- Work
- Mutual college friends

Exercise 8.1 Creating Personal or Clinical SBE

Directions: Using the information from the SBE (Figure 8.1), draw your personal SBE from your own life, or from a clinical case. Circle the domain that you are using to map the SBE resources. For example, if you want to look at the *family and community networks, institutional networks, cultural conditions, and environmental/geographic changes over time*, which you have in your family, you would circle the family choice in the center circle.

Fill in the blank SBE below using the example above for reference.

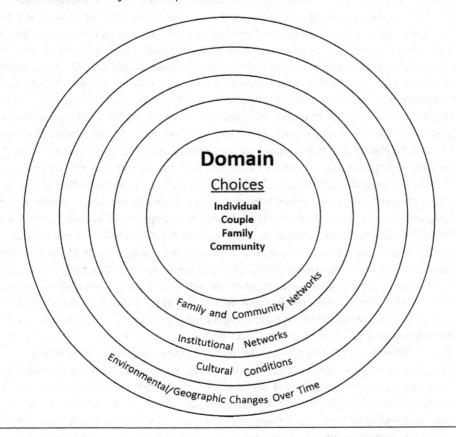

Applications of the SBE

The SBE reveals ways in which the client-system interacts with the community, mapping strengths, resources, and needs (McCormick, Stricklin, Nowak, & Rous, 2008). Philadelphia had been a mecca for developing and expanding family therapy practice to work with challenged children and their families. Speck (1967) and Speck and Attneave (1973) created a methodology for working with social networks that included 20–40 participants and several (3–5) family network therapists to search for ways to develop resources to work with family members struggling with extensive mental health needs. Compher (1989) began extending the work of various family therapy pioneers within the child welfare system in Philadelphia. Jones and Lindblad-Goldberg (2002), also in Philadelphia, established Ecosystemic Structural Family Therapy (ESFT). Lindblad-Goldberg and Northey (2013) further detailed the clinical and theoretical components of ESFT, a model now considered evidence-based, which rests on the foundation of Structural Family Therapy pioneered by Minuchin (1974). These multidimensional family therapy models will also benefit by using the IA and the Attachment Theory construct to deepen assessment of the client-system within the Contextual Domain.

Before conducting any assessment, it is essential to consider both the unique cultural experience(s) of each individual within the client-system, as well as the larger cultural context in which the system is embedded. Failing to recognize and inquire about such information can have a significant effect on one's clinical work, in particular, the TxP. Using attachment theory as a construct for developing a TxP requires attention to the multicultural context of the client-system. Attachment theory provides flexibility to normalize attachment styles, patterns, and scripts based on a multicultural perspective (Kietaibl, 2012). When multicultural considerations fail to be assessed or included as part of the early attachment assessment, some of the clinical implications can include: missing key information in the assessment process, not collecting enough data and/or the right kind of data around the presenting issues, having difficulty joining with the client-system, and may even result in the client-system not participating either partially or fully in therapy.

Further, it is important to inquire about the client-system's definition of "family" as this can affect who is included in the construction of genograms, timelines, and maps. Traditional blood-related definitions of families are outdated (Lamanna & Reidman, 2012). Failure to inquire into the client-system's definition of who constitutes their family places a therapist in a position of assuming and imposing their own definition and one's imposed definition may not be culturally sensitive to the unique culture of the client-system. This is problematic as family therapists have an ethical responsibility to be sensitive to the unique culture of each client in order to provide assistance in a nondiscriminatory manner (AAMFT, 2012). Thus, family therapists need to be attentive to how their definition of family may be too inclusive or not inclusive enough depending upon the client-system with which they are working (Green & Twist, 2005). For instance, a therapist with a relatively narrow definition of family that only includes people legally and/or biologically connected to each other may fail to recognize family members that a client-system views as family through a broad definition such as through fictive, relational, cultural, economic, religious/spiritual, and/or chosen connections.

Some client-systems may have much broader definitions than others. For instance, in client-systems where members come from African American descent, it is not uncommon to have a definition of family that includes fictive, play, or church family members (Hines & Boyd-Franklin, 2005). In families of indigenous descent (e.g., Native Americans, American Indians, Alaska Natives), there are multiple ways to define who is a member of a particular tribal nation and family. An example is, the United States Department of the Interior Indian Affairs currently recognizes 566 tribes, which means that any indigenous persons outside of the federally recognized tribes are not considered by the dominant government to be of native ancestry. Furthermore, while Indian Affairs leaves it up to each tribe to determine tribal membership of individuals, the government has generally set forth the following guidelines for who is considered Native American and as such "family," which include the person being of lineal descent to someone named on the tribe's original list of members, or to someone who descends from someone whose name appears on the original list. This differs from how specific families or tribal groups may define family, which is often by those who are in close relation to them regardless of genetic or legal ties, and/or by those who have undergone ceremonial pathways to be inducted into a particular tribal group (Sutton & Broken Nose, 2005). Thus, these are two very different definitions of who is part of one's tribe and relatedly family. By inquiring into the definition of family of the client-system, one can construct the SBE more appropriately.

Similarly, client-systems in which members happen to identify as sexual and/or gender orientation minorities (e.g., gay couples, lesbian-headed families, bisexual couples, heterosexual parents with a transgender child, asexual partners, etc.) it is not uncommon to have a definition of family that includes fictive or chosen family members (Ariel & McPherson, 2000; Bepko & Johnson, 2000). According to research conducted by Blumer and Murphy (2011) these family members typically include sexual orientation majority and minority friends, members of one's family of origin or procreation, coworkers, neighbors, mental health providers, as well as former partners, and reportedly act as an essential supportive network to recognize and include in therapy. Moreover, in multi-partnered configurations, it is common to have multiple partners involved in intimate and even parental relationships. Thus, therapists must realize that committed couples may be living together in a different arrangement than a male and female heterosexual monogamous legal marriage. Domestic partnership, common law marriage, and other forms of commitment are all recognized in order to understand the couple and family system of the client.

Summary

This chapter explored the SBE, which provides a format for investigating the contextual domain. This domain includes contextual, multicultural, and community supports, as well as socioeconomic, political, and geographical aspects of the client-system. For example, spiritual communities are a resource for finding meaning and community through times of adversity and should be included in the assessment if they are a part of the client-system. Additionally, collective healing is an important possibility to explore through the SBE in this domain. The SBE allows the therapist to engage with the family on extrafamilial sources of resilience and bonding that may help them to feel supported by their community. It also stresses the importance of therapists understanding the complex healthcare, community mental health, and social institution systems.

Note

1 Yale Book of Quotes attributes "it takes a village" only back to 1989.

References

American Association for Marriage and Family Therapy. (2012). *AAMFT code of ethics*. Retrieved from www.aamft.org/iMIS15/AAMFT/Content/Legal_Ethics/code_of_ethics.aspx

Ariel, J., & McPherson, D. W. (2000). Therapy with lesbian and gay parents and their children. *Journal of Marital and Family Therapy, 26*, 421–432.

Bepko, C., & Johnson, T. (2000). Gay and lesbian couples in therapy: Perspectives for the contemporary family therapist. *Journal of Marital and Family Therapy, 26*(4), 409–419.

Blumer, M. L. C., & Murphy, M. J. (2011). Alaskan gay male's couple experiences of societal non-support: Coping through families of choice and therapeutic means. *Contemporary Family Therapy, 33*(2), 1–18.

Compher, J. V. (1989). *Family-centered practice: The interactional dance beyond the family system*. New York, NY: Human Sciences Press.

Green, M. S., & Twist, M. (2005). The importance of self-awareness for practitioners working with gay and lesbian headed families. *National Council on Family Relations Report, 50*, F19–F20.

Jones, C. W., & Lindblad-Goldberg, M. (2002). Ecosystemic structural family therapy. In F. W. Kaslow (Ed.), *Comprehensive handbook of psychotherapy: Interpersonal/humanistic/existential* (Vol. 3, pp. 3–33). Hoboken, NJ: John Wiley & Sons Inc.

Hines, P. M., & Boyd-Franklin, N. (2005). African American families. In M. McGoldrick, J. Giordano, & N. Garcia-Preto, (Eds.). *Ethnicity and family therapy* (3rd ed., p. 87). New York, NY: Guilford Press.

Lamanna, M. A., & Riedmann, A. (2012). *Marriages and families: Making choices in a diverse society* (11th ed.). Belmont, CA: Cengage Learning.

Lindblad-Goldberg, M., & Northey, W. F. (2013). Ecosystemic structural family therapy: Theoretical and clinical foundations. *Contemporary Family Therapy, 35*(1), 147–160.

McCormick, K. M., Stricklin, S., Nowak, T. M., & Rous, B. (2008). Using eco-mapping to understand family strengths and resources. *Young Exceptional Children, 11*(2), 17–28.

Minuchin, S. (1974). *Families and family therapy*. Cambridge, MA: Harvard University Press.

Toni Morrison in *Essence*, July 1981 - Morrison, T. (1981) as cited in Doyle, C. C., Mieder, W., & Shapiro, F. R. (Eds.). (2012). *The dictionary of modern proverbs*. Knopf Doubleday Publishing Group.

Speck, R. V. (1967). Psychotherapy of the social network of a schizophrenic family. *Family Process, 6*(2), 208–214.

Speck, R. V., & Attneave, C. L. (1973). *Family networks*. New York, NY: Pantheon.

Sutton, C. T., & Broken Nose, M. A. (2005). American Indian families: An overview. In M. McGoldrick, J. Giordano, & N. Garcia-Preto (Eds.), *Ethnicity and family therapy* (3rd ed., pp. 43–54). New York, NY: Guilford Press.

9 The Attachment-Based Case Formulation

Exploring the Four Domains, Developing the Four Therapeutic Styles, and Identifying Clinical Goals and Tasks

Overview

The *Focused Genogram Workbook* (FGW) introduces the Intersystem Approach (IA) Case Formulation (CF) Assessment. The CF provides a comprehensive and systemic clinical assessment guide. The attachment-focused maps and timeline tools in *Focused Genograms*, 2nd edition (FG2) (2017) provide a comprehensive clinical assessment package to explore the complexity of family systems and dynamics. In exploring individual assessment, the Internal Models Maps (IMMs) are applied. The CF form was first utilized in the original volume of *Treating Couples: The Intersystem Model of the Marriage Council of Philadelphia* (Weeks, 1989). The CF form has been used by clinicians for decades to systematically organize information about the client-system using the IA framework. A CF approach is different from an intake form. CF uses a particular theory – here, the IA – to conceptualize a case in its entirety. As a result of the FG2, the CF form has been expanded to include the IA's newest construct of attachment theory and DeMaria's addition of therapeutic posture (TxP). The attachment construct is present in all the domains of the IA. The FG maps and timelines have been expanded to include attachment theory and integrated into the CF form as a visual notation of the client-system's attachment presentations.

The aim of the CF form is to structure and document the comprehensive assessment data presented by the client-system and to plan therapeutic interventions. With the IA as a guide, the therapist intervenes throughout all domains, both immediately and continuously. The first step is identifying the client's attachment childhood patterns as early as possible using the IMM. The FG maps, timelines, and FGs provide information that can help the therapist create the attachment-focused therapeutic alliance, TxP. TxP, combined with clinical goals and tasks, provides a foundation for effective clinical practice. The FG Roadmap in Chapter 1 illustrates the mapping and timeline techniques developed in FG2. The CF Assessment mirrors these domains and provides an opportunity for the clinician to complete an assessment using these attachment-focused tools.

Objectives

1. Complete an assessment within the CF for each IA domain of the client-system using maps, timelines, and narratives, with a particular focus on attachment patterns.
2. Create a plan for forming TxP using the attachment information gathered in the IMM, and applying the TxP Styles, within the CF.
3. Within the CF, address the link between assessment in the four domains and the presenting problem, and then establish treatment goals.

The Attachment-Based CF Assessment

CF is an essential skill for systemic therapists (Schwitzer & Rubin, 2012). The FG CF provides a comprehensive model for clinical assessment and attends to key concepts of the IA (Weeks & Fife, 2014). With the various elements of the CF, the clinician has an organized method for focusing on the unique experiences of the particular client-system that provides a comprehensive and organized treatment plan. This format of the CF also helps therapists expand their clinical range and flexibility because it accentuates the multitude of possible inroads and perspectives in any case. Assessment as part of an integrative systemic approach to treatment necessarily requires that the therapist develops an understanding of the identified or presenting problem within the meta-theoretical framework of the IA. Thus, it requires a perspective which focuses on the larger context of the person's family system.

The CF, which is the initial data collection and assessment procedure with the client, is an important companion to the Clinical Mind Map (CMM) and expands the practitioner's perspective on developing a comprehensive plan for assessment and intervention. The goal of the CF is to collect information in the process of strengthening the therapeutic alliance and to anticipate potential ruptures in the therapeutic relationship. The CF provides an attachment-based format that guides the clinician's gathering of pertinent and crucial information about each unique client-system. As part of the FGW, the CF organizes information using the IA meta-framework with specific attention to the attachment theory construct that guides assessment and helps the student and the practitioner attend to contradictions within the presenting problem.

Developing the Attachment-Based CF

The first and most immediate purpose of FGs is to provide therapists with a way to assess the presenting problem and other aspects of the client-system. Strategically, the aim of using a CF form is to identify the presenting problem(s) and its roots. Most client-systems present with multiple problems and may not understand how those problems are related. For example, one couple presented with problems of parenting, money, control, lack of communication, inability to resolve conflict, and low desire. The husband wanted to work on the low desire problem first. It will be clear to most clinicians that this is probably the last problem that can be solved. Certainly, the couple must learn to communicate and resolve conflicts constructively before approaching any of the other problems. The therapist helps the couple understand that problems must be sequenced and collaborate in developing an overall plan of the order in which problems are treated. The CF aids the therapist in understanding the historical and etiological relationship between the problems.

Further, in order to implement TxP, the therapist must make a preliminary assessment for the attachment style of each member of the client-system. With this knowledge, the therapist begins to join and accommodate each individual client's needs within the system based on their attachment style and needs. As the clinician's awareness of each person's internal working models (IWMs) grows, the clinician begins to adopt and adapt their TxP accordingly, shifting the TxP styles as the TxP evolves.

In treatment planning, we advocate for an intentional development of TxP for each individual in the client-system based on their IWM as early in the joining process as possible. The CF serves as a tool for the information gathered by the IMM, CIM, FCM, and timelines. Inherent in these tools is information about the attachment styles and behaviors of each member of the client-system, which contributes directly to the TxP adapted by the clinician. Therefore, the CF form provides the structure that organizes the relevant information for the TxP as well as the larger more comprehensive treatment plan. In this revised edition, a new IMM, CIM, FCM, and SBE are added to the CF form that provides the underpinning for the formation of the TxP.

Next, we provide a blank CF form, followed by a completed example. Each section of the CF form addresses a different IA domain and contains the appropriate maps and timelines. The example uses a couples therapy case; this CF provides additional insight into the flexibility and comprehensiveness possible when using the form (Figures 9.1–9.6). *This case is a compilation of cases; no one person described is an actual person.*

Attachment-Focused Assessment: The CF

Date of Initial Interview: _____

DEMOGRAPHIC ASSESSMENT

Family Name:_____

Partner's Name:_____   Age:_____ Race:_____

- *Ethnicity:*_____   *Religion:*_____

- *Gender:*_____   *Sexual Orientation:*_____

- *Ability: (Physical and Mental)*_____   *Socioeconomic Status (Class)*_____

- *Primary Language:*_____   *Education Level:*_____

Partner's Name_____   Age:_____ Race:_____

- *Ethnicity:*_____   *Religion:*_____

- *Gender:*_____   *Sexual Orientation:*_____

- *Ability: (Physical and Mental)*_____   *Socioeconomic status (Class)*_____

- *Primary Language:*_____   *Education Level:*_____

Years in Relationship_____/Committed/Married: _____

   Children:

- Name(s) and Age _____

   Number and name that resides with you? _____

Other Family in the Home: _____

Referred by and Reason for Referral: _____

Precipitating Event: _____

Previous Therapy Experience: _____

Initial Impressions and Reactions of Previous Therapist: _____

Presenting Problem(s):
   *Provide a concrete description including the **who, where, what, how,** from each member's view.
   How is the problem maintained in the system?*

History of the Problem(s): *Abbreviated form of the above.*

Solutions Attempted: *Including previous therapy(ies).*

Changes Sought By Clients: _____

INDIVIDUAL ASSESSMENT

Name: Partner (A)_____

Diagnostic and Statistical Manual (DSM) Diagnosis *(if applicable):* _____

Medications *(if applicable):* _____

Name: Partner (B)_____

Diagnostic and Statistical Manual (DSM) Diagnosis *(if applicable):* _____

Medications *(if applicable):* _____

Traumatic experiences: *(if applicable – physical, sexual, emotional, other):*

    Partner (A) _____

    Partner (B) _____

Cognitive, emotional, behavioral, and personality considerations:

    Partner (A) _____

    Partner (B) _____

    Attachment Styles IMM(s)[1]

Partner (A): _____   **Partner (B):** _____

Individual Timeline[2]

Partner (A): _____

Partner (B): _____

COUPLE INTERACTION PATTERN ASSESSMENT

How They Met: _____

Attraction, Affection, Friendship, Social

CIM (the Loop)[3]: _____

Relationship Experiences Timeline[4]: _____

THE FAMILY-OF-ORIGIN INTERGENERATIONAL ASSESSMENT

Partner A, Partner B, Adult Child(ren), Related Family Members as Indicated

Family Connections Map (FCM)[5]: _____

Family Timeline: _____

The Current Family Map: _____

Basic Genogram: *Identify key words or themes*
Attachments Genogram[6]: *Identify key words or themes*
Themes and Patterns: *Fairness, Gender, Sexuality, Abuse/Violence/Trauma, Addictions; Other FG Variations*

CONTEXTUAL DOMAIN ASSESSMENT

Ecomap: _____

Identify intergenerational family attachment narratives for the individual/couple related to their contextual experiences:

TxP

Partner (A): *IMM patterns; CIM style; FCM script:* _____

Partner (B): *IMM patterns; CIM style; FCM script:* _____
TxP Styles:

Partner (A) TxP Styles: _____

Partner (B) TxP Styles: _____

Self of the Therapist: Below list *your* <u>strengths</u> and <u>weaknesses</u>. *State how you can get support and information.*

TREATMENT PLAN

Client(s) Goals: _____

See Phases of Treatment below to make goals relevant to the current phase of treatment.

TREATMENT STRATEGIES

Domain _____ **Problems** _____ **Change Strategies** _____

Individual(s)

Couple: Partner(s)

Intergenerational/FOO

Contextual

TREATMENT PHASES[7]

Phase 1: Establishing Collaborative Therapeutic Alliance
Phase 2: Resolving Presenting Problem and Reducing Relationship Conflict
Phase 3: Promoting Behavior Change, Vulnerability, and Empathy; Further Identifying Individual, Relationship, Intergenerational, and Contextual and Cultural Challenges
Phase 4: Consolidating and Strengthening Relational Changes, Reevaluating Goals, and Updating Treatment Tasks and Strategies

PROFESSIONAL CONSIDERATIONS

- What ethical and/or professional issues exist or may exist with this case (i.e., divorce and custody potential, possible unavoidable dual relationships, etc.)
- Does this patient have the potential for suicide? What are the indicators?
- Will there be collaboration with outside entities throughout the duration of this case?

END FORM

_____

_____

Notes

1. IWMs identify childhood attachment patterns with parental figures.
2. Use Individual Timeline to address current stressors and lifestyle changes (new job, move, death, divorce, child leaving home, etc.). Also include relevant childhood/adolescent experiences.
3. See Chapter 6 of this workbook to identify the ten Steps of the Loop (CIM).
4. Use the Relationship Experiences Timeline to address infidelity, current and previous romantic relationships, marriage(s), cohabitation, broken engagements, other significant losses.
5. Provide the FCM questionnaire to clients to determine their family attachment script. Circle the appropriate square and write the initials of the individual whose family of origin falls in that square.
6. The Attachments Genogram was featured in FG2.
7. For consideration in treatment planning.

CF: Couple Case Example

The case presented is of a cohabiting couple, struggling with communication issues, breakdowns in trust, and complex grief, resulting from a miscarriage. The case illustrates the depth of assessment that is possible with the FG maps and timelines across all the domains of the client-system using the IA. Particularly, take note of the IMM's contribution to the formation of the TxP in the initial stage of treatment and beyond. The maps and timelines provide layers of attachment information that contribute to the current interaction patterns of the couple, and their underlying insecurities to be targeted with focused interventions described in the Treatment Plan. While it is up to each individual clinician when to complete the assessment, we recommend that it be initiated over the first two to three sessions and updated throughout the treatment process, to enhance and modify the strategic clinical tasks which promote change.

EXAMPLE CF

DEMOGRAPHIC ASSESSMENT

Family Name: n/a

Partner's Name: James   *Age:* 32   *Race:* Caucasian
- *Ethnicity:* German   *Religion:* Lutheran
- *Gender:* Male   *Sexual Orientation:* Heterosexual
- *Ability: (Physical and Mental):* Normal   *Socioeconomic status (Class):* Middle
- *Primary Language:* English   *Education Level:* Bachelor's degree

Partner's Name: Celia   *Age:* 28   *Race:* Caucasian
- *Ethnicity:* Italian   *Religion:* Roman Catholic
- Gender: Female   *Sexual Orientation:* Heterosexual
- *Ability: (Physical and Mental):* Normal   *Socioeconomic status (Class):* Middle
- *Primary Language:* English   *Education Level:* Bachelor's degree

Years in Relationship//Married: 3 years dating, 1 year cohabitating

Children: n/a

Other family in the home: n/a

Referred by and reason for referral: James initiated therapy after becoming suspicious that Celia might be having an affair.

Previous therapy experience: No prior history of therapy.

Initial Impressions and Reactions: James and Celia both seemed distant and self-protective. James wanted to "figure out what's happening and solve the problem." From the beginning, they were blaming and critical with each other and had limited emotional vocabulary when describing themselves and the relationship.

Precipitating event: The precipitating event was that James noticed Celia spending more time with her friends after work. He also thought he saw text messages on her phone from her male colleague. This led him to suspect that Celia may be cheating on him.

Presenting Problem(s): *Provide a concrete description including the* who, where, what, how, *from each member's view.*
The problem as it was presented in the first session by James, was that Celia is spending too much time with friends and maybe getting too close with a male colleague. Celia did not agree that her behavior was problematic. Instead, she said that James was demanding and she did not know how else to have fun and connect with people.

In the second session, Celia revealed that she was resentful of James because he seemed to quickly dismiss the emotional impact of her miscarriage nine months ago. The miscarriage had occurred in the fourth month of pregnancy. Though they both agreed they were not ready for a baby, James had moved on after little overt grieving and Celia did not feel like he was there for her when she needed him to be. Since then, she has felt distant and angry with him.

How is the problem maintained in the system?
Celia and James are both feeling isolated and suspicious of one another. These feelings have driven them to defend themselves instead of expressing their feelings in a vulnerable way. They are both fearful of abandonment, loneliness, and inadequacy, leading them to minimize or avoid their feelings and pursue one another in maladaptive ways.

History of the Problem(s): *Abbreviated form of the above.*

As presented by the clients, their relationship felt good in the beginning, but living together and the miscarriage have created problematic communication patterns, especially around the expression of feelings, and each of their desire to create a greater sense of intimacy.

Solutions Attempted: *Including previous therapy.* No solutions have been attempted. They do not try to talk through their difficulties and have not had any prior counseling.

Changes Sought by Clients: James and Celia want to communicate better and be closer. In their words, the couple wants to "understand each other" and "figure this out."

INDIVIDUAL ASSESSMENT

Name: James

DSM Diagnosis (if applicable): Explore Depression in James's personal life

Medications (if applicable): n/a

Name: Celia

DSM Diagnosis (if applicable): Adjustment Disorder and/or Complex Grief (Provisional)

Medications (if applicable): n/a

Traumatic experiences (if applicable - physical, sexual, emotional, other):

No trauma in James's history to the best of the clinician's knowledge as of session 4. Though he has experienced the miscarriage, he has not articulated that this feels like a loss to him because he was not sure of his desire to be a parent at this time.

Celia stated she was subject to corporal punishment by her father as a child until she was 14. The father was also emotionally abusive to her mother at times. In adulthood, the miscarriage was traumatic for Celia, as it happened in the fourth month when she had already begun to bond with the fetus and feel like a mother. The loss of that potential role, as well as the perceived unavailability of James, left Celia feeling lonely on top of the grief.

Cognitive, emotional, behavioral, and personality considerations: The most notable considerations here are that both partners are highly intelligent and capable, but have not developed emotional language or tolerance for negative emotions. They both seem to have difficult and feisty temperaments and they do not take responsibility for their actions.

Attachment Patterns: *Develop the <u>Internal Models Map</u> (IMM) to identify each person's <u>Childhood Attachment Patterns with parental figures</u>. The IMM includes the attachment dynamic between the parents, which will be addressed in the next section of the CIM.*

IMM(s):

A.P.: _____avoidant_____   **A.P.: _____disorganized____**

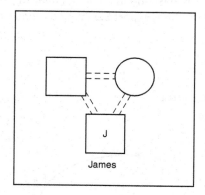 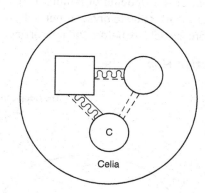

Figure 9.1 Celia and James's IMMs.

Explanation of IMMs:

- *James's childhood attachment patterns are avoidant with both parents. James's parental relationship was dismissive as is the couple relationship dynamic.*
- *Celia's childhood attachment patterns with her father are disorganized because he was physically unavailable and threatening as well as emotionally unreliable and emotionally abusive throughout her childhood.*
- *Celia's childhood attachment patterns with her mother are avoidant, who was physically available but emotionally unreliable. Celia's parental relationship with the father is disorganized as a consequence of her father's physical and emotional abuse toward her mother.*

Recent Significant Changes:

<u>Use Individual Timeline</u> *to address stressors and lifestyle changes (new job, move, death, divorce, child leaving home, etc.). Also, include relevant childhood/adolescent experiences.*
    James timeline points:

- *Memories of baseball and Boy Scouts, his dad wasn't really involved (~ age 4–8)*
- *Grandparents died when James was young (before age 13)*
- *James went to college for engineering when he was 18*
- *He graduated from college with honors and his dad told him he loved him.*
- *James quickly got a job (age 22) – 10 years at the same job*
- *James was promoted 3.5 years ago*
- *Met Celia 3 years ago*
- *Moved in with Celia 1 year ago*
- *Miscarriage 9 months ago (now age 32)*

Celia's timeline points:

- *Earliest memory of physical affection from mom, around age 4. Physical affection is rare.*
- *Two siblings are 3 and 5 years younger than her, Angelo and Josephine*
- *Celia remembers the use of corporal punishment from ages 5–10*
- *She hit puberty at age 13 and was allowed to help her mom at their store*
- *Age 18 Celia went to college and felt a sense of freedom*
- *Serious relationship age 19–21*
- *Worked in sales age 22–present (age 28) at different companies*
- *Met James age 24, moved in age 27, miscarriage 9 months ago*

COUPLE PATTERN ASSESSMENT

How they met: *Attraction, Affection, Friendship, Social*

The couple met at the wedding of a mutual friend. They describe immediate chemistry, but have never shown much physical affection to one another outside of sex. They report being good friends in the beginning and having a strong social life, before the miscarriage.

Couple Interaction Map

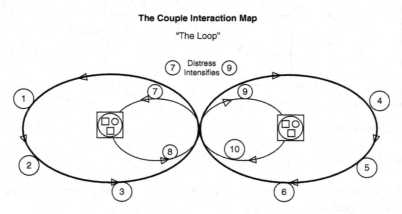

Figure 9.2 Celia and James's CIM General.

Summary

James's emotional allergy makes him demanding toward Celia to make up for the emotional neglect in his childhood. James is then dismissive of his own feelings when they have significant mutual distress (i.e., the miscarriage). He then withdraws emotionally from Celia, feeling unloved, and his anxiety intensifies; he becomes emotionally distant and unavailable.

When Celia is distressed, her emotional allergy leads her to distrust James. She appears dismissive, however, her underlying disorganized attachment with her father fuels her impulses to seek closeness, which is then countered by her impulse to avoid conflict and connection. Celia then becomes hyperactivated, becomes demanding, and withholds affection.

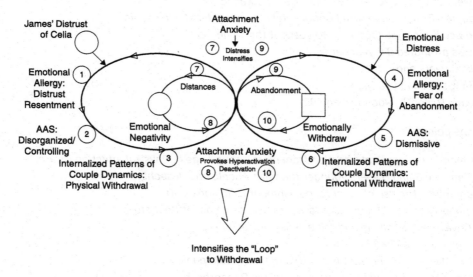

Figure 9.3 Celia and James's CIM Detailed.

In Detail, with Each Step Explained

(See Chapter 6 for the Couple Interaction Map worksheet and more details)

Step 1: James believes that Celia must be having an affair with her coworker, which triggers **Celia's emotional allergy** of distrust, and leads to resentment toward James.

Step 2: Celia appears to be controlling, simply stating that he "can't really think that I'd do that."

Step 3: Celia's internalized patterns of her parental couple dynamic was one in which her father was critical and abusive toward her mother, and consequently, she responds avoidantly to her father as her mother would toward her father.

Step 4: Celia's controlling behavior triggers **James's emotional allergy** of feeling that his thoughts and feelings are unimportant, with an underlying fear of abandonment.

Step 5: James responds to Celia by dismissing her plea that she is not having an affair. He withdraws from Celia for not admitting that she cheated on him.

Step 6: James attempts to hold Celia accountable but he is emotionally disconnected while at the same time reaching out to her with distrust.

As the clinician's therapeutic bond becomes more secure with James and Celia, they will each be able to address each of their attachment anxieties. The clinician will be able to help minimize emotional hyperactivation and/or support connection rather than deactivation. The couple must be willing to explore deeper emotions in order to resolve the negative interaction patterns during the session. The therapist will then help them work through steps 7-10 as each partner becomes more vulnerable and each begins to explore how they get stuck in the Loop.

Step 7: Celia feels increased attachment anxiety. Celia then becomes increasingly distant and controlling toward James as her emotional allergy intensifies.

Step 8: This interaction triggers Celia's disorganized attachment with her father, with whom she would sometimes defend herself and sometimes retreat from. Celia is now replaying her childhood attachment pattern with her father. The replay of her childhood experience arouses her emotional negativity with James.

Step 9: James becomes angry, feeling old fears of abandonment that he has lived with throughout his life. His attachment anxiety leads to even increased anxiety.

Step 10: James becomes increasingly emotionally withdrawn and avoidant as he was with his father and his mother as well. Feeling unloved, James's avoidant attachment with his mother leads to doubt and misgivings about pursuing Celia.

Relationship Experiences Timeline

<u>Use the Relationship Timeline</u> to address previous romantic relationships, marriages, cohabitation, broken engagements, significant loss).

James Timeline points:

- *Kissed a girl at an eighth-grade dance*
- *Girlfriend at 11th grade*
- *A two-year relationship in college 18-20*
- *Girlfriend 22-23 (when first started working)*
- *Single but dating casually age 24-28*
- *Met Celia age 28, moved in age 31, miscarriage age 31*

Celia timeline points:

- *Noticed liking boys around age 12-13*
- *Relationship age 19-21 in college, serious but unhealthy*
- *Single 21-24*
- *Met James age 24, moved in age 27, miscarriage 9 months ago*

INTERGENERATIONAL FAMILY ASSESSMENT

Basic Genogram:

Basic Family Genogram

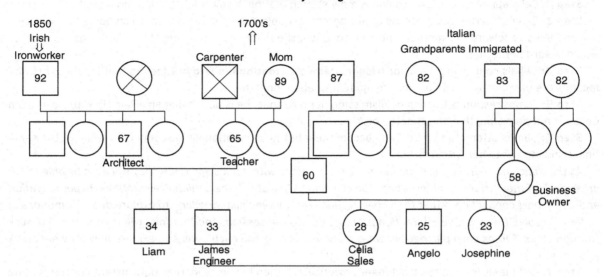

Figure 9.4 James and Celia's Basic Genogram.

Themes and Patterns:

Note: These themes will appear as treatment continues and can be pursued with FGs at any time.

Fairness, Gender, Sexuality, Abuse/Violence/Trauma, Addictions; Other FG Variations

Gender roles were pertinent in both partners' FOOs, particularly masculinity for James. For James, a Fairness FG may be warranted because of his emotional allergy of feeling like he needs to earn love and be "good enough." For Celia, themes of trauma suggest an Abuse, Violence, Trauma-Focused Genogram to further explore the intergenerational patterns of disorganized attachment.

The Current Family Map

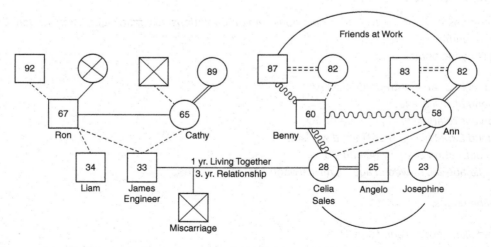

Figure 9.5 James and Celia's Basic Family Maps.

James's family is currently distant and gets in touch for holidays. James calls his mother more frequently. Celia's family is still very much in her life, but she is not sure whether she feels close all the time.

Family Connections Map

Table 9.1 James and Celia's FCM

F L E X I B I L I T Y		Disengaged	Distant	Connected	Enmeshed
	Chaotic	UNPREDICTABLE **Disorganized**	Distant Chaotic **Dismissive**	Connected Chaotic **Preoccupied**	OVERINVOLVED **Disorganized**
	Flexible	Disengaged Flexible **Dismissive**	**Secure**	**Secure**	Enmeshed Flexible **Preoccupied**
	Structured	Disengaged Structured **Dismissive**	**Secure**	**Secure**	Enmeshed Structured **Preoccupied**
	Rigid	UNINVOLVED **Disorganized**	Distant Rigid **Dismissive** **JAMES**	Connected Rigid **Preoccupied**	CONTROLLING **Disorganized** **CELIA**
				C O N N E C T I O N	

Table 9.1 shows James and Celia's locations on the FCM. James would fall in the Dismissive (distant-rigid) section and Celia would fall in the Disorganized (controlling) section. James describes his relationship with his mother as avoidant, as she was focused on herself and her own needs; he describes the family as generally rigid with rules and roles, and generally distant because people were focused on self-sufficiency. Celia's family was controlling because there was little flexibility with an excessive level of closeness in their relationships that led to rigidity, strictness, and extreme closeness mixed with suspicion.

Family Timeline

James's timeline points:

Themes: being self-made, building a professional life, less of a coherent family story because of being a disengaged family

- *Birth of James's brother*
- *James's birth*
- *Grandparents lived with James when their spouses died, between ages 9 and 13 for him.*
- *James's dad retired when James was 24*
- *James's mom retired when he was 31, and she asked for grandkids as he moved in with Celia*

Celia timeline points:

Themes: enmeshment, not sticking up for yourself especially against men

- *Grandparents immigrated from Italy in the 1920s*
- *Grandparents set up a tailor/seamstress shop and parents knew each other as children*
- *Parents married, dad went into sales and mom stayed at home with Celia (new baby)*
- *Mom opened a boutique when Celia and her siblings were young*
- *Celia's mom took care of her aging parents while running the shop, Celia tried to help when she was 13. Her dad was unhappy at his job and finances were tight.*
- *Celia felt free when she went to college.*

CONTEXTUAL ASSESSMENT

Ecomap: *Show resources and relationships with the community, schools, spiritual resources, cultural entities, government agencies, and any other relevant people or organizations outside the family. Stories of survival, lessons learned, hardship, particular people who were there for you, etc.*

Include culture, societal values, race and ethnicity, oppression, political unrest, man-made and natural disasters, religious teachings and values, socioeconomic context including financial hardship and unemployment, housing and social environment (others living in the home, proximal social environment, etc.

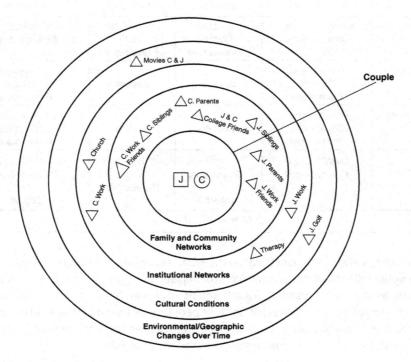

Figure 9.6 Celia and James's SBE.

Points on Celia's SBE:

- Siblings
- Work friends (controversial if these are helpful because James thinks there is an affair)
- Parents
- Church/Spirituality
- Therapy
- Yoga
- The Movies – their first date and a mutual hobby
- Mutual college friends

Points on James's SBE:

- Siblings
- Work friends (controversial if these are helpful because James thinks there is an affair)
- Parents
- Therapy
- Golf
- The Movies – their first date and a mutual hobby
- Work
- Mutual college friends

Identify intergenerational family attachment narratives for the individual/couple related to their contextual experiences:

Celia's immigrant grandparents and Italian heritage play a role in the family attachment narrative. The trauma of immigration, experiencing the Great Depression as new Americans, and particularly the failure of men in the family as providers during that time, may have led Celia's paternal grandfather to pass his own disappointment in himself on to his son. This son, Celia's father, was critical and emotionally abusive to his wife and daughters. Having an unpredictable father may have led Celia to the disorganized attachment pattern she has now and is playing out with James. Celia's maternal legacy of being vocal and self-sufficient have contributed to the empowerment and resiliency of women in her family, allowing Celia to continue to work toward her own self-sufficiency and have moderately healthy relationships despite her disorganized tendencies.

To James, being American has meant being traditional and self-sustaining. Despite feeling like he was not ready for fatherhood at the time that Celia had the miscarriage, it seems relevant to explore James's thoughts on fatherhood in the context of his gender and ethnicity. His values may reveal important information about the difficulties of the miscarriage for him or his mis-attunement to Celia's needs during the aftermath. In addition, the ties between emotions and manhood have yet to be explored through James's family attachment script and narrative. His IMM, CIM, and FCM suggest that he minimizes and avoids his feelings due to the lack of any acceptable or satisfactory means of expression and support he experienced throughout his upbringing.

TREATMENT PLAN

Client(s) Goals:

For the first session the goal was to determine if Celia was violating boundaries (cheating or too friendly with a coworker) by James's account. Celia was interested in appeasing James by coming to therapy but was not admitting whether or not she was cheating on James. In the second session the goal widened to include their need for better connection and understanding. Celia also revealed some of the grief she had not expressed about the loss of her pregnancy and her feelings of betrayal about James's emotional reaction.

Therapeutic Posture

Through the process of asking questions, and demonstrating interest, compassion and empathy as applicable, identify each individual's attachment pattern/style presentation within the initial interview(s). List the IMM, CIM primary style/pattern, and FCM styles.

James

IMM pattern: avoidant with dad and avoidant with mom

CIM style: dismissive

FCM script: dismissive (low connection and low flexibility)

Celia

IMM pattern: disorganized with dad, avoidant with mom

CIM style: disorganized

FCM script: controlling (disorganized)

Table 9.2 TxP Styles

TxP		TxP Styles within TxP			
		Validation	**Guidance**	**Reassuring**	**Challenging**
Childhood attachment styles – foundations for TxP	**Secure**	X	X	X	X
	Ambivalent		X	X	
	Avoidant	X			X
	Disorganized	X	X	X	X

Table 9.2 depicts the most effective TxP Styles (Chapter 3 in this book) to use with each attachment pattern in an individual's IMM.

Identify which TxP styles will be used in the beginning phase of treatment to establish a safe and familiar emotional environment for each individual in the treatment based on the maps above (particularly, the IMM).

James TxP Styles: **Validation and Challenging**

Celia TxP Styles: **Guidance, Reassurance, Validation, Challenging** (depending on her presentation at any time). Her tendency toward avoidance with females suggests that a Validating and Challenging posture would be indicated with a female therapist.

What are your therapeutic goals?

The first goal is to create safety by showing empathy, pacing, emotional tracking, and ensuring that disagreements do not escalate. The next goal is observing the pattern of interaction and gathering the history, as chronicled in this form. The later goals will include utilizing TxP, creating experiential opportunities for reconnection, processing the trauma of the miscarriage together, and fostering closeness so that if a relationship is developing outside of Celia and James's relationship, then they will confide in each other before acting out.

Self of the Therapist (SoT): Below list *your strengths* and *weaknesses*. Then *write a statement* on how you can gather support and additional aspects of the case. A more complete assessment of your SoT can be undertaken in Chapter 4 with the SoT Project.

As a therapist, I am adept at staying present with whatever is happening in the room. I tend to give attention and support "fairly" while maintaining a connection with both clients (in a couple). Sometimes I may hesitate to challenge someone who is thinking or behaving in an unhelpful way because I don't want to hurt their feelings while they are struggling. I can monitor this tendency to want to protect clients in myself using mindfulness, and talking with my supervisor (Table 9.3).

Table 9.3 Treatment Strategies

Problems	Change Strategies
Individual	
1. James avoiding vulnerability	Help verbalize emotions (empathic conjecture), guidance, reassurance
2. Celia unexpressed grief and trauma around miscarriage	Help her explore the grief around the miscarriage
Couple	
1. Unexpressed grief about the miscarriage	Help the couple process the loss, including loss of hopes, dreams, potential roles; help them support each other during the grieving
2. Distance and insecurity around Celia's work relationships	Explore appropriate boundaries with work people; couple contract about an acceptable depth of friendship with people of the opposite sex?

Intergenerational/FOO	
1. Unhealthy arguing patterns: James - preoccupied and passive aggressive, Celia - disorganized and fearful	Explore these patterns through the genogram and their effect on the couple currently; develop and practice other ways to fight (see #2)
2. Experiential bonding	Deepen the emotion and practice empathic listening to increase compassion and empathy
Contextual	
1. Trauma narrative in the FOO (Celia)	Rework family attachment narrative - retelling and witnessing
2. Disconnection from culture and social network	Deepen connections with friends and community through outings, events, and processing of those experiences in therapy

(Add more lines if needed)

Treatment Phases - See Chapter 3

For Consideration in Treatment Planning

Phase 1: Establishing Collaborative Therapeutic Alliance.

Phase 2: Resolving Presenting Problem and Reducing Relationship Conflict.

Phase 3: Promoting Behavior Change, Vulnerability, and Empathy; Identifying Individual, Relationship, Intergenerational, and Contextual and Cultural Challenges.

Phase 4: Consolidating and Strengthening Relational Changes, Reevaluating Goals, and Updating Treatment Tasks and Strategies.

PROFESSIONAL CONSIDERATIONS

What ethical and/or professional issues exist or may exist with this case (i.e., divorce and custody potential, possible unavoidable dual relationships, etc.)

There are no foreseeable dual relationships, divorce or custody issues, or other concerns at this time.

Does this patient have the potential for suicide? What are the indicators?

No potential for suicide has been observed in the assessment process.

Will there be collaboration with outside entities throughout the duration of this case?

Not at this time.

END of Sample

Summary

The Attachment-Based CF Form is a theory-based comprehensive assessment tool that utilizes the FG Tools to create a detailed assessment of the client-system. This chapter is instrumental in showing the reader, who might be new to the IA, how the FG assessment tools and principles of the IA coalesce to form a complete and holistic picture of the client-system. The CF is useful because, unlike other assessments that focus on one portion of the client-system, the CF form directs that information on every domain of the client-system. A comprehensive and all-encompassing assessment tool such as this ensures that the clinician maintains a systemic and integrative view of the case. The addition of the attachment construct, as you can see, has increased the scope of the assessment and strengthened the relationship between the domains, for an intensive assessment and an enhanced treatment potential.

Furthermore, the clinician can integrate treatment strategies and interventions into the CF form in such a way that each of the domains can be targeted, as well as the overall client-system. For example, some work may be oriented toward the individuals and others may be focused on the couple-as-couple. This method of treatment planning encourages an integrative approach to the intervention that is the purpose of the IA. It also aids in the implementation of TxP and an intentional and systematic use of interventions that fit within the treatment planning section of the CF form. As resistance or bumps in the road happen the therapist can refer back to the CF form and update the information for each of the domains. The therapeutic process is developmental and should be an organic process. Assessment and treatment are not finite and distinct processes. They are continuous and reciprocal processes that relate back to the dialectical nature of therapy.

The CF provides a structure for gathering pertinent and crucial information about the client-system with specific focus on the attachment theory construct across the four domains of IA. A comprehensive assessment provides a foundation for using various clinical strategies and techniques based on a comprehensive understanding of attachment styles, interaction patterns, family scripts, and attachment narratives. In our roles as faculty and supervisors within graduate and postgraduate programs, we find that most practitioners will naturally begin to seek a meta-framework, such as ours, to broaden, strengthen, and transform their clinical practice. As we mentioned earlier, therapists usually become eclectic in their approach, but some want a more systematic approach that is integrative. We recognize, and appreciate, the lofty goal that we have established for the field and ourselves. However, our combined clinical experience, theoretical understanding, and research-based approach to practice, suggests that the attention to each of the domains within the IA will help practitioners develop their own unique applications of the client-system. Integrative approaches continue to be an evolving and steady development across professional domains (Gelso, 2011). Recently, literature has emerged on the importance of integrative approaches to therapy, such as the IA (Weeks & others), the Internal Family Systems (Castonguay, Eubanks, Goldfried, Muran, & Lutz, 2015; Schwartz, 1997).

In the context of systemic-relational therapy supervision and training, we encourage all clinicians to conduct an FG CF with clients on a regular basis. It is also possible, however, to make use of various parts of the assessment, piece-by-piece, like using the Basic Genogram only to conduct a thorough intergenerational assessment. Utilization of each part of the assessment as a whole or separately is possible because the assessment and approach are remarkably adaptable, based on the clinical setting, clinician, and clinical model.

What is most important is that practitioners explore the varied dimensions of their clients' life experiences in a focused way. In practice, the various questions on the CF may be sketched out after the first few meetings. Then as therapy proceeds, the therapist can return to different aspects of the client-system in order to gain a more in-depth understanding.

References

Castonguay, L. G., Eubanks, C. F., Goldfried, M. R., Muran, J. C., & Lutz, W. (2015). Research on psychotherapy integration: Building on the past, looking to the future. *Psychotherapy Research, 25*(3), 365–382.

DeMaria, R., Weeks, G. R., & Twist, M. L., (2017). *Focused genograms: Intergenerational assessment of individuals, couples, and families*. New York, NY: Routledge.

Gelso, C. J. (2011). Emerging and continuing trends in psychotherapy: Views from an editor's eye. *Psychotherapy, 48*(2), 182–187.

Schwartz, R. C. (1997). *Internal family systems therapy*. New York, NY: Guilford Press.

Schwitzer, A. M., & Rubin, L. C. (2012). *Diagnosis and treatment planning skills for mental health professionals: A popular culture casebook approach*. Thousand Oaks, CA: SAGE Publications.

Weeks, G. R. (Ed.). (1989). *Treating couples: The intersystem model of the marriage council of Philadelphia*. New York, NY: Brunner/Mazel.

Weeks, G. R. & Fife, S. (2014). *Couples in treatment: Techniques and approaches for effective practice* (3rd ed.). New York, NY: Brunner-Routledge.

Part IV

The Evolving Focused Genograms

10 The Basic Genogram

A Comprehensive Update with Markie L. C. Twist and Rita DeMaria

Overview

The Basic Genogram (BG) is an important first step in developing a complete picture of the client-system. It includes the basic family structure and functioning, as well as themes of marriage/partnering and dissolution, adoption, birth order, and contextual aspects. The BG provides the format that is used with all the other Focused Genograms (FGs), such as the Attachments FG, Gender FG, and the Abuse, Violence, and Trauma FG, among others. These were laid out in *Focused Genograms, 2nd Edition*. In particular, the Attachments FG is a key organizing genogram that provides foundational information for working with all the attachment functions in each domain of the client-system. In other words, the BG serves as the first layer of a multi-layered assessment process that is comprehensive and integrative. The Attachments FG and others are more specific to a given client-system as assessment evolves.

This chapter introduces a comprehensive BG, an essential first step as part of an initial interview. Gaining information about the client's relational context is an important part of joining and establishing a therapeutic alliance. The BG is a diagnostic and therapeutic process that is structured through a set of questions which explore particular aspects of the family system and the intergenerational transmission of family patterns, dynamics, and forces that mold the client's personality and behavior. The purpose of the BG is to begin the process of developing a comprehensive individual, couple, and family assessment that explores the structure and functioning of any given family system. The subsequent specific topics presented include birth order, adoption, health and illness, marriage and partnering patterns, and contextual considerations. Specific questions related to each of these topic areas serve as a guide for the practitioner. Thus, each topic for the BG has been deconstructed to help the therapist explore more fully.

Individual development cannot be overlooked in systemic practice just as couple and family relationships cannot be overlooked in individual treatment. Weeks and Wright (1979) explored the dialectics of the family life cycle and emphasized the importance of the individual-biological and the individual-psychological dimensions of human development. Behavior problems in childhood have continued to escalate prompting the American Academy of Pediatrics to establish a Family Task Force (Schor, 2003). These areas are crucially important to explore with the Timeline because the child's level of development and adaptability is important in determining the potential and actual effects of these influences on the child and the client-system. These life challenges have increased for many families given the complexity of contemporary life.

The heterosexual couple/family life cycle is well known in family therapy literature (Carter & McGoldrick, 1999, 2005; McGoldrick & Carter, 2003; Monte, 1989) with its six stages: (1) the young unattached adult, (2) the newly married couple, (3) the couple/family with young children, (4) the couple/family at midlife (with adolescents) and aging parents, (5) the stage of launching children and moving on, and (6) the couple/family in later life. Changes across time can be anticipated transitions or unanticipated crises and traumas. The Group for the Advancement of Psychiatry (Fleck, 1989) refined these stages more discreetly to include the following: marriage, reproduction, pregnancy, infancy, family formation, nurturance, toddler family, grade school, adolescence, young adulthood, midlife stages, aging, and dying.

From generic, as well as male and female perspectives, Sheehy (1984, 1995, 1996, 1998, 2006) has examined the adult life cycle in depth. Harrar and DeMaria (2007) proposed stages of love, commitment, and marriage for couples that cover the couple relationship life cycle over time. DeMaria has further refined various strategies of love and marriage to explore the seven stages: passion, realization, rebellion, cooperation, reunion, completion, and explosions. All of these stages are useful markers for developing the timeline, because each stage has unique challenges and stresses. Assessing and clarifying the impact of deviations and traumatic experiences is an important part of the assessment process. Unfortunately, developmental issues often are overlooked in family systems assessments.

Objectives

1   Identify the topics that are included in the BG, noting the questions provided in each section (Exercises 10.1–10.7).
2   Demonstrate how the topic questions become useful while developing the BG (Exercise 10.8).

Developing and Reintroducing the BG

The BG is the foundation for all themed FGs because it establishes the unique structure and functioning of the client-system. Constructing a BG is not a rigid process, it is a systematic method for gathering information about the family system. As information is gathered as part of the initial interview process, the therapist identifies topics and questions that influence personal development and relationships. Based on research and clinical expertise, constructing genograms that include information for four or more generations is recommended, especially for assessment of issues related to contextual experience and ethnicity (Hardy & Laszloffy, 1995; Hoopes & Harper, 1987; McIntosh, 1998) and/or genetic pedigree or medical background (Wattendorf & Hadley, 2005). For example, in African American families the legacy of slavery is much more salient four generations back and still influences the family, but the latest generation may only be aware of its effects indirectly (Black & Jackson, 2005). The same is often true for Jewish families with a history of experiencing the Holocaust (Rosen & Weltman, 1996). Many clients may not have information going back several generations, however, there are often stories and beliefs about the earlier generations with important historical narratives that have been created and established. The exploration of these narratives is of great value in helping individuals, couples, and family members of the current generation develop transformative narratives for themselves to alleviate the effects of transgenerational trauma (Hollander-Goldfein, Isserman, & Goldenberg, 2012).

As part of the compilation of information gathered during exploration of the BGs and FGs, the Family Timeline identifies expected and situational transitions for members that the clinician and clients may see as important events in how they function or fail to function. The expected transitions may be more complex than what the literature has suggested. Family life may not be so consistently progressive or linear. Often childbearing and child-rearing extend over many years, with overlapping cycles of toddlers, grade school-aged children, adolescents, and emancipated children. Moreover, situational transitions can occur if there are crises or developmental disruptions such as suicide, illness, miscarriages, accidental death and injuries, and unanticipated retirements or job loss. Situations like divorce, teenage pregnancies, and geographic moves can affect family life and family functioning.

Strengths of the BG

The Circumplex Model has been a core for the assessment of family functioning (Olson, 1999, 2011). Briefly, the Circumplex Model utilizes the Family Adaptability and Cohesion Scales instrument to determine a family's levels of flexibility and cohesion. The flexibility continuum can range from rigidity to chaos and refers to the adaptability within the family over developmental transitions and crises. The cohesion continuum ranges from disengaged to enmeshed and encompasses the boundaries within the family. These reliable and valid scales were developed to assess the family dynamics and devise treatment goals.

Within the Circumplex Model, enmeshed family systems are frequently characterized by extreme emotional connectedness and loyalty, whereas disengaged family systems are characterized by emotional separateness and lack of support (Olson, 1999). From an individualistic, dominant United States (US) contextual perspective, enmeshed and disengaged family systems have been viewed as unhealthy, and families with a balance of separation and connection have been considered optimal or healthy (Manzi, Vignoles, Regalia, & Scabini, 2006; Olson, 1999). Further, it has been the historical belief that a person existing within an enmeshed family system is less able to fully achieve differentiation of self (Bowen, 1978) or separation-individuation (Rice, Cole, & Lapsley, 1990), which in turn leads to problems such as inhibition to psychological autonomy, youth problems, and problem internalization, as well as difficulty achieving and maintaining psychosocial maturity (Barber & Buehler, 1996; Barber, Olson, & Shagle, 1994).

More contemporary scholars are beginning to note that this characterization of problems related to enmeshment must be considered within the context of contextual and gender considerations (Barrera, Blumer, & Soenksen, 2011). Johnson (1986) has emphasized the significance and importance of attachment bonds as a primary relationship need, in particular, she emphasized that dependency and love relationships have been pathologized with terms such as "enmeshment." Instead, she encourages the use of the term "effective dependency" to underscore the human need for connection and understanding. Similarly, Bograd (1988) emphasized the importance of interdependent relational systems that allow for boundaries that are clear enough to allow for both relational cohesion and individuation. Findings from a recent study, involving 188 late adolescents/young adults in a college context, confirm this more contemporary understanding (Barrera et al., 2011). In this study, participants who came from a more enmeshed family system and/or who identified as allocentric (defined as the individual cultural self-construal of a person existing in a larger cultural context that is collectivistic in nature [Triandis & Gelfand, 1998]) displayed higher levels of separation-individuation than their peers coming from disengaged, connected, or separated family systems (Barrera et al., 2011).

Barrera et al. (2011) hypothesize that a possible explanation for these findings is that individuals within enmeshed family systems, and those who embrace collectivist values, may be better able to separate as they have a secure and connected familial base from which to do so. In other words, they feel safe in their secure family base to explore and define who they are as individuals (Byng-Hall, 1999) while remaining connected to the family system. This lends support to the idea of a both/and understanding of what is healthy in terms of family systems functioning. Kagitcibasi (2003) suggested that healthy separation-individuation in adolescence/young adulthood can occur through processes of autonomy and disconnection, as well as those of relatedness and connectivity. Barrera et al. (2011) further proposed that healthy separation-individuation, in fact, might best occur through ongoing processes of autonomy and disconnection, particularly in the case of persons coming from those identifying as females, or of multiracial backgrounds, or Asian descent. These findings underscore the importance of including attachment theory as a critical part of the Intersystem Approach (IA) when considering the functioning of family systems.

The BG Topics and Questions

The focused questions of the BG yield a tremendous amount of data for the practitioner to consider as the treatment process proceeds, all of which can help to conceptualize the client-system. Each aspect of BG (and those topics not included here) can be explored in greater detail through the construction of the other appropriate FGs.

In this section, we provide a selected review of pertinent issues that are addressed by the BG. Reflecting the biases of the authors, salient aspects of theory and research have been selected that may be helpful to both beginning and experienced clinicians, and include the following areas of focus:

- Marriage, Partnering, Dissolutions, and Divorces (couple)
- Birth Order and Adoption (individual)
- Health Patterns (individual)
- Contextual (family/contextual)

The purpose of the BG is to gather and identify key features of the client-system from the individual, couple, or family perspective(s) in the initial interview. The goal is to begin to identify the client's concerns and the attachment styles that are observable. The initial interview is an important opportunity to learn about the client-system's current relational context and brief history. It is important to note previous treatment, medications, and other considerations as the interview begins. If the client-system has been in previous treatment it is helpful to inquire about how the client benefited from previous experiences.

The BG Topics and Questions: Marriage/Partnering, Dissolutions, and Divorces; Birth Order, Adoption, and Health Topics; and the Contextual Considerations for the Client-System (Figure 10.1).

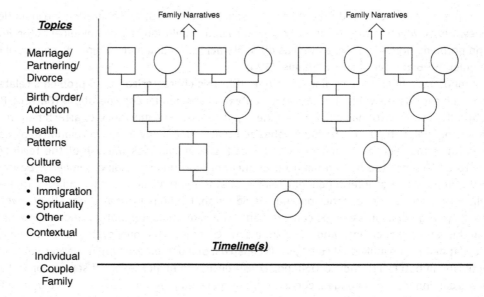

Figure 10.1 The Basic Genogram with Topics.

Marriage/Partnering, Dissolutions, and Divorces

Many families experience separation and dissolution. For instance, the current rate of divorce in the US is 3.2 per 1,000 (Centers for Disease Control and Prevention, 2014). The process of ending a relationship can often create havoc within a family. In instances where the erosion of a marriage occurs, which usually takes place over a period of years, the parties typically first experience ambivalence toward the marriage and emotional turmoil. With the marital breakup, there is often a tremendous amount of anger as each partner strengthens their commitment to divorce. As the divorce proceeds, sadness, loss, and grief mix with the anger as the reality of the family break-up takes hold. Children usually struggle with intense loyalty conflicts that can be exacerbated if parents want a child to "take sides" – referred to as "parental alienation syndrome" (Gardner, 1987) by some. Patterns of unrequited love, loss, abandonment, or divorce are important. It is remarkable how many people recreate their parents' patterns in this area. For example, a person deciding to divorce at 40 often has a father or mother who did so as well. Sometimes a person whose parents endured a difficult marriage and did not divorce feels compelled to divorce to prove they are not like the parent. A parent whose great love was an affair partner, rather than a spouse, leaves the child questioning whether real intimacy is possible within marriage. Managing dissolutions can be even more complex when the partners are of the similar gender, particularly as many currently lack legal recognition and support around marital and divorce practices, as well as clear relationship role models to which they can identify within their FOO (Blumer, 2008; Blumer & Green, 2011).

Divorce is never a complete emotional break, and families often contend with the dynamics of previous partnerships, as well as face economic disparities. For instance, female single-parent families often suffer more than their two-parent heterosexual and male-single parent household counterparts in terms of economic deprivation due to the gender inequities that continue to remain in place in the US (Twist, 2006). The legal, spiritual, domestic partnership, civil union, plural, or common-law marriage of two (or more) individuals forms the core of the family structure. Thus, exploring patterns of marriage and/or partnering, as well as when there are disruptions to such family formations like divorces and dissolutions, are important to examine and can influence the basis of family stability and attachment processes. In this section we provide an overview of marriage and/or partner patterning, dissolutions, and divorces. With the many forms of partnering that exist today, exploring partnering patterns can be quite a complex undertaking. The partnering lens provides a way to examine these patterns through the composition of a BG. Romantic love, sexuality, infidelity, and common couple violence patterns were presented in greater detail in *Focused Genograms*, 2nd Edition.

Marriage/Partnering, Divorce, and Dissolution Questions

1   What are the patterns of marriage and/or partnering (e.g., legal, spiritual, domestic, civil, plural, common-law marriages) and dissolutions (e.g., divorce, separation, uncoupling) in the family system?
2   If there are dissolutions, what are the known circumstances surrounding the ending of the relationship?
3   What types of partnering are there in the family system?
4   Have family members participated in premarital counseling or marital/couples therapy?
5   What kinds of stresses have resulted for the family if there has been dissolution?
6   How have parents worked out custody and visitation?

Exercise 10.1 Marriage/Partnering, Divorce, and Dissolution

Directions: Read the questions. List below the ones that appear most important to you? Why do you think this is so?

_____

_____

_____

_____

Birth Order

Many clinicians believe that identifying and exploring birth order and sibling roles is an essential part of family systems intervention. Toman (1989), who conducted research on family constellation patterns and their effects, emphasizes the importance of family dynamics over personality dynamics. Perlmutter (1988) encourages clinicians to explore sibling bonds and roles rather than assume that the ecology of the sibling subsystem is simply a reflection of parental functioning. Indeed, it is more often the case that it is the sibling subsystem that often serves as a template for future partnered and friend-based relationships.

Although his model was neither systematic nor comprehensive, Adler was the first to recognize the psychological effects of birth order (Toman, 1992). Since this time birth-order effects, or the patterns that tend to emerge in relation to the order in which children enter family systems, have received ongoing scholarly and clinical attention. Stewart and Stewart (1995) examined trends in birth-order research and found that through the 1970s to the mid-1980s topics such as achievement, intelligence, personality, and psychopathology received attention. They found that birth-order research evolved toward increased emphasis on cross-cultural factors, parent-child interactions, development, and family relations. Hoopes and Harper (1987) suggested that intergenerational family structure, process, as well as child and family development are significant influences on sibling positions and experiences. To elaborate, they suggested that siblings are influenced by the unresolved emotional issues of their parents, the unique family environment at the time they were born, and the roles that are associated with their birth order position. Additionally, the spacing, gender, addition or deletion of siblings, and identifying characteristic of the particular position are also important to the experience of each sibling.

A few things are important to note about these observations on sibling relationships. Some scholars have critiqued notions of sibling rivalry as being culturally bound to the dominant western culture. Observations of such dynamics between siblings do not appear present in situations when siblings are relating in oppressed cultural contexts like in economically disadvantaged and/or ethnic minority families. Indeed, in these cultural contexts the sibling relationships are typically characterized by high degrees of closeness and interdependency because of the need for survival.

Birth Order Questions

Sibling position and role, often referred to as *birth order*, affects individual development and personality in a number of ways, as well as future involvement in relationships. The questions that follow focus attention on this area of family life.

1   What is your birth order in your FOO?
2   What is the spacing between siblings? Was spacing planned? Were there large periods of time between siblings?
3   Are there half-siblings, step-siblings, and blended family siblings?
4   What is the gender of each sibling? Was there an expressed preference for a specific gender of a child?
5   What are the similarities and differences among the siblings?
6   Which siblings are more emotionally close to one another and which are more emotionally distant from each other?
7   Who is like one's parent(s), grandparent(s), aunt, uncle, or any other family member(s)?
8   How did you experience favoritism in your family?
9   Was there sibling rivalry or conflict that was experienced? How was this managed by the siblings? By parents?
10   Was there sibling support or encouragement that was experienced? How was this expressed by the siblings? By parents?
11   What is the birth order of your parent(s)? What effect do you think that has had on them?
12   What is the birth order of your partner(s)? What effect do you think this has had on your relationship?

Exercise 10.2 Birth Order

Directions: Read the questions. List below the ones that appear most important to you? Why do you think this is so?

_____

_____

_____

_____

Adoption

Adoption is another aspect of family structure and process that is examined through the construction of a BG. The role of adoption is important to explore in assessment, especially as the prevalence of adoption is on the rise, particularly in terms of instances of international and/or same-gender-headed household adoptions (Nickman et al., 2005).

Identifying the effects of age at adoption can be an important part of the assessment process. For instance, most scholars have reported that those adopted at earlier ages (typically 15 months of age and below) tend to experience little to no disruption, feel well-adjusted and have high self-esteem (Benson, Sharma, & Roehlkepartain, 1994; Nickman et al., 2005). In addition, parents of children adopted at these younger ages frequently report feeling deeply committed, and solidly attached to their children (Benson et al., 1994; Nickman et al., 2005). However, children adopted at older ages, particularly boys, are more likely to experience placement disruption, which is usually attributed to them having been more traumatized by things like malnutrition, social instability, abuse and neglect, and drug and alcohol exposure before placement with their adoptive families (Nickman et al., 2005). Researchers have identified variables associated with successful later-age adoption, including being female, being placed with one's biological siblings, being adopted by one's long-term foster parent(s), and/or being adopted by parents who have strong parenting skills (Nickman et al., 2005).

Currently, 2% of children under the age of 18 are adoptees in the US (Nickman et al., 2005). The historical, contemporary, social, and legal context of adoption has affected the ways in which these issues are addressed within the family. Because adoption has a lifetime impact on all the members of the family, it is important to assess the ways in which adoption shapes family development. Stressors for adoptive families often involve negotiation of the misinformation and stigmatization around adoption, knowledge of adoption processes, challenges regarding rights and legalities around adoption, and decisions regarding participation in private, open, semi-opened, and/or closed adoption processes (Hartman & Laird, 1990; Hartmann, 1993).

Adoption Questions

Adoption is another facet of birth order, as well as the overall family dynamics. The following are questions to consider when examining the effects of adoption.

1 What information is known about the biological donors? What beliefs exist about their circumstances, if known?
2 What are the differences and similarities between the culture of the adopted family and the culture of the biological donor family?
3 If infertility was a factor, how was it addressed?
4 What was the decision-making process? Were family reactions explored?
5 What kind of process (e.g., open, semi-open, private, closed, public, etc.) around adoption has taken place?
6 Were there difficulties with other children in the family (e.g. school problems, secrecy, inheritance issues, behavior problems)?
7 What was the age of the adopted members at the time of adoption?
8 How has the family managed any stigmatization around the adoption?
9 With regard to the adoption, what were some of the positives experienced within the family?
10 What are the history and family patterns around adoption?

Exercise 10.3 Adoption

Directions: Read the questions. List below the ones that appear most important to you? Why do you think this is so?

_____

_____

_____

_____

Health Assessment

Health is a factor that often is overlooked unless there is a serious or terminal illness that affects family functioning. Both psychiatric and physical illnesses are important components of the health-and-illness focus of the BG. Also included in conducting a health and illness assessment is the completion of a basic drug and alcohol use screening (see Chapter 11 for the Addictions Genogram). Unfortunately, a comprehensive theoretical overview and related assessment aimed at exploring illnesses, diseases, and genetic disorders is beyond the scope of this text. In the briefest sense, assigning death dates and causes of deaths of family members is essential to include in the BG. Asking questions about when a family member became mentally ill is also important information. For example, in one family the father had a history of severe depression from the age of 22. As his children approached this age, they all feared that depression might "capture" them. In addition, Eunpu (1997), a genetics counselor among other things, developed questions appropriate in cases of genetic illnesses and diseases that are useful regardless of the specific health problem.

The health assessment must also consider acute or chronic illnesses that have caused significant distress or readjustment to family life. The cohesion and flexibility of the family may be exemplified in stories about these incidences and how the family has coped with them. These health and medically focused questions are not always asked but are important because interactions with the medical world may affect families in a multitude of ways, both positive and negative. There may also be thematic significance in the Family Attachment Narrative (Vetere & Dallos, 2008) in reference to health or illness. Some themes may include resilience, strength or weakness, dependability, and mortality.

Health Questions

1 What are the patterns of illness (mental, genetic, physical) in the family? Did your parents' health affect the way they related to you? To others?

2   What messages did you receive from family members about illness in general, and/or certain medical diagnoses?
3   What are the known causes of death? Are there mysteries about how family members died?
4   Who was regarded as afflicted (sick or ill) in your family? Who believed themselves to be affected?
5   What were the attitudes of family members to those who were or are affected?
6   What is the meaning of doing something different regarding the genetic risks in your family (e.g., having or not having testing, terminating a pregnancy)?
7   What about the meaning of doing something different regarding the environmental risk factors in your family (e.g., eating less red meat, exercising, drinking less alcohol)?
8   What health conditions do you have if any, and what are the consequences for you?
9   Do you have health fears or concerns for your mortality?
10   Is your health affecting the way you relate to others?

Exercise 10.4 Health

Directions: Read the questions. List below the ones that appear most important to you? Why do you think this is so?

_____

_____

_____

_____

Contextual and Clinical Considerations for the BG

Race, Ethnicity, and Immigration

Cultural background and experiences determine attitudes and beliefs about life and what political, social, and economic options and opportunities people are likely to have are particularly important during the initial interviews. The cultural questions begin with an overview of racial cultural experience and then are expanded to include ethnicity and immigration, religious orientation, and socioeconomic status.

Cultural experiences organize attitudes, beliefs, feelings, and behaviors both personally and intergenerationally. These attitudes, beliefs, and behaviors are particularly evident in prejudices, biases, and bigotry that exist among and between various cultural groups. A cultural sense of self is important to a healthy self-esteem. Hardy and Laszloffy (1995) believe that cultural experience is the broadest multidimensional experience for understanding self and others. Questions around culture are a way of bringing these hidden values, expectations, and assumptions out into the open for review, clarification, and modification. The purpose of these questions is to examine the impact of race, immigration, and ethnicity, religious orientation, and socioeconomic class upon individuals. Culture defines some of the most important parameters within which family systems and individual personalities develop.

Cultural is often used as a broad umbrella term used to encapsulate different dimensions of one's individual and/or collective identity. Such dimensions include one's race, ethnicity, socioeconomic status, religious or spiritual orientation, etc., and the intersection of each of these dimensions. Cultural identities usually contain in them inherent strains and contradictions so that even those who are a part of the privileged, dominant majority identified in a particular time and space still experience areas of choice and areas of stress. Kirk and Okazawa-Rey (2003) coined the term "social location" to describe this interplay between multiple parts of who we are, or our social locations, and how these locations situate us so that we and those around us know who we are in relation to each other across varying contexts. Certain social locations are more salient at times than others based on the context and degree to which we (and other people) highlight them. Our social locations are composed of dominant and subordinate parts of our identity. Depending on the context, some social locations may be dominant, majorized, and/or privileged while others may be subordinate, minoritized, and/or oppressed (Kirk & Okazawa-Rey, 2003). For instance, a male-identifying, college instructor, who is European American, outwardly identifies as bisexual, and lives on the western coast of the US may experience privilege with regard to many parts of his social location like being educated, male, and racially White, yet, may experience marginalization in being bisexual depending on the community he is in on the West Coast (Blumer, Haym, Zimmerman, & Prouty, 2014).

In the US, "mainstream" or dominant culture, primarily European American culture encompasses a number of general beliefs, such as that individual rights and responsibilities take precedence over duty to extended family; progress, optimism, and future orientation are central values; and consumerism and enjoyment of material advantage are good things. The US still values family ties very highly, in spite of its commitment to individual choice. However, a person may belong to one or many different cultures by birth (e.g., Italian American), by marriage (e.g., a Caucasian American who marries a Vietnamese American), or by choice (e.g., a fundamentalist religious group, Civil war enthusiast). The culture may be all-encompassing, or partial, and may have values different from the mainstream culture. Fundamentalist religious groups of all persuasions place loyalty to church and community over self-determination. In the US, most people belong to a number of subcultures. The clinician can and must consider the areas where facets of a client-system's identity are representative of the interplay of power, oppression, and privilege, expanded upon by Kimberlé Crenshaw (1989), when exploring the experience of the multidimensional cultural identity. Intersectionality compounds disadvantages and highlights oppression and discrimination, and encapsulates the unique experience of any given individual client-system.

Cultural questions are a method of uncovering and addressing the influences of cultural biases. Cultural differences impact family dynamics in many ways. Cultural influences affect marital and/or partner relationships, parent-child relationships, and expectations about kinship and community. The clinician's attention to the cultural dimensions of the client's social experience often is perceived as validating and affirming and is an important part of building rapport. In general, multicultural counseling is associated with positive treatment outcomes (Yutrzenka, 1995). Indeed, if there are obvious cultural differences between the clinician and the client-system, asking questions around cultural considerations can be essential in developing an atmosphere of empathy, especially in the context of research demonstrating that clients are more satisfied with their therapeutic experience when their therapists are of a similar racial background (Coleman, Wampold, & Cassali, 1995). It is not only clients who report differences in the therapeutic experience in relation to shared or differing ethnic or racial backgrounds. Researchers have found that therapists who see themselves as racially similar to their clients (rather than racially different) report a higher understanding of the client problem, believe the client's change is more positive, and report that their clients are more likely to maintain change after therapy has concluded – all in comparison with clients they perceive as racially different (Murphy, Faulkner, & Behrens, 2004). Sensitivity to cultural themes and biases is a part of becoming a culturally informed clinician, and can also help the clinician overcome transferential and countertransferential roadblocks (Murphy, Park, & Lonsdale, 2006). If the client is uncomfortable, in any way, about discussing racial, ethnic, religious, or socioeconomic issues, the clinician can use the opportunity to talk with the client about their comfort level. There may be questions or beliefs that the client has that, when addressed, strengthen the therapeutic alliance.

Race, Ethnicity and Immigration Questions:

The questions in this section begin with those focused on race and racial experiences, and then they are expanded to include ethnicity and immigration queries.[1]

1   What do you know about your family's migration patterns? If they came as a family, who in the family wished to emigrate, and who did not?
2   How do family members define themselves racially and/or ethnically and how do you define yourself?
3   If other than Native American or American Indian, under what conditions did different family members (or their descendants) enter the US? In what years did they arrive?
4   Were there ties to the homeland? Where and how were they maintained?
5   If more than one group makes up the culture of origin, how were the differences negotiated in the family? What were the intergenerational consequences?
6   What are the ways in which pride and shame issues of each group are manifested in the family system?
7   Describe the relationship between the group cultural identity/ies and your individual cultural identity/ies. What were or are the group's experiences with oppression? What were or are the markers of oppression?

8   What significance do race, skin color, and hair play within the group?

9   What prejudices or stereotypes does this group have about itself? What prejudices and stereotypes do others hold about the group? What prejudices and stereotypes does the group have about other groups?

10   What role (if any) do names play in the group? Are there rules, mores, or rituals governing the assignment of names? What about play or nickname usage and patterns?

11   What occupational roles are valued or devalued by the group?

12   How does this group view outsiders in general, mental-health professionals, and other professions?

Exercise 10.5 Race, Ethnicity, and Immigration

Directions: Read the questions. List below the ones that appear most important to you? Why do you think this is so?

_____

_____

_____

_____

Religious, Spiritual, and/or Philosophical Orientation

Religion, spirituality, and/or life philosophy are powerful lenses to explore through questions regarding culture. Clinicians tend to leave the religious and spiritual dimension outside of the practice setting (Raider, 1992). In many families, religion plays a central role in the family's values, traditions, and rituals. Marriage, parenting, community service, and attitudes toward work, money, and productivity can be significantly influenced by religious beliefs. Many religions are, in fact, practiced as a way of life (e.g., Islam, Buddhism). Populations of various religious groups are concentrated in certain areas of the world, and thus those that immigrate to the US from these places bring their religious origins with them.

Raider (1992) has suggested that the therapist, through specific questioning, can help the client assess ways in which religion influences their family structure, their family processes, their family boundaries, and their family system equilibrium or integration. In order to enhance the power of the religious-orientation genogram, additional questions can be asked about family traditions and rituals. Careful assessment in these areas may uncover hopeful and helpful supports or guidance for the individuals and the family as they work together at problem-solving and decision-making.

While 84% of the world population identify with a religion, one of the largest groups is the non-religiously affiliated – a group on the rise (Hackett & Naylor, 2014). The unaffiliated group includes those who indicate no religion, identify as atheists or agnostics, and/or hold spiritual beliefs that are not necessarily linked to any established faith. The unaffiliated make up 16.3% (1.1 billion) of the world population, and are on the rise in Europe and North America, yet the majority, 62%, are concentrated in China (Hackett & Naylor, 2014). In addition, in the US there are generational differences associated with being unaffiliated. Those of younger-age cohorts are higher in count than those of older-age cohorts with a breakdown as follows: 32% of 18-29-year-olds, 21% of 30-49-year-olds, 15% of 50-64-year-olds, and 9% of those 65 years and above (Funk & Smith, 2012). As the cohort's age in the US, as well as the number of people of Asian descent, particularly Chinese, increases, perhaps we will see even more people identifying as unaffiliated. Yet, historically in the process of assimilating and acculturating to the dominant US culture many Asians who immigrate to the US have frequently become members of Christian faiths.

In general, understanding the diverse nature and contradictions of Christianity, Judaism, Islam, Buddhism, and other religious influences provides a broad context for understanding a particular family system in political, social, and historical perspectives. Although it is beyond the scope of this text, the clinician needs to have a basic understanding of the major religions and their influences on family systems. Although religions share many similarities, there are significant differences. Religions vary on whether they emphasize faith or specific deeds, what behaviors are valued (self-abnegation versus achievement, pacifism versus warfare to spread God's word), and what traditions are established and observed. They also vary in how much of a place they give to psychological issues. For example, is psychotherapy acceptable or should prayer suffice? In clinical practice with couples struggling with one partner's extramarital affair, the clients' religious and spiritual orientations have important implications for dealing with forgiveness. Forgiveness is a very different process in Jewish and Christian traditions, for example. One's religious orientation can even influence whether people define intimate relationships with more than one person as an affair or as a normative relational orientation (Blumer et al., 2014). For instance, it is not uncommon for Bedouin-Arabian Islamic practitioners to have family structures that include a husband with typically four wives (Al-Krenawi & Graham, 2006).

Family rituals and traditions have various levels of importance within family systems and often are tied to religious, spiritual, and/or philosophical beliefs (e.g., Christmas, Hanukkah, Ramadan, etc.). Other rituals and traditions can have ethnic origins. In order to provide the family with meaning and significance, such rituals and traditions are often repeated and coordinated allowing for a sense of predictability, continuity, connection, and identity as well as a way to enact values (Doherty, 1997). Doherty (1997) identified rituals of connection, celebration, and community. Rituals such as these can play a mediating role in families in terms of alcohol use and related patterns (Kiser, Bennett, Heston, & Paavola, 2005; Steinglass, Bennett, Wolin, & Reiss, 1987; Wolin & Bennett, 1990). More specifically, research by Wolin and Bennett (1984) demonstrated that planning and maintaining family rituals like family dinners, holidays, and other family celebrations are associated with significantly less transmission of alcohol drinking.

Religious, Spiritual, and/or Philosophical Orientation Questions

1   How important is religious or spiritual practice or affiliation?
2   What religious or spiritual affiliations exist within the family?
3   Is there a conflict within the family about religious or spiritual practices?
4   How do religious, spiritual, and/or life philosophy beliefs influence self-esteem, partnering, marriage, parenting, sexuality, and familial responsibilities and loyalties?
5   What are the unique features of the religious, spiritual, or philosophical orientation(s) of the family?
6   Have family members married outside the family faith or belief system? What were the consequences?
7   Is religious, spiritual, or philosophical affiliation a source of strength in the family system or a source of conflict?
8   How is family membership defined by the family's religions, spiritual, or philosophical orientation?
9   To what extent does the family's religion, spirituality, and/or life philosophy influence the degree of permeability of the family's boundaries with the neighborhood, community, and outside environment?
10 To what extent does the family's religion, spirituality, and/or life philosophy emphasize tradition, stability, and order?
11 How does the family system celebrate rituals of connection: family meals, rising and retiring, coming and going, going out and going away, couple(s) rituals?
12 How does the family system observe the rituals of celebration and community, special-person rituals, community rituals, lifespan rituals, religious rituals, rites of passage rituals, etc.?

Exercise 10.6 Religious, Spiritual, and/or Philosophical Orientation

Directions: Read the questions. List below the ones that appear most important to you? Why do you think this is so?

_____

_____

_____

_____

Socioeconomic Status

Socioeconomic status (SES) and experience influence important areas of life. SES is a complex process and involves more than just a family or individual's financial status. Instead, SES is helpful when conceptualized as having differing, yet interrelated components – social position and economic status. For example, a person can come from a FOO where the economic status is lower in income, but their social experiences are characterized as more middle class. They may partner with someone whose economic background is of an upper income and upper social status. If these two people have a child, their SES is not neatly a middle-class status as if the upper- and lower-class experiences simply create a splitting of the differences in the next generation, but rather the child's SES will be an intersection of that of their parental units. Thus, they will embody components of the varied FOO SES experiences. They may economically be middle class, and socially upper class in areas like education and travel, but be lower class in terms of patterns around health, nutrition, and divorce.

Ross (1995) calls attention to the importance of attending to issues of social class within the family system. She identifies three patterns of social class tension: one family member achieving significantly more or less than others within the family system, marrying someone who is "up" or "down" in social class, and divorce and remarriage, causing class differences between children and parents. Ross notes that upward or downward mobility of individual family members can be the basis for many tensions within the individual and the family and that, too often, these tensions go unacknowledged by clinicians. Social-class tensions affect individuation and differentiation, identity, and attitudes toward financial success. The social-class lens focuses the therapist to consider the influence of these tensions. With the most recent "great recession" (as it has been called in the US), which began in approximately 2008 and is slowly dissipating, exploration of SES may be more critical now, and for subsequent generations, than at any other point in recent history (Blumer, Nemecek et al., 2014). The last major recession of this kind, the Great Depression (1929–1939), was primarily tied to changes in weather conditions like droughts, which resulted in job loss, and unemployment, and the related experience of poverty for many individuals and families (Jackson & Warr, 1984). This affected people's social experiences in myriad ways. For one, the rate of only-child families was higher than at any other point in US history – with 25% of families being comprised of only children.

The most recent recession has been economically similar, yet different. First, unemployment numbers have remained higher for longer than in previous recessions (Tasci & Mowry, 2009). Second, this recession was tied to an unprecedented number of housing foreclosures, which contributed to increased levels of personal and familial stress related to things like forced relocation. The social effects of this more recent recession have also been similar to, yet different from the last. For example, it has been similar in terms of the number of only child families also increased to roughly 25%, different in that the number of families not having children also increased. There have also been resulting shifts in gender roles and power dynamics in families, as many of the labor force that lost their jobs were men, which placed them in the role of becoming the home- and child-care providers while their wives maintained or acquired jobs outside the home (Blumer, Nemecek et al., 2014).

Socioeconomic Questions

Social class is an important aspect of American life, yet it is frequently overlooked in the clinical setting. Yet socioeconomics cut across all aspects of one's life and their intergenerational story. Thus, questions around socioeconomics are essential to include in BG construction.

1   What did you learn from your parents about social class? With what class did your parents identify themselves? How did this fit or not fit with what they modeled for you by their behavior, where they lived, whom they associated with, and so forth?
2   Would your parents agree or disagree with your perceptions? How important was social class to them and to your siblings in the neighborhood in which you grew up?
3   Do you think your family was more or less concerned about social class than other families? How might things have been different in your family if different economic possibilities had been available to it?
4   Do different members of your family belong to different social classes? Have members of your family changed class (up or down) due to marriage, making or losing money, illness, or bad luck?

5 When you were growing up, what messages did peers pass on about social class? What ideas about social class do you want to pass on to the next generation? How are these the same or different from what your parents taught you?

6 Think back to when you first visited, lived in, and worked in a neighborhood of a different social class. How did you think about social class differently/act differently after that?

7 How have recessions affected your FOO? Family of procreation? Family of choice? Neighborhood? Community?

8 What are the FOO and procreation experiences with relocation and moving? What have been the reasons behind the moves? Have the moves been within a state, across states, across countries, etc.?

Exercise 10.7 Socioeconomic

Directions: Read the questions. List below the ones that appear most important to you? Why do you think this is so?

_____

_____

_____

_____

Further Considerations for Exploring Race, Ethnicity, and Immigration Factors

Race

Race is an extraordinarily complex issue in the US, which is one of the most racially diverse and racially conscious countries in the world. Physical-trait differences in skin color or clear differences in features are the usual basis for differentiating race, but, in fact, race is, to a surprising extent, a social construction. Social construction of racial identity is fluid and affects a person's power and privilege throughout the IA. Moreover, although race is a social construction the effects of race and related racism are very real. People of Caucasian European descent are privileged in the US while People of Color, or those defined as People of Color, have fewer opportunities and less access to power. For example, by the end of the American Civil War there was so much intermingling of Caucasians and African Americans (primarily due to white slave owners having sex with their slaves) that a socially constructed definition was created during the post-Civil War period: anyone with one eighth (or even one sixteenth or one thirty-second, depending on the state) of African heritage was considered Black. Many such people, of course, had Caucasian skin and features. Fear of "racial impurity" was so strong that it was a crime to "pass." The ability to "pass" and the concept of "passing" demonstrates the power of the social construction of race.

The ongoing changes to racial categories employed by the United States Census Bureau with each iteration of the Census further demonstrate the reality of race as a social construction (Blumer, 2014). In the 1790s the options for racial categories on the US Census were White and other. By 1920 the categories were White, Black, Mulatto, Indian, Chinese, Japanese, Filipino, Hindu, Korean, and other. In 1960 the categories were White, Negro, American Indian, Japanese, Chinese, Filipino, and other. In the most recent Census (2010) the racial classification included White, Black or African American, American Indian or Alaska Native, Asian, and Native Hawaiian or Other Pacific Islander. The United Nations views the construction of race as so problematic on a global scale that it dropped the use of the term in 1950 in favor of ethnicity, of which the organization estimates there are over 5,000 different distinct ethnic groups worldwide.

South America is a particularly interesting example of the interaction between race and ethnicity. Many South Americans are multiracial and multiethnic, the result of the mixing of indigenous peoples, African slaves, and European conquerors. However, those with mostly European heritage are still privileged. Many White North Americans tend to label anyone with a Spanish accent from Central and South America, Cuba, or Puerto

Rico as "Hispanic" or "Latino," which erases specific differences of race, class, and ethnicity. For example, a Puerto Rican man states that he defines himself as Puerto Rican but does not think of himself as a Person of Color. However, while in the US he identifies himself as a minority and identifies with People of Color. A socio-economically privileged Argentinian woman identifies herself as White and upper class. She is troubled that in the US, when among people who do not know her, she is treated with disrespect and seen as a Person of Color, which she attributes to their perception of her accent. The term *Latino* or *Latina* tells very little about the specifics of class, race, or country. Thus, in asking queries around race, the therapist must explore the person's own construction of their cultural identity, as well as how they experience racial and cultural biases.

In the US, race is often a code word for Black–White relations, which have their roots in slavery. There are people alive in this country whose grandparents or great-grandparents were slaves or shareholders so that this heritage is still very real and alive today. The most obvious markers of segregation – the separate water fountains, the segregated neighborhoods, the laws against interracial marriage – were still the norms in the childhood for one of our co-authors in *Focused Genograms*, 2nd Edition (Gerald Weeks), for instance. The consistent prejudice and discrimination against African Americans and the impact of slavery have made it difficult for African Americans to experience equality and equity in the US. Such discrimination and prejudice are ultimately rooted in White privilege and the dominance that comes with this unearned power. Some scholars hypothesize that such race-based discrimination in the US continues in part because this privilege that White North Americans' hold has hurt their capacity to understand racism (Jealous & Haskell, 2013). Thus, one way of diminishing racial discrimination is to help White people to see and acknowledge their skin and related privilege, and own the implications of this privileged position for themselves and People of Color (Case, 2013). Indeed, in the US, "white skin" is privileged in a variety of ways, one of which is that one's actions are not considered to be a reflection on one's race. For People of Color, the anticipation of and vulnerability to prejudice are daily facts. One of the most confusing situations to a Person of Color is that, in these days in which segregation laws do not exist but racism does, many situations are ambiguous. For instance, advancements, problem relationships, or poor performance reviews may be about performance or related in some way to racial biases.

Despite often-hostile environments, many People of Color do well in this country. This is due to both their own abilities and the abilities of their families to help them deal with prejudice and discrimination in a nonrestrictive way. Unfortunately, mainstream prejudice often is integrated into individuals and family life (like in the form of internalized racism), so that in some African American families light skin and straight hair are preferred and light-skinned children are treated better than dark-skinned ones (Pinderhughes, 1989). It is important to understand how the family supports the child in developing a positive racial identity and teaches them to deal with the daily problems of living in a highly stressful situation. Class also impacts the family. Middle-class African American families, like other middle-class families, live in a different situation than those in poverty. Gender is also a factor. The experiences of African American women are different from those of African American men. Black men are perceived as more dangerous, and often have fewer academic and work opportunities, than women (Boyd-Franklin, 1989). Yet, on average, African American men continue to economically outearn their female counterparts (Hegewisch, William, Hartman, & Hudiburg, 2014).

Ethnicity and Immigration

Cultural genograms (Hardy & Laszoloffy, 1995; Shellenberger et al., 2007) have emphasized the importance of cultural genograms for family therapists and health care providers. Cultural genograms typically focus on traditional information on the family background but also cultural values around ethnicity, immigration, health beliefs, and behaviors, and prevention practices. Ethnicity involves the classification or affiliation a person experiences with a particular group, and often includes a sense of belonging. It is used to describe one's identification or allegiance with a group of people of shared social and/or cultural heritage. One's ethnic group will have common customs, characteristics, languages, foods, dressing rituals, and appearances. In the US, many people have this type of dual identity – a sense of roots connected to the area of emigration as well as an allegiance to mainstream values. A vast number of Americans are within four or five generations of immigration experience and have some connection to their country (or countries) of origin. The process of acculturation – that is, the switch to predominant allegiance to and expression of the dominant culture – is difficult and normally takes a family about three generations.

The circumstances of immigration are often important themes in the BG and should be explored in detail. These patterns suggest that clinicians cannot overlook the immigration and ethnicity of a family system and its impact on current family functioning. The major trends that have emerged since the 2014[2] Census continue to be that the Asian American population is growing faster than any other population. Additionally, those identifying as more than one race are a population that is growing at a rate much more rapidly than those identifying as one race alone. These trends are expected to continue. Moreover, the Census Bureau estimates that current minority groups will comprise more than half of the US population by 2044, a phenomenon they call the "majority-minority crossover." Thus, at some point in this century, it is likely that White European Americans will constitute the minority of people in the US (Olmedo, 1994). These facts have important implications. For one, there are differences in the legacies that are passed down through generations. Next, there are cultural intersections (i.e., ethnicity, race, education, socioeconomic level, gender, sexual orientation, etc.) between variables that emerge for each person. Thus, changes in immigration patterns and cultural intersections affect different generations of a family system and each individual within a family system.

For a number of reasons few families in this country will be able to go beyond constructing genograms that include more than four generations. For one, the majority of immigration to the US occurred in the late 1800s and early 1900s, so tracking patterns before this time can be difficult, given that family histories often went unrecorded. Second, the immigration records for many non-White American people are difficult to accurately track, because of the circumstances under which their families came to the US, like through slavery, indentured servitude, and/or through wartime and refugee experiences. Third, the records of many indigenous people to the US were not documented in written format, nor maintained, and/or were destroyed. In other instances, the situation is such that in immigrating, a cutoff for a family from its ethnic roots occurs. Thus, the circumstances that led to immigration becomes a family myth, usurped in the process of acculturating and assimilating to the dominant culture, or simply lost to memory. By being knowledgeable about immigration patterns, clinicians can be more focused on asking cultural questions around immigration. A basic knowledge of history helps the process as well. If a client does some background research on their family, they often find out where the family tree stops. Asking historical questions during this process often can help the client gain a richer understanding of the impact of immigration on the family system.

In general, researchers have found that having a greater understanding of one's ethnic identity helps foster a sense of self-actualization (Helms, 1993). Clients often report that getting and giving cultural history reconnects them to their ethnic origins. The therapeutic alliance is strengthened by increased empathy between clinician and client. Clients often state that learning about their family heritage is a significant and important experience as part of the treatment process. In addition, when clinicians attend to their own ethnic identity it improves understanding of why "-isms" persist, and creates more of an opportunity to work toward combating and changing "-isms" in ourselves, our clients, and the community at large (Case, 2015; Jealous & Haskell, 2013; Murphy et al., 2006).

Immigration patterns are considered carefully by asking cultural questions around immigration. The US is an ethnically diverse nation, and this diversity will be evident in many genograms. The majority of Americans are descended from Europeans who came to the US to obtain religious and/or political freedom and economic opportunities.

Exercise 10.8 BG Topics

Directions: After exploring the multiple aspects of the BG and its various Topics, list below how each of these topics' questions might become useful to you as a clinician and why?

- Marriage, Partnering, Dissolutions, and Divorces (couple)

_____

_____

_____

- Birth Order and Adoption (individual)

  _____

  _____

  _____

- Health Patterns (individual)

  _____

  _____

  _____

- Contextual (family/contextual)

  _____

  _____

  _____

Summary

The basic family genogram was used in a variety of ways in the pioneering days of family therapy which began around the 1940s, which was also around the time period when child development centers also emerged. Coincidentally, penicillin was discovered and used to improve the odds of recovering from infections and much more, which also led to increases in longevity. The history of increasing lifespans is a fascinating story. As people lived longer, family stories became more available and extended family members had the possibilities of getting to know others in their extended family system. The topics in the BG relate to essential information that family members typically want to know more. The more knowledge and understanding, the more likely individuals could make more sense out of their own life experiences and their unique family systems. We have described a variety of topics and tools – the maps and timelines – that become the starting point from which you can deepen assessment.

As *the* classic inclusion in the assessment process, the BG focuses on overall family structure and functioning. Due to its broad scope, the BG becomes the template for constructing each themed FG. The BG assesses marriage/partnering and/or dissolution, birth order, adoption, health, and multiple aspects of contextual factors. Questions within each section will help the clinician begin to focus the assessment within each area, but are not exhaustive and the clinicians can add their own questions, as well. These details are crucial to understanding the particular idiosyncrasies of the client-system's life experiences in all domains: individual, couple, family, and contextual. In conjunction with the attachment-based maps and timelines, the BG aids the clinician in gathering basic information foundational to relevant themed FGs.

Notes

1 For additional exploration, see Hardy and Laszloffy (1995) and Shellenberger et al. (2007).
2 www.census.gov/content/dam/Census/library/publications/2015/demo/p25-1143.pdf.

References

Al-Krenawi, A., & Graham, J. R. (2006). A comparison of family functioning, life and marital satisfaction, and mental health of women in polygamous and monogamous marriages. *International Journal of Social Psychiatry, 52*(1), 5-17.

Barber, B. K., & Buehler, C. (1996). Family cohesion and enmeshment, different constructs, different effects. *Journal of Marriage and the Family, 58*(2), 433-441.

Barber, B. K., Olsen, J. E., & Shagle, S. C. (1994). Associations between parental psychological and behavioral control and youth internalized and externalized behaviors. *Child Development, 65*(4), 1120-1136.

Barrera, A. M., Blumer, M. L. C., & Soenksen, S. (2011). Revisiting adolescent separation-individuation in the contexts of enmeshment and allocentrism. *New School Psychology Bulletin, 8*(2), 70-82.

Benson, P. L., Sharma A. R., & Roehlkepartain E. C. (1994). *Growing Up Adopted: A Portrait of Adolescents and Their Families.* Minneapolis, MN: Search Institute.

Black, L., & Jackson, V. (2005). Families of African origin: An overview. In M. McGoldrick, J. Giordano, & N. Garcia-Preto (Eds.). *Ethnicity and family therapy* (3rd ed., pp. 77-86). New York, NY: Guilford Press.

Blumer, M. L. C. (2008). Gay men's experiences of Alaskan society in their coupled relationships, Doctoral dissertation, Thesis/Dissertation ETD, Temple University in Philadelphia PA.

Blumer, M. L. C. (2014, January). *Overview of race and ethnicity for family therapists.* On-demand Online Educational Webinar, American Association of Marriage and Family Therapy, Alexandria, VA.Blumer, M. L. C., & Green, M. S. (2011, September). *The role of same-sex couple development in clinical practice.* Workshop presented at the annual conference of the American Association for Marriage and Family Therapy, Fort Worth, TX.

Blumer, M. L. C., Haym, C., Zimmerman, K. J., & Prouty, A. M. (2014). What's one got to do with it? Considering monogamous privilege. *Family Therapy Magazine, 13*(2), 28-33.

Blumer, M. L. C., Nemecek, R. T. L., Hertlein, K. M., Rogers, K., Weeks, G. R., Peterson, C. M., & Fife, S. T. (2014). Counseling the unemployed: Exploring MFT trainees' perceptions of a pilot clinical program. *The American Journal of Family Therapy, 42*(3), 205-216.

Bograd, M. (1988). Enmeshment, fusion or relatedness? A conceptual analysis. *Journal of Psychotherapy and the Family, 3*(4), 65-80.

Bowen, M. (1978). *Family therapy in clinical practice.* New York: Rowman & Littlefield Publishers, Inc.

Boyd-Franklin, N. (1989). Five key factors in the treatment of black families. *Journal of Psychotherapy & the Family, 6*(1-2), 53-69.

Byng-Hall, J. (1999). Family therapy and couple therapy: Toward greater security. In J. Cassidy & P. R. Shaver (Eds.), *Handbook of attachment: Theory, research, and clinical applications.* (pp. 625-645). New York, NY: Guilford Press.

Carter, B., & McGoldrick, M. (1999, 2005). *The expanded family life cycle: Individual, family, and Social Perspectives.* Needham Heights, MA: Allyn & Bacon.

Case, K. (2013). Beyond diversity and whiteness: Developing a transformative and intersectional privilege studies pedagogy. In K. Case (Ed.), *Deconstructing privilege: Teaching and learning as allies in the classroom* (pp. 1-14). New York, NY: Routledge.

Case, K. (2015). White practitioners in therapeutic allyance: An intersectional privilege awareness training model. *Women and Therapy, 38,* 263-278.

Centers for Disease Control and Prevention. (2014). *National marriage and divorce rate trends.* Retrieved on June 10, 2016 from. https://www.cdc.gov/nchs/nvss/marriage-divorce.htm

Coleman, H. L. K., Wampold, B. E., & Casali, S. L. (1995). Ethnic minorities' ratings of ethnically similar and European American counselors: A meta-analysis. *Journal of Counseling Psychology, 42,* 55-64.

Crenshaw, K. (1989). Demarginalizing the intersection of race and sex: A black feminist critique of antidiscrimination doctrine, feminist theory and antiracist politics. *University of Chicago Legal Forum, 1989,* Article 8, 139-167.

Doherty, R. W. (1997). The emotional contagion scale: A measure of individual differences. *Journal of Nonverbal Behavior, 21,* 131-154.

Eunpu, D. L. (1997). Systemically-based psychotherapeutic techniques in genetic counseling. *Journal of Genetic Counseling, 6*(1), 1-20.

Fleck, S. (1989). *Psychiatric prevention and the family life cycle. By the Committee on Preventive Psychiatry, Group for the Advancement of Psychiatry.* New York: Brunner/Mazel.

Funk, C., & Smith, G. (2012). *Nones on the rise: One-in-five adults have no religious affiliation.* Washington, DC: Pew Research Center.

Gardner, R. A. (1987). *The parental alienation syndrome and the differentiation between fabricated and genuine child sex abuse.* Cresskill, NJ: Creative Therapeutics.

Hackett, C., & Naylor, J. (2014). *Many religions heavily concentrated in one or two countries.* Washington, DC: Pew Research Center.

Hardy, K. V., & Laszloffy, T. A. (1995). The cultural genogram: Key to training culturally competent family therapists. *Journal of Marital and Family Therapy, 21*(3), 227-237.

Harrar, S., & DeMaria, R. (2007). *The 7 stages of marriage: Laughter, intimacy and passion today, tomorrow, forever.* Pleasantville, NY: Reader's Digest.

Hartman, A., & Laird, J. (1990). Family treatment after adoption: Common themes. In D. M. Brodzinsky & M. Schechter (Eds.), *The psychology of adoption* (pp. 221-239). Oxford: Oxford University Press.

Hartmann, E. (1993). *Boundaries in the mind: A new psychology of personality.* New York, NY: Basic Books.

Hegewisch, A., Hartman, H., Williams, C., & Hudiburg, S. (2014). *The gender wage gap: Differences by race and ethnicity.* Washington, DC: Institute for Women's Policy Research.

Helms, J. E. (1993). More psychologists discover the wheel: A reaction to views by Penn et al., on ethnic preference. *Journal of Black Psychology, 19*(3), 322-326.

Hollander-Goldfein, B., Isserman, N., & Goldberg, J. (2012). *Transcending trauma: Survival, resilience, and clinical implications in survivor families.* New York, NY: Routledge.

Hoopes, M. H., & Harper, J. M. (1987). *Birth order roles & sibling patterns in individual & family therapy.* Rockville, MD: Aspen.

Jackson, R. & Warr, B. (1984). Unemployment and psychological ill-health: The moderating role of duration and age. *Psychological Medicine, 14,* 605-614.

Jealous, A. T., & Haskell, C. T. (2013). *Combined destinies: Whites sharing grief about racism.* Washington, DC: Potomac Books.

Johnson, S. M. (1986). Bonds or bargains: Relationship paradigms and their significance for marital therapy. *Journal of Marital and Family Therapy, 12,* 259-267.

Kagitcibasi, C. (2003). Autonomy, embeddedness and adaptability in immigration contexts. *Human Development, 46*, 145-150.

Kirk, G., & Okazawa-Rey, M. (2003). Identities and social locations: Who am I? Who are my people? In *Women's Lives: Multicultural Perspectives* (3rd ed., pp. 59-110). New York, NY: McGraw-Hill.

Kiser, L., Bennett, L., Heston J., & Paavola, M. (2005). Family ritual and routine: Comparing clinical and non-clinical families. *Journal of Child and Family Studies, 14*(3), 357-372.

Manzi, C., Vignoles, V. L., Regalia, C., & Scabini, E. (2006). Cohesion and enmeshment revisited: Differentiation, identity, and well-being in two European cultures. *Journal of Marriage and Family, 68*(3), 673-689.

McGoldrick, M., & Carter, B. (2003). The family life cycle. In F. Walsh (Ed.), *Normal family processes: Growing diversity and complexity* (pp. 375-398). New York, NY: Guilford Press.

McIntosh, P. (1998). *A personal account of coming to see correspondences through work in women's studies.* Presented at the Virginia Women's Studies Association conference, Richmond, VA.

Monte, E. P. (1989). The relationship life-cycle. In G. R. Weeks (Ed.), *Treating couples* (pp. 287-316). New York, NY: Brunner/Mazel.

Murphy, M. J., Faulkner, R. A., & Behrens, C. (2004). The effect of therapist-client racial similarity on client satisfaction and therapist evaluation of treatment. *Contemporary Family Therapy, 26*(3), 279-292.

Murphy, M. J., Park, J., & Lonsdale, N. J. (2006). Marriage and family therapy students' change in multicultural counseling competencies after a diversity course. *Contemporary Family Therapy, 28*, 303-311.

Nickman, S. L., Rosenfeld, A., Fine, P., MacIntyre, J. C., Pilowsky, D., Howe, R., ... Sveda, S. (2005). Children in adoptive families: Overview and update. *Journal of American Academy of Child and Adolescent Psychiatry, 44*(10), 987-995.

Olmedo, E. (1994). *Testimony of Esteban Olmedo to the subcommittee on health and the environment.* United States House of Representatives Committee on Energy and Commerce. Reprinted in CSPP Visions 7:15-17.

Olson, D. H. (1999). Empirical approaches to family assessment. *Journal of Family Therapy, 22*(4), 447-449.

Olson, D. H. (2011). FACES IV and the Circumplex model: Validation study. *Journal of Marital & Family Therapy, 37*(1), 64-80.

Perlmutter, M. S. (1988). Enchantment of siblings: Effects of birth order and trance on family myth. In M. D. Kahn & K. G. Lewis (Eds.), *Siblings in therapy: Life span and clinical issues* (pp. 25-45). New York, NY: Norton.

Pinderhughes, C. A. (1989). Expressively black: The cultural basis of ethnic identity. *The Journal of Nervous and Mental Disease, 177*(8), 503-504.

Raider, M. (1992). Assessing the role of religion in family functioning. In L. A. Burton (Ed.), *Religion and the family: When God helps* (pp. 165-183). New York, NY: Haworth Press.

Rice, K. G., Cole, D. A., & Lapsley, D. K. (1990). Separation individuation, family cohesion, and adjustment to college: Measurement validation and test of a theoretical model. *Journal of Counseling Psychology, 37*(2), 195-202.

Rosen, E. J., & Weltman, S. F. (1996). Jewish families: An overview. In M. McGoldrick, J. Giordano, & J. K. Pearce (Eds.), *Ethnicity and family therapy* (2nd ed., pp. 611-630). New York, NY: Guilford.

Ross, J. L. (1995). Social class tensions within families. *The American Journal of Family Therapy, 23*(4), 338-350.

Schor, E. L. (2003). Family pediatrics: Report of the task force on the family. *Pediatrics, 111*(6 Pt 2), 1541-1571.

Sheehy, G. (1984, 1995, 1996, 1998, 2006). *Passages.* NY and London: Random House.

Shellenberger, S., Dent, M. M., Davis-Smith, M., Seale, J. P., Weintraut, R., & Wright, T. (2007). Cultural genogram: A tool for teaching and practice. *Families, Systems, & Health, 25*(4), 367-381.

Steinglass, P., Bennett, L. A., Wolin, S. J., & Reiss, D. (1987). *The alcoholic family.* New York, NY: Basic Books.

Stewart, A. E., & Stewart, E. A. (1995) Trends in birth-order research: 1976-1993. *Journal of Individual Psychology, 51*(1), 21-36.

Tasci, M., & Mowry, B. (2009). *The labor market in this downturn: A historical comparison.* (Economic Trends, 6.05.09, 27-29). Retrieved from Cleveland Fed Digest, Publications - Economic Trends, Discontinued 2016; Website: https://www.clevelandfed.org/our-research/publications.aspx

Toman, S. (1989). Issues of a nontraditional student: The case of Fabian. *The Career Development Quarterly, 38*(1), 25-27.

Toman, S. (1992). The career dilemma of an artistic client: The case of Rachel. *The Career Development Quarterly, 41*(1), 27-29.

Triandis, H. C., & Gelfand, M. J. (1998). Converging measurement of horizontal and vertical individualism and collectivism. *Journal of Personality and Social Psychology, 74*(1), 118-128.

Twist, M. (2006). A response to the Babies and Bosses Report: The effects of policy on therapy and the influence of therapists on politics. *Journal of Feminist Family Therapy: An International Forum, 17*, 67-77.

Vetere, A, & Dallos, R. (2008). Systemic therapy and attachment narratives. *Journal of Family Therapy. The Association for Family Therapy, 30*, 374-385.

Wattendorf, D. J. & Hadley, D. (2005). Family history: The three-generation pedigree. *American Family Physician, 72*(3), 441-448.

Weeks, G. R. & Wright, L. (1979). Dialectics of family life cycle. *The American Journal of Family Therapy, 7*(1), 85-91.

Wolin, S. J., & Bennett, L. A. (1984). Family rituals. *Family Process, 23*, 401-420.

Wolin, S. J., & Bennett, L. A. (1990). Family cultural and alcoholism transmission. In R. L. Collins, K. E. Leonard, & J. S. Searles (Eds.), *Alcohol and the family* (pp. 194-219). New York, NY: Guilford Press.

Yutrzenka, B. A. (1995). Making a case for training in ethnic and cultural diversity in increasing treatment efficacy. *Journal of Consulting and Clinical Psychology, 63*, 197-206.

11 The Addictions Focused Genogram

A Companion for Comprehensive Clinical Assessment with Markie L. C. Twist

Overview

The Addictions Focused Genogram (AdFG) is included in the Focused Genogram Workbook (FGW) because of the significant importance of identifying substance and behavioral addictions throughout the intersystem approach (IA) domains. In this workbook, the Basic Genogram and the AdFG are important throughout an assessment with any given client-system. In this workbook, the AdFG incorporates attachment patterns, styles, and narratives into a comprehensive individualized and intergenerational assessment of addictions. This is an expansion of the initial screening provided in the Basic Genogram, and is useful with many client-systems. The Family Connection Map (FCM) is an important resource for the clinician and for the clients. The objective of the AdFG is to structure treatment to meet clients' needs and to facilitate systemic change.

This FGW chapter emphasizes the crucial importance of assessing for addictions issues thoroughly in the early phase of treatment. Thus, in this chapter we will provide a brief overview of the varied definitions of addictions, and the different kinds of addictions, theoretical considerations of addictions with attention to the role of attachment, and an overview of the relationship between addictions and family systems and sociocultural groupings. The chapter provides ways to construct genograms and ask related focused genogram (FG) questions that focus on addictions. It is important to note too, that the bulk of the information contained within this chapter, will be weighted toward the manner in which addiction is conceptualized via the American Psychiatric Association (APA) in the fifth edition of the *Diagnostic and Statistical Manual of Mental Disorders* (*DSM-V*; APA, 2013) in order to meet current diagnostic criteria and the needs of both clinicians and clients for treatment. However, there will be some information provided on addictions in this chapter that are being considered for inclusion in future iterations of the DSM but are not contained within the current edition.

Objectives

1   Construct the AdFG using the Case Study Observations within the AdFG, noting the questions provided in each section (Exercise 11.1).
2   Evaluate the content of the myriad variations of Addiction Questions (Exercises 11.2-11.5).

Exploring the AdFG

Addictions, which affect individual health, as well as relational functioning, can pervade and demolish family life. The consequences of addictions include lowered self-esteem, increased risk-taking behaviors, financial disaster, relational stress and dissolution, career and work difficulties, loss of friends, and loneliness. The development of an AdFG is very useful in detailing intergenerational patterns of addiction and identifying vulnerabilities to a variety of addictions. Griffiths (2005) proposed that many addictive behaviors have commonalities, and that an eclectic approach may be the most useful framework for understanding addiction. Morgenstern and Mckay (2007) highlight 25 years of psychotherapy research on addiction emphasizing the limitations of current approaches to treatment and suggested that the field begins "rethinking the paradigms that inform behavioral treatment research for substance use disorders" (p. 1377). The IA, now incorporating attachment theory as an

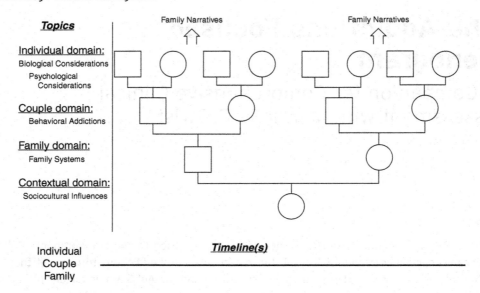

Figure 11.1 Addictions Focused Genogram with Topics.

integrational construct, is an important addition to helping client-systems with substance-related and behavioral addictions. Destructive habits of living form the rubric for ongoing suffering for those who are addicted and their families. The comprehensive assessment provided by the IA and the attachment-based focused genograms provides therapists a map for initiating treatment.

Most professionals see the etiology of addictions as biopsychosocial. Our focus on the IA's four domains – individual, couple/partner(s), family, and context – for assessment and treatment of addictions is consistent with this professional perspective. However, it is important to note that the AdFG is not a comprehensive medical, psychological, or behavioral assessment for any given client-system. We include the AdFG as an FG in this edition because of the fact that addictions interfere with healthy family function at all levels – the individual, the couple (as partners and parents), the entire family system, and the community. The themes for the four domains are (1) individual biopsychosocial considerations and addictions, (2) couples/partners and behavioral addictions, (3) family systems and addictions, and (4) sociocultural considerations and addictions. We provide questions for the clinician as a guide to exploring the themes for each of these domains. These questions may lead the client to feel more fully understood, which may help the development of a systemic therapeutic alliance. Figure 11.1 shows the AdFG template. The AdFG includes the following topics: biological and psychological considerations, behavioral addictions, family systems, and sociocultural influences.

Incorporating an Attachment Focus on Addictions

We see our work as influenced by, as well as adding to the work of our predecessors. Bradshaw's (1988, 1996) seminal work on "the family" brought the destructive forces of addiction on individuals into the light of day. Bradshaw's book was presaged by the conceptual model of Stanton et al. (1978), which focused on the experiencing of heroin addiction as a family phenomenon, and a harbinger of Stanton, Todd, and associate's (1982) *Family Therapy of Drug Abuse and Addiction*. Liddle and his associates (1999, 2003, 2010) followed the lead of Stanton and others to develop Multidimensional Family Therapy for adolescent drug abuse. In Beattie's (1986) *Codependent No More*, the role of codependency and the challenges of life with family members experiencing addiction was the focus. Later, Elliott (1991) developed and tested a measure of codependency – the Friel Codependency Inventory – which appears to reveal codependency as an independent construct for family members. It is important to note though that there is a real danger in perpetuating the idea that all family members with substance use addiction experiences have codependency within their family system, because researchers have found that linkages between codependency and substance use addiction may be mediated through general mental and relational health functioning of family members (Cullen & Carr, 1999; Knudson & Terrell, 2012). Indeed, in families where there is a lack of clarity of roles, warmth, support, and appropriate affective expression and family members have mental health issues, people may take on more codependent roles to caretake, and may not take on such roles in families where this is substance use addiction in which these other issues are not present (Cullen & Carr, 1999; Knudson & Terrell, 2012). Regardless, the impact of addictions on families and communities has been widely recognized, especially by social epidemiologists (Galea, Nandi, & Vlahov, 2004). Finally, Griffiths (2005) highlights that there are commonalities among substance and addictive behaviors. The IA provides a systemic model that integrates elements of all the theories mentioned above, and adds the concept of attachment bonds within the scope of addictions.

Attachment theory is a backdrop for this chapter because addiction by its nature disconnects individuals from themselves, couples/partners from each other, and family members, generally resulting in dismissive adult attachment patterns. However, in some families where one or more family members are experiencing addiction, the family system becomes chaotic, controlling, rigid, and/or uninvolved, thus leaning toward disorganized attachment patterns. Addiction has been described as an attachment disorder (Flores, 2004), the foundation of which is a disconnection from human relationships. Similarly, addiction is also considered a relationship between the person living with the addiction and the object of the addiction, destructive to self and others. Codependency is a widely used term to describe the dysfunctional emotional connections between the person experiencing the addiction, their family members, and their community (Beattie, 1986). Codependency can be viewed as a preoccupied adult attachment style, whereby family members, with good intent, enable the addicts in their lives to continue their interpersonal disconnection from friends, families, and community. At best, those who are living with addiction display dismissive attachment styles, but often they reveal underlying disorganized and disoriented adult attachment.

Defining Addiction and Applying Attachment Theory

In considering various definitions of addiction, first and foremost one has to understand that what is viewed as an addiction is socially constructed, fluid, and considered in context (Juhnke & Hagedorn, 2006). For instance, when viewed in context, what is considered the purpose of drug use and whether it is problematic or not has varied over time and space. For instance, in the Neolithic period of our world, 8500-4000 B.C., over 4,000 plants were used for inducing altered states of consciousness, relieving pain, and performing spiritual rituals, and there was no perceived concern for such usage being problematic (Inaba & Cohen, 2007). But, by the next global age of people – civilizations of ancient times (4000 B.C.-A.D. 400) – despite the heavy use of various drugs across cultures, including alcohol, the first warnings of overindulgences began to appear (Inaba & Cohen, 2007). In addition, what has been defined as addiction is influenced by legal and political systems, popular opinion, biological and medical knowledge, war, globalization, and technology. At present, for instance, various groups of laypeople and professionals consider all sorts of behaviors and substances to be addictive like alcohol, tobacco, coffee, gambling, shopping, sex, food, video games, Internet, work, caffeine, anger, illicit drugs, prescription drugs, nicotine, cell phone, e-mail, eBay, online gambling, cybersex, online pornography, television, exercise, and Facebook.

In the context of substance use and addiction, related terminology includes dependence, tolerance, and withdrawal. Dependence on a substance or behavior develops over a long period of time and involves the compulsive use of a substance or engagement in a behavior, and includes associated symptoms of tolerance and withdrawal. Tolerance is a state of physical habituation to a drug or behavior, resulting from frequent use or engagement in the behavior, such that higher doses over time are needed to achieve the same effect. Withdrawal includes a cluster of symptoms that occur when a dependent person abruptly stops using a particular substance or stops engaging in particular behavior following heavy, prolonged use or engagement. In terms of withdrawal symptoms from any substance, frequently they are the opposite of the intoxication associated with said substance (Juhnke & Hagedorn, 2006). Thus, it is important for clinicians to have a general level of understanding of the different types of substances that exist and the related effects of each. It is also essential for clinicians to have an understanding of the different kinds of behavioral activities that may put people at risk for the development of an addictive disorder.

Lay definitions of addiction include the following: (1) an abnormal love and trust relationship with an object or event in an attempt to control that which cannot be controlled, and (2) an increasing desire for something with an accompanying decreasing ability to satisfy that desire (Juhnke & Hagedorn, 2006). The way that addiction is defined in the current *DSM-V* is as an addictive disorder in the revised chapter of "Substance-Related and Addictive Disorders." Substance use disorder includes substance abuse and substance dependence as being a single disorder, but on a continuum from mild to severe. Substance use disorder includes substances like alcohol, opiates, cocaine, and other physically addicting substance. Each specific substance is then addressed as a separate use disorder (e.g., alcohol use disorder, stimulant use disorder, depressant use disorder, etc.). It is also important to note that not all substance use is considered disordered. In other words, whether the drug use is disordered or not is related to determining a person's amount, frequency, and duration of use, and the effect of said use on one's life and relationships with others. This means that when making a diagnosis of a substance use disorder, a clinician needs to understand the level of use. Commonly there are five levels of use: abstinence, experimentation, social or recreational use, abuse, and addiction (Juhnke & Hagedorn, 2006).

Other than substance use disorders, Gambling Disorder is the only disorder recognized as an Addictive Disorder in the *DSM-V*. Gambling Disorder was included based on research findings that determined that engagement in problematic gambling is similar to partaking in problematic substance use in terms of clinical expression, brain origin, comorbidity, physiology, and treatment (Rathus, Greene, & Nevid, 2006). In future iterations of the DSM, other addictive disorders or behavioral addictions may be added like out-of-control sexual behavior (OCSB) and/or technology-related addictions, but only with more research to support their inclusion as issues that result in clinically significant impairment or distress.

Moreover, an addiction has been said to reveal and/or create other mental health issues (Real, 1997). Indeed, dual diagnosis – meaning diagnosis of an addiction and a mental health issue – is an expectation, not an exception (Minkoff, 2003). It is estimated that 45% of people with an addiction have a co-occurring mental health disorder (Substance Abuse and Mental Health Administration [SAMSHA], 2010). However, frequently mental and relational health practitioners do not conduct adequate assessment around addiction-related issues; resultantly too often, those people who are dual-diagnosable receive treatment for only one or the other of these issues (Smith, Twist, & Hertlein, 2015). Many practitioners believe that addictions must be treated before other mental and relational health issues can be addressed. Unfortunately, those experiencing co-occurring disorders receive only an estimated 34% of mental health treatment, while 2% receive drug rehabilitation treatment, and 12% receive treatment for both disorders (SAMSHA, 2010). Yet, professionals trained and licensed/certified in both mental health and addiction recovery fields treat both issues, and do so in a way that is appropriately balanced; working on each disorder as they coexist, thus treating both diagnoses as primary ones (Minkoff, 2003). Because addictions issues are often intergenerational in nature, some questions from Addiction Genograms should be done routinely, even if not obviously directly linked to the presenting problem. Many relational and mental health problems often seen in clinical practice are co-occurring with client-systems living with addictions.

Biological and the Psychological Aspects of Addiction

Biological Considerations

Biological etiology can include many areas—here we focus on the role of genetics and neurotransmitters. There have been demonstrated links between genetic factors to various forms of use and abuse of substances such as alcohol, opiates, and nicotine. From twin studies and research involving families, we have found that genetic factors are believed to play a moderate role in male alcoholism and a modest role in female alcoholism, for instance (Rathus et al., 2006). However, it is important to keep in mind that ultimately our genes interact with our environment like our family and cultural systems, so it is hard to tease apart how much of these latter influences on addictions to substances are genetic versus systemic.

In terms of the consideration of neurotransmitters, many psychoactive drugs produce a pleasurable effect by increasing levels of the neurotransmitter dopamine in the brain's pleasure or reward circuits – the network of neurons responsible for the pleasurable feelings we experience from sexual stimulation or winning a sporting bet or even connecting with a new partner(s) via online dating. Chronic use damages brain circuits that produce feelings of pleasure. As a result, it may make it hard for the brain to produce these feelings from other natural activities on its own, and then the client is in need of dopamine, which is a necessary component to alleviate depression, anxiety, and other disturbing feelings (Rathus et al., 2006). These changes to the dopamine system may explain the intense cravings and anxiety that accompany drug withdrawal and the difficulty people have maintaining abstinence. The biochemical bases of drug use and abuse are complex and appear to involve other neurotransmitters besides dopamine. For example, we have natural opiates that run through our bodies like endorphins. These help us with comfort and ease from pain. When we take opioids outside of what our bodies naturally produce, our body becomes habituated to this use and stops producing our natural endorphins. This could account for some of the withdrawal symptoms, and some medical providers believe, with heavy repeated use of opioids, that even after stopping such use the natural endorphins will not return (Rathus et al., 2006). Such providers see this as akin to the diabetic not producing insulin. Thus, the diabetic needs external insulin, as do people no longer produce endorphins need endorphins in the form of opiates like methadone. This is why methadone maintenance may be a part of the biological recovery from an addiction to opioids.

Once an addiction has reached the level of tolerance, and even before, it is important to consult a medical professional regarding cessation of substance use. Withdrawal symptoms can be uncomfortable, and sometimes even deadly. This biological component may necessitate the use of medications to help the client through withdrawal. Medication-supported recovery is a more prolonged method of recovery, and involves giving the client regular doses of medications such as methadone, naltrexone, naloxone, buprenorphine and buprenorphine/naloxone for opiate abuse as well as disulfiram and acamprosate for alcohol abuse. Please note that, as mentioned with the concept of dual diagnoses, medically supported recovery does not treat the concurrent mental health challenges that addicts may face. In many instances, psychotherapy and medication, such as antidepressants, are also an integral part of recovery.

Psychological

Attachment theory research suggests that an insecure attachment style is a factor in addiction. In particular, an anxious-ambivalent attachment style has been shown to lead to high-risk drinking with potentially adverse consequences as a result (Molnar, Sadava, DeCourville, & Perrier, 2010). Indeed, researchers suggest that almost 50% of those experiencing alcohol addiction struggle with obsessive drinking and thoughts of drinking, as well as drinking urges and behaviors. Such obsessions, thoughts, and related thoughts are common in people with anxious-ambivalent attachment styles (Wyrzykowska, Głogowska, & Mickiewicz, 2014).

At the same time, other psychological etiologies of addictions are conceptualized via principles of learning like social learning theory, operant conditioning and observational role modeling. Learning theorists propose that addiction-related behaviors are learned (and can be unlearned) via operant conditioning and role modeling. In terms of observational learning, this theory may partially explain why there is an increased risk of developing an addiction to substances or certain behaviors in adolescents raised in families who show a history of such problems. This modeling may set the stage for observant children of family members to use in adulthood.

Using operant conditioning as an explanatory model, it has been suggested that the pathway for addiction begins via social influence, as well as through pathways like trial and error and social observation (Rathus et al., 2006). Once the individual begins using drugs/alcohol and/or developing an addiction, the substances and/or behavioral addictions provide their own reinforcement for the ongoing compulsions. For instance, one of the primary reinforcers for using alcohol is relief from states of tension or unpleasant states of arousal. Indeed, the tension-reduction theory proposes that the more often one drinks to reduce tension or anxiety, the stronger or more habitual the habit becomes. Rather than learning to resolve problems, people use drugs as a form of self-medication, and then find themselves adding to their problems by now having a substance-related issue on top of the problems they already had and from which they were attempting to escape. After one becomes physiologically dependent, negative reinforcement comes into play in terms of maintaining the habit. In other words, people continue to use drugs and alcohol to gain relief from unpleasant withdrawal symptoms, which acts as a negative reinforcer in resuming drug use (Rathus et al., 2006).

As psychological factors can be a part of creating addictions, so too can psychological models be a part of creating solutions to addictions. Indeed, researchers have demonstrated varied treatment results via psychologically based interventions. For instance, Morgenstern and McKay (2007) noted four paradigms of psychotherapy, three of which are useful with individuals experiencing addictions. The three paradigms are (1) Motivational Interviewing, (2) Cognitive behavioral therapy, and (3) Twelve-Step Programs. A fourth paradigm is Behavioral Couple Therapy, which is discussed in the next section involving the couple/partner domain.

Attachment and Addictions

Assessment and treatment for addictions are complex because there are multiple forms of addictions. Attachment theory, through the lens of the IA, provides a comprehensive assessment methodology. Flores (2001, 2004) proposed addiction as a disorder in self-regulation and suggested that addiction is an attachment disorder. Flores provides extensive scholarly and clinical insights as to why certain vulnerable individuals so desperately need to substitute addictive behavior for human connections. Through his and other work, attachment bonds and processes in relationships have been shown to play a key role in addiction. In this context, addiction is believed to be a form of failed attachment transition from childhood to adulthood (Höfler & Kooyman, 1996), and/or the manifestation of a reparative effort of prior attachment abuse in childhood (Stosny, 1995), and attachment injuries (Johnson, Makinen, & Milliken, 2001) in couple/partnered relationships. Attachment abuse for children and adolescents result in the social, emotional, and physical deprivation of secure family bonds. Attachment injuries in the form of emotional abandonment and isolation during vulnerable times in an individual's life create relational impasses for a couple bond (Johnson et al., 2001).

Indeed, in several different studies insecure attachment has been positively correlated with drug addiction (Caspers, Yucuis, Trotman, & Spinks, 2006; Edwards, Eiden, & Leonard, 2004; Finzi-Dottan, Cohen, Iwaniec, Sapir, & Weizman, 2003; Jaeger, Hahn, & Weinraub, 2000; McArdle, Ferrer-Caja, Hamagami, & Woodcock, 2002). In one such study comparing both husbands using heroin and male multidrug users, both were primarily characterized by an avoidant attachment style (Finzi-Dottan et al., 2003). In another study, insecure attachment predicted maladaptive emotional regulation, which then leads to increased substance use and abuse (Caspers et al., 2006). Borhani (2013) explored links between substance abuse, emotional distress, and interpersonal problems, which showed a correlation between substance abuse and insecure attachment styles.

Two inpatient studies of patients living with an addiction to alcohol were studied in Europe and provided an interesting cultural lens, as well as a cross-cultural study of secure and insecure attachment. First, a study by deRick and Vanheule (2007) was able to distinguish secure and insecure attachments within the population of inpatients experiencing addiction to alcohol, and their findings suggest consideration of differential assessment and treatment planning for these groups in treatment. Second, Wyrzykowska et al. (2014) studied cisgender men and women experiencing addiction to alcohol. They found differences between attachment styles for people experiencing addiction and those not experiencing such an addiction. The participants experiencing addiction were more likely to display both dismissive and preoccupied attachment behaviors leading to reinforcement of their insecure attachment bonds. Additionally, in this study they found no correlation for either group (those experiencing alcohol addiction and those not) with the experience of alcohol addiction in one's parent(s).

An insecure attachment style, specifically an avoidant one, as defined via Hazan and Shaver's (1987) "Adult Attachment Questionnaire," is frequently assigned to people living with alcohol addiction. Schindler et al. (2007) sought to look more closely at disorganized attachment style and found that fearful attachment,[1] as assessed by Bartholomew (1990), was frequently found in those who have a dual diagnosis. However, fearful attachment did not predict the severity of the addiction itself. Juen, Arnold, Meissner, Nolte, and Buchheim (2013) found DD adult attachment style in a variety of clinical groups, particularly among those experiencing bipolar disorder (BPD) and posttraumatic stress disorder (PTSD). Those with BPD, along with those who were addicted, struggle with self-other boundary confusion, and those with PTSD struggle to maintain emotional equilibrium during assessment. These studies are crucially important for understanding the distinctions between avoidant and disorganized attachment styles in people living with addiction.

The inclusion of attachment theory in the AdFG underscores the relational and systemic impact of addiction on client-systems. Addiction weakens any opportunity for secure attachment with parents, partners, and family members. Consequently, primary attention for an attachment-informed practice is to support, engage, and direct individuals living with addiction toward treatment of the addiction or addictions. TxP, as we have previously described, provides a guide to supporting this population of client-systems toward recovery, regardless of the lens used for assessment. Family members who are not engaged in addiction can benefit from an attachment focused approach to helping them with a variety of issues, including enabling and attending to their own codependency and unmet attachment needs.

AdFG Case Example

We begin this chapter with a case example to illustrate the usefulness of the AdFG. A college student named Elia is forced into therapy by her parents after being caught under the legal drinking and smoking of marijuana age on campus. She has been caught more than once, and her school has threatened to place her on a disciplinary leave of absence. In therapy, she reports caring deeply about her future, feeling anxious about being kicked out of school, yet not wanting to give up the partying lifestyle because it "helps not to think so much about stuff." She claims to drink only on weekends at first, but by the end of the first session, she has reported that she drinks on weeknights and that she has spent more money on alcohol than she would like to admit.

This individual domain information helps the clinician understand Elia's potential addiction. Further, considering this example throughout the other domains may give you a better idea of how to conceptualize this case. With this limited information, we might already guess that Elia has an avoidant attachment pattern due to her desire to handle stress through avoidance of the stressors. Continuing to learn about Elia's other domains through this FG assessment will give you clues as to her attachment disruptions, as well as other factors of her potential addiction.

To continue with this example, let's introduce Elia's boyfriend, John. John came in for a session at the therapist's request, because addictions sometimes distort personalities and relationships. Elia and John appear to be passionately in love. They sit next to each other on the couch and hold hands. On second look, the therapist spots a potential codependent dynamic. John looks to Elia before answering any of the therapist's questions, even ones about himself or his experiences. Sometimes Elia jumps in to answer questions directed at John. But John doesn't seem to notice these issues. He says, "I just want to support Elia, if she actually has a problem."

With this observed couple dynamic, we might conclude that John is enabling Elia by indulging in her behaviors, and not holding her accountable in the relationship. Continue with this example in the next domain to understand more about Elia's family-of-origin history and some of the ways this dynamic may be a repetition of what she experienced in childhood. Still, we are looking for the presence of an addiction, its degree of severity, and what is reinforcing it in the client's life and environment.

Developing an understanding of Elia's family will provide more insight into Elia's attachment framework, which has been tied to addictive behaviors specifically in college students like Elia (Labrie & Sessoms, 2012). When asked about her family, Elia first dismisses the topic, stating that she "had a fine childhood" and that her parents are currently just "worried" about her. (This reinforces the clinician's suspicion that she had an avoidant attachment pattern.)

Further questioning, using the probes in the AdFG, revealed a hidden addiction. Elia said that her mom had a stressful job, and always drank a bottle or more of wine after work. She began to put the pieces together that her mom was using alcohol to handle stress (much like Elia was doing in college) and that Elia's father enabled her mother by not addressing his issues with the drinking. Though Elia's mother was a "functioning alcoholic," Elia noted that she did not feel like her mother was ever "fully there" for her and her brother. Elia felt that much of the conflict in the family was under the surface, and that everyone pretended things were fine until there was some crisis, like when her brother failed out of medical school for cheating last spring.

Using the AdFG topics and questions, Elia began to see how she was creating this unhealthy dynamic in her own life, by using drinking to cope, refusing to deal with her drinking until it reached this crisis, and by disallowing John from standing up to her about her drinking.

For Elia, the college context was a catalyst for her to develop unhealthy drinking habits based on her family-of-origin learnings and avoidant attachment. College students tend to view drinking and partying as something fun and carefree, and it is acceptable - even socially encouraged - to blackout or drink excessively. For Elia, this encouraged her to avoid her stress and made her problems with drinking worse. Luckily, though, consequences served as a healthy boundary which brought her to therapy to work on establishing healthy habits in her life.

> ## Exercise 11.1 Constructing the AdFG
>
> *Directions*: Use the detailed clinical example above to construct an AdFG in the space provided. Keep in mind the topics on the left side of the template.
>
> What questions did you think you might want to ask Elia and John? In the rest of the chapter, we will address addictions in each domain and suggest some questions for you to build on what you write here.
>
> _____
>
> _____
>
> _____
>
> _____
>
> _____

The Basics of Assessment for the AdFG

The Individual Domain

The themes of the individual domain assess the biological and psychological aspects of substance use addiction. Although biological considerations are sometimes overlooked in assessment of client-systems, the AdFG emphasizes a biological theme, as an important first step in assessing the individual domain.

Biological and Psychological Considerations and Addictions Questions

The individual domain includes biological, psychological, and systemic considerations. There is a range of key questions that provide guidance and direction while exploring patterns of addiction within the individual domain. The biological aspects of addictions require core questions around individual substance use addictions that follow below and are influenced by the "Michigan Alcoholism Screening Test" (Selzer, 1971):

1   Do you drink or use recreational, illicit, and/or prescription drugs? If so, exactly how often? (A journal will need to be kept if still using)
2   Are you concerned about the amount of time and energy you devote to thinking about or doing drugs, and/or other behaviors that seem excessive?
3   Have you experienced any physical and/or psychological discomfort or pain in moments where you have not used a substance? If so, what was this experience like for you? How did you manage it? If not, why do you think this is the case?
4   Are other people, especially family members, concerned about the amount of time and energy you devote to thinking about or doing drugs or drinking?
5   Are there times when you do not want to use a substance, but do so anyway? What do you think causes you to use the substance in these instances where you do not resist doing so?
6   How does or has your substance use impacted you and your relationship with your partner(s)? How has or does your substance use impact you and your relationship with your child(ren)? How does your substance use affect your relationships with other family members?
7   How does your substance use affect you in your life – financially, emotionally, physically, socially, work/career/friendships? Does your substance use interfere with school, work, friendships, and/or other activities you have enjoyed?
8   Do other people tell you that your substance use is interfering in your relationship with them, your life, or your work?
9   Do you have family members who struggle with substance use addiction? What is your perspective on their problem?

10 Have you ever tried to get help for using substances? How, when, where, who? Do your family members, partner(s), friends, and/or fictive family members know that you are or have struggled with substance use?

Exercise 11.2 Biological and Psychological Considerations and Addictions

Directions: Read the questions. List below the ones that appear most important to you. Why do you think this is so?

_____

_____

_____

The Couple Domain

There are three types of behavioral addictions besides substances: gambling, OCSB, and out-of-control technology-related behavior. Gambling Disorder is the only behavioral addiction classified in the *DSM-V* as an addictive disorder. There are diverse ranges of addictive behaviors that impact the couple's relationship such as sports betting, shopping, working, and of course, drug and alcohol abuse. These particular behavioral addictions typically result in significant negative effects upon partners or spouses. Partners in an addictive or codependent relationship becomes entangled in negative interaction patterns such as enabling, denial, acting out, regressive behaviors, and compartmentalization.

The focus of the couple domain is examining who and how the behavioral addictions impact their intimate partnership. In this domain, we attend to a few more behaviors that are sometimes conceptualized as behavioral addictions; these include, in particular, the abuse of technology and sexual acting out. Although addictions to substances wreak havoc on the individual, as well as the couple/partnered relationship, behavioral addictions are even more particularly damaging to the relationship.

Codependency and enabling become the standard for interaction on a daily basis. The couple/partnered relationship often bears the primary stress of day-to-day management of daily life that is overshadowed by the addictions. Often couples break up or divorce when challenged by ongoing substance abuse or behavioral addictions. Various couple therapy approaches can be very useful when recovery begins for the addicted partner, and when both partners engage in treatment that specifically meets the unique needs for their relationship. In a review of controlled studies of couples therapy outcomes, O'Farrell and Clements (2011) emphasized that couple and family therapy helped family members and supported the person experiencing addiction to alcohol to enter treatment. In addition, it was found that Behavioral Couples Therapy is more effective than individual treatment, particularly for women, gay, and lesbian people experiencing alcohol addiction (Fals-Stewart, O'Farrell, & Lam, 2009).

Gambling Disorder

Prior to 1989, Nevada and New Jersey were the only two states in the United States with commercial casino gambling. In the past 30 years, however, the number of states with commercial and racetrack casinos has increased tenfold. During this same period, the prevalence rate of gambling disorder in the country has remained steady, with only about 1-3% of the population having gambling behaviors problematic enough to meet the criteria of an addiction disorder (Rathus et al., 2006). A gambling disorder is characterized by an urge to gamble despite harmful negative consequences or desires to stop. Symptoms of a gambling disorder include tolerance and related withdrawal – the former meaning that over time it requires larger or more frequent wagers to experience the same rush, and the latter meaning that restlessness or irritability becomes associated with attempts to cease or reduce gambling (Rathus et al., 2006). Other symptoms include the use of gambling to escape problems, chasing of gambling losses with more gambling, and hiding and lying about one's gambling (Rathus et al., 2006). The effects of a gambling disorder can be devastating on the individual who experiences the addiction, as well as on persons close to them. The person with a gambling disorder may commit unlawful acts in order to obtain gambling money or to recover gambling losses, and thus, may turn to family and friends for bailout assistance from the legal or financial consequences (Rathus et al., 2006).

In general, partners struggle with the challenges of living with a gambler. The loss of financial resources, friends, and social support along with stress-related physical challenges deplete the emotional resources for the partner. Partners of gamblers often reach out to medical providers, attorneys, mental and relational health providers, and religious leaders for help and for feelings of being lost and alone (Lorenz & Shuttlesworth, 1983). Shame minimizes the likelihood of the person experiencing a gambling disorder, or their partner(s), in participating in receiving help and support. In recent years, various states have established statewide gamblers aid services and certified gambling therapists are also becoming more available. Many couples do divorce as a result of the significant impacts of gambling. Gambling, alcohol addiction, sexual infidelity, and other acting out behaviors often impact the overall partnered relationship, as well as children, and other family members.

Out-of-Control Sexual Behavior

Acting out sexual behaviors have many characteristics of a behavioral addiction. Yet, sexual addiction was not included in the *DSM-V* due to controversy among many in the sexology and medical fields. Additionally, a review of the literature suggests that there is no evidence-based treatment for sex addiction, consequently, this particular addiction is not included as a psychiatric diagnostic category (Derbyshire & Grant, 2015). Also, the term "sexual addiction" has become a pejorative and viewed as condemning. Regardless of the term that is used to describe OCSB,

> sexual addiction/hypersexual disorder is [often] used as an umbrella construct to encompass various types of problematic behaviors, including excessive masturbation, cybersex, pornography use, sexual behavior with consenting adults, telephone sex, strip club visitation, and other behaviors.
>
> (Karila et al., 2014, p. 1).

Moreover, often OCSB leads to sexual infidelity/promiscuity and interferes in one's sexual relationships.

One of the most common questions asked around OCSB is whether it is a problem on the extreme end of the "normal" range of sexual behaviors, or if it is a distinct behavior that is qualitatively different from what is the norm, but in ways that are problematic (Bancroft & Vukadinovic, 2004). Leading clinicians in the field in this area, Braun-Harvey and Vigorito (2016), begin with the assumption that OCSB can be both/and or either/or because their way of seeing OCSB is tied to how the specific individual envisions their behavior. More specifically, they suggest that OCSB is a sexual health problem only if the sexual urges, thoughts, or behaviors feel out of control to that specific individual. Moreover, a problem with sexual health means a problem with one's state of physical, emotional, mental, and social well-being in relation to sexuality; it is not merely the absence of disease, dysfunction, or infirmity (World Health Organization [WHO], 2010).

In order for an individual to be sexually healthy it requires a positive and respectful approach to sexuality and sexual relationships, as well as the possibility of having pleasurable and safer sexual experiences that are free of coercion, discrimination, and violence. In order for an individual to attain and maintain sexual health, rather than suffer from OCSB, the sexual rights of all persons must be respected, protected, and fulfilled (WHO, 2010). Some of the functions of OCSB include behaviors that are engaged in as a way to control anxiety, stress, isolation, and/or solitude (Rathus et al., 2006). In addition, individuals oftentimes have feelings of low self-esteem, remorse, and fear of being found out in their OCSB (Rathus et al., 2006). Finally, the individual with OCSB continues the behavior despite any adverse consequences experienced (Rathus et al., 2006). Consequently, OCSB is helpful to explore as a lifestyle choice or as an aspect of other psychological and/or relational issues.

Out-of-Control Technology-Related Behaviors

Issues with technology have yet to be diagnosable by the APA. Yet, people can and often do, struggle with excessive, and potentially addictive, technology issues and its effects on relationships (Hertlein & Blumer, 2013). Up until the last few years, this problem has been invisible in the mental health community. With the rapid spread of technology, more people are now being adversely affected and becoming aware that technology can have both positive and negative impacts. Some of the various technological mediums that people experience issues with include, but are not limited to, video/online gaming, smartphones, Internet, and television. Technology is also used to support an addiction to pornography, video sex chats, and a range of other sexual behaviors.

Defining technology-related issues is essential for proper assessment. Internet addiction shares definitional similarities to other behavioral addictions such as gambling disorder (Cravens, Hertlein, & Blumer, 2013). Indeed, Internet addiction is defined as a preoccupation with the Internet in which someone has developed a tolerance for their time online, has tried to stop but cannot, becomes irritable when they try to stop, and staying online longer than originally planned (Beard & Wolf, 2001). One of the key criteria in considering Internet addiction is the number of hours spent online (Widyanto & Griffiths, 2006), with problematic usage ranging from 8 to 38 hours per week (Beard & Wolf, 2001). Problematic video and online gaming is defined as excessive gaming. Gaming addiction has been shown to produce neuroimaging results that appear congruent with other substance and behavioral addictions (Kuss, 2013). With the advent of non-substance addiction disorders in the *DSM-V*, Petry et al. (2014) propose an international consensus for the inclusion of an Internet gaming disorder. The number of hours spent engaging in gaming is also an essential part of the assessment process with regard to problematic video and online gaming behaviors (Cravens et al., 2013). Expanded awareness is necessary for clinicians to attend to out-of-control technology-related behaviors (Blumer, Hertlein, Smith, & Allen, 2014).

Questions for Behavioral Addictions

1   Do you struggle with behaviors like gambling, sexuality, and/or gaming? If so, how frequently?
2   Are you concerned about the amount of time and energy you devote to thinking about behaviors like gambling, sex, gaming, and/or other behaviors that seem excessive?
3   Are other people, especially family members, concerned about the amount of time and energy you devote to thinking about doing or actually doing things like gamble, have sex, and/or game?
4   Are there times when you do not want to engage in one of these behaviors, but do so anyway? What do you think causes you to do these behaviors in these instances where you do not resist doing so?
5   How do or have these behaviors impacted you and your relationship with your partner(s)? How have or do these behaviors impact you and your relationship with you child(ren)? How do these behaviors affect your relationships with other family members?
6   How do these behaviors affect you in your life – financially, emotionally, physically, socially, work/career/friendships? Are these behaviors interfering with school, work, friendships, and/or other activities you have enjoyed?
7   Do other people tell you that (name problem) is interfering in your relationship with them, your life, or your work?
8   Do you have family members who struggle with controlling behaviors like gambling, sex, or gaming? What is your perspective on their problem?
9   How do you feel about your engagement in certain behaviors (e.g., gambling, sex, gaming, etc.) most of the time? Have you ever tried to not partake in these behaviors? If so, how was this experience? If not, how come?
10   Have you ever tried to get help for behavioral issues? How, when, where, who? Do your family members, partner(s), friends, and/or fictive family members know that you are or have struggled with behavioral issues like gambling, sex, and/or gaming?

Exercise 11.3 Behavioral Addictions

Directions: Read the questions. List below the ones that appear most important to you? Why do you think this is so?

_____

_____

_____

_____

The Intergenerational Domain

The themes of the intergenerational domain assess the family system with concentration on the patterns, rules, and roles around the addictions in family systems. The role of family systems in substance and behaviorally related addictions is complex and influences such behaviors in myriad ways, like genetic predispositions, as well as influences in modeling behaviors of or for family members. Labrie and Sessoms (2012) explored impacts of parental attachment to risky drinking among college students. They found that students having a stronger secure attachment relationship with one's mother decreased the likelihood of engagement in risky drinking behaviors while in college, and insecure maternal attachment bonds for both cisgender-identifying sons and daughters increased the likelihood of more drinking and related consequences, with sons at greater risk of experiencing such consequences. This finding, like others in this text, contributes to greater attention of how attachment bonds influence intergenerational patterns carried from one generation to the next.

Assessment of addictions needs to include the person or people living with the addiction, as well as members of their relational systems and current treatment or medical providers involved. This provides a comprehensive picture, as well as a broad and specific context of the problem. The AdFG is part of a comprehensive package of FGs that promote an integrative and comprehensive assessment. When conducting an assessment, it is important for clinicians to consider who will be included and in what way in the assessment; for instance, it could be the case that the person experiencing the addiction is present in the session, but it may also be the case the person is not, and instead it is the person's partner(s) or members of their relational systems. Families with a hidden addiction are typically characterized by a history of substance use and abuse intergenerationally. These families often present with (1) an over-functioning parent and a complimentary uninvolved parent, (2) role reversals resulting in childhood parentification, (3) denial of the addiction, (4) isolation within the family system, (5) patterns of physical abuse and incest, (6) scapegoating of members, and (7) an irrational fear of teen and adolescent addiction.

Working with families with younger children, it is important to consider when, if even at all, to include the children, who may or may not be living with the addict and in the family system. Roberts and McCrady (2003) provide a range of guidance for family interventions. For example, involving the children can help by bringing a taboo topic into the open so that children can recognize that the adult in their lives experiencing addiction is doing something that changes them, and their behavior. Children can also become educated on addiction, and can be reassured that a problem previously hidden or not open for discussion is no longer hidden and is now open for dialogue. The choice to not involve children in the assessment process is when there is the potential for (1) boundary issues between parents and children to be violated in destructive ways by a full discussion around the addiction and (2) any extensive discussion of addiction issues that may involve the addressing of other personal or intimate couple issues that may be inappropriate for children to be privy to; (3) if there is violence in the family, it might not be safe to ask children to discuss the parental addiction.

There is a high degree of overlap in addiction behaviors and patterns among family members and throughout the entire client-system. Research suggests that one child in every four (28%) is exposed to substance abuse addiction in their families of origin (Roberts & McCrady, 2003). Consequently, there has been a steady upsurge of individual use, and family continuance of use, and we now have third- and fourth-generation alcohol and opiate users (Bepko & Krestan, 2002). Many parents of the so-called "Baby Boomer" generation have faced widespread drug and alcohol use by their teenage and young adult children. Moser and Jacob (1997) studied child outcomes related to the gender of a parent experiencing alcohol addiction. They found that when both parents or mothers only were experiencing alcohol addiction, children struggled to maintain sobriety in contrast to when said child did not have a mother who was living with alcohol addiction. In addition, family members experiencing addiction are at risk for many other likely co-occurring problems like domestic rape, common-couple violence, domestic violence, sexual abuse, interpersonal violence, relational conflict, infidelity, jealousy, economic insecurity, divorce, and fetal alcohol effects (Roberts & McCrady, 2003).

The rules of family systems experiencing addiction include those that are both spoken and unspoken. Some of the common unspoken rules in family systems experiencing addiction include, not talking about the addiction and other painful or problematic issues, holding unrealistic expectations, believing it not okay to be selfish or to think of oneself and one's own needs, the open expression of feelings is not permitted, role modeling of inherent hypocrisy (e.g., do as I say, not as I do), believing it is not okay to play as children or even be playful in adulthood, and the need to maintain things as they are in terms of appearance (e.g., don't rock the boat) (Galvin, Bylund, & Brommel, 2007). In addition to these family rules, there are multiple kinds of roles that exist in systems. A role can be defined as recurring patterns of behavior developed through the interaction that family members use to fulfill family functions. Roles are bound to the communication process, and one learns how to assume their place within a family from the feedback provided by family members (Galvin et al., 2007). There are commonly repeated roles that we often see enacted in families where addiction is being experienced; however, these can also be common roles in families not experiencing addiction. One of the commonly different experiences with roles, however, in addiction-oriented families is that they tend to experience greater role rigidity. In addition, Wegscheider-Cruse (1981) originally identified six common roles associated with members in families experiencing addiction. These roles include the family hero, family mascot, dependent/chief enabler, scapegoat, lost child, and addict.

Family Systems and Addictions Questions

In addition to the questions listed below regarding family systems and addictions, the FCM[2] can be a very useful tool for attachment focused assessment:

1   Is substance use, and/or behaviors like gambling, sex, and technology use a problem in your family system, and/or for certain members within your family system? How widespread is the problem? If yes, how has the problem been addressed?
2   Have family members participated in any sort of treatment, therapy and/or counseling to get help for these kinds of problems (i.e., substance use, gambling, sex, technology)? If yes, how was this helpful (or unhelpful)? If not, how come?
3   Have any members of your family system ever attempted to control their and/or your substance and/or behaviorally related habits (e.g., switching types of alcohol, setting rules, promising to cut down, taking away one's smartphone, limiting one's Internet access, etc.)?
4   If someone has a problem in the family, how does everyone deal with it? If someone in the family is engaging in substance use and/or behavioral addiction behaviors, how does everyone deal with it? What is helpful and unhelpful about the way problems of any kind are dealt with in the family?
5   In cases where there is a substance use and/or behavioral addiction is it kept a secret, ignored, a source of conflict, a mark of pride, a stressor for you and other family members, or something else?
6   To what extent do you feel you have a voice in your family system? When are times that you feel heard? To what extent are you are never heard by other family members or discounted in your thoughts and feelings?
7   How does your family communicate (also think about how people communicate in relation to substance use and/or behavioral habits)? Is communication calm, controlled, hostile, limited, confusing, or is there another word you would use?
8   How does your family deal with conflict (also think about how conflict in relation to substance use and/or behavioral habits manifests and is managed)? Do you resolve differences together? Is there one person in charge of solutions? Do some family members "go along to get along"? Do some "check out"?

Exercise 11.4 Family Systems and Addictions

Directions: Read the questions. List below the ones that appear most important to you? Why do you think this is so?

_____

_____

_____

_____

The Contextual Domain

The theme of the contextual domain assesses the sociocultural aspects of addiction. Sociological explanations for the etiology of addictions are rooted in the understanding that a condition of being human is needing to cope with life and addictions are one way through which people cope (Juhnke & Hagedorn, 2006).

Socioculturally speaking, the use of substances and participating in certain behaviors is in part determined by where each of us lives, whom we worship with, and the overall social or cultural norms that regulate our behavior (White, 1996). Thus, cultural attitudes can encourage or discourage binge drinking. For instance, college students drink more heavily than non-college students (Quinn & Fromme, 2011). What makes addiction so challenging to overcome from a cultural point of view, is that addiction becomes a way of life, a means of organizing one's daily existence, and a way of viewing events and the people in one's world (White, 1996; Williams & Edison, 2009).

Addiction thrives in a social network in which group norms promote excessive substance use and/or addictive behaviors (White, 1996; Williams & Edison, 2009). White's work (1996) and text exploring cultural attention to addiction and recovery is an important perspective. Each social network is like a tribal group of users – who are bonded by use that mirrors one's own use, and are typically composed of a small group of users who can nurture one's use, and often overlap with other groups to create a broader social networking of users who share common attributes and goals. Within these groups, people fall into certain typologies of addicts: (1) the acultural addict, a person who initiates and maintains use in isolation of others; (2) the culturally enmeshed addict, a person who is a full member of the subculture of use and has lost connection to or has never been in the dominant culture of abstinence or moderation around use; and (3) the bicultural addict, a person who simultaneously lives in dominant or mainstream culture, as well as the subculture of use. Additionally, within these groups people hold various key cultural roles which benefit each individual member and the group as a whole. These roles can vary based on the substance being used and/or the addictive behaviors being engaged and can include dealers, high priests, storytellers, jailhouse lawyers, ambassadors, gangsters, non-addicted hustlers, working-class addicts, high-class addicts, weekend players, pseudo-junkies, pledges, marks, the man, snitches, protectors, cultural rejects, and profiteers.

Thus, there is a whole array of social influences, and by-products tied to the person experiencing addiction, and includes things like the addictive behaviors or substances themselves, as well as foods, music, dress, literature, work activities, values, sexualities, and symbols associated with the addiction. Some of the influential substances include celebrated drugs, which are those that have been heavily integrated into major societal rituals and/or mainstream culture, and therefore are metaphorically and sometimes literally blessed for social consumption. Also included are tolerated drugs, which are those that are not punished by society, but have some stigma and/or ridicule affiliated with their use. Thus, society discourages their use, but does not prohibit them. There are also instrumental drugs, which are those that can be legally obtained only under special conditions and for clear purposes (e.g., medically prescribed psychotropics and/or pharmacologics). Finally, there are prohibited drugs, which for the most part are viewed as having no utilitarian value and are thus perceived as disruptive to society's values and order even if they offer some instrumental value (White, 1996). A tremendous amount of resources are utilized in many places around the globe to eliminate availability to these substances and severe punishment is enforced for partaking in their use.

Some of the sociocultural literature associated with addictions can include (1) law books, which provide information on drug control laws, rights of the arrested, etc.; (2) recipe books that have as their focus procedures for creating, processing, growing, manufacturing, purifying, packages, and/or testing substances; (3) technical books that discuss substances and their related effects; and (4) first-person accounts of addiction (White, 1996). Work activities associated with addictions involves the selecting of an occupation well suited for use; myriad believable stories to explain one's tardiness or absence from work; the use of manipulation of supervisors through stories, crying, rage, and/or blackmail; the use of accidents, medical leave, disability benefits, and/or workman's compensation in creative and useful ways; frequent job changes to avoid detection; use of substance or engagement in behaviors while at work; finding ways to avoid being tested for substance use; avoiding the consequences of addiction through expertise of personnel policies and/or grievance procedures; and lastly, the tendency to quit out of moral outrage before the person can be terminated (White, 1996).

There are also sociocultural rituals, values, and symbols associated with substance use and addictive behaviors. Some of the rituals associated with use and addictive behaviors include pre-engagement rituals (e.g., preparation, buying, measuring, growing, etc.), engagement rituals (e.g., smoking, drinking, eating, "shooting-up", listening to music, logging on to the computer, etc.), and post-engagement rituals (e.g., cleaning, sleeping, eating, chilling, etc.) (White, 1996). When considering rituals, it is important to think of the who, what, when, where, and how around them. The values of use and addictive behaviors are concentrated on the following areas: the addictive substance or behaviors comes first over everything else, distrust in others, avoidance of responsibility, risk-taking, thrill-seeking, being image-focused, and/or a lack of feelings and emotions (White, 1996). Some of the symbols associated with substance use or addictive behaviors include the substance or item itself, affiliated brands or containers, related paraphernalia, and/or demarcations, tattoos, brandings, or markings on the body or clothing that signal cultural belonging, affiliation, and/or values of use (White, 1996).

Sociocultural Considerations and Addictions Questions

1   What do substances or addictive behaviors like gambling, sex, or gaming do your family, friends, work colleagues, and community use and/or engage?
2   What attitudes do you think you have learned about substance use, and other addictive behaviors such as gambling, sex, online gaming from family, friends, and others?
3   When were you first exposed to substance use and/or behavioral-habitual experiences? By whom? Was it in secret or shared with others?
4   How is engagement in substance use and/or addictive behaviors viewed by you, your partner(s), family, friends, and community?
5   Are substance use and/or addictive behaviors seen as a part of "fitting in" to a group, or are they viewed negatively by members with whom you associate?
6   What values regarding your substance use and/or behaviors such as excessive gambling, sex, or use of technology (name behavior) guide your family and/or community? Do you think your use of one of the substances and/or behaviors is part of what is expected in your cultural group?
7   What consequences have been established in your community, your workplace, etc. for substance use and/or behaviorally habitual behaviors? How does the legal system attend to substance use and behavioral addictions?
8   What support systems exist for medical, psychological, family, and social support in your community, particularly with regard to assistance in managing substance use and/or behavioral addictions?

Exercise 11.5 Sociocultural Considerations and Addictions

Directions: Read the questions. List below the ones that appear most important to you? Why do you think this is so?

_____

_____

_____

_____

Closing Considerations

Assessment of Dual Diagnosis

Dual diagnosis of addiction and mental health disorders is the expectation, and not the exception when working with client-systems who present with addiction issues (Minkoff, 2003). Although in this chapter we have focused on primarily assessment of the addiction side of dual diagnosis, it does not mean that clinicians should not be assessing for and treating mental health issues concurrently. Indeed, when assessing for addiction, there are many things to consider – the themes in the sections noted above are some of the areas that need to be considered, as well as the mental health of the individual and members within the family system. Thus, the Case Formulation in Chapter 9 of this text, which focuses on *DSM-V* mental health diagnoses, can help the practitioner assist the individual and client-system that is coping with addiction, and mental health issues. The Case Formulation includes all the FGs, and the mapping and timeline tools – all of which will be helpful in getting a complete picture of the mental health issues, which, when paired with an AdFG, provides a relatively comprehensive assessment of clients experiencing dual diagnosis.

Summary

Addictions to substances and/or behaviors can ravage individuals, and their relationships. They can exist alone, or in combination with mental health concerns that warrant a dual diagnosis and dualistic treatment attention. In this chapter, we looked at different types of addiction and the attachment implications that have been explored in the literature. Insecure attachment is inevitable within addiction and family life, and provides a new lens to help client-systems recover from the impact of addictions.

The shift in diagnostic language and criteria in the *DSM-V* has begun to include substance use and abuse on a continuum. Behavioral addictions like gambling are also entering the picture for the first time. Conceptually, addiction is thought of as a relationship to a substance instead of or in addition to a relationship with people. Consequently, it is possible to think of an addiction as an attachment relationship, and to examine the consequences of the relationship with substances on the addict's other relationships.

In this chapter we also explored the systemic and sociocultural dynamics, rules, roles, and patterns common in families and relational groups experiencing addictions. In the IA domains, we examined these principles through a discussion of the etiology and effects of addiction on the individual, couple, family, and contextual domains. Finally, and perhaps most importantly, we reiterate that a thorough, systemic assessment is needed when working with addicts, including medical attention in some instances. In closing, it is our belief that people experiencing addiction, and their families, can get the help they deserve, and can achieve recovery, if they receive thorough care and are held accountable for changing their share of the dynamics.

Notes

1 Fearful attachment is another term used to describe disorganized attachment. See Chapter 2 to review our discussion of attachment terminology.
2 For more detail, see Chapter 7.

References

American Psychiatric Association [APA]. (2013). *Diagnostic and statistical manual of mental disorders* (5th ed.). Washington, DC: Author.
Bancroft, J., & Vukadinovic, Z. (2004). Sexual addiction, sexual compulsivity, sexual impulsivity, or what? Toward a theoretical model. *Journal of Sex Research, 41*, 225–234.
Bartholomew, K. (1990). Avoidance of intimacy: An attachment perspective. *Journal of Social and Personal Relationships, 7*(2), 147–178.
Beard, K., & Wolf, E. (2001). Modification in the proposed diagnostic criteria for Internet addiction. *Cyberpsychology and Behavior, 4*, 377–383.
Beattie, M. (1986). *Codependent no more: How to stop controlling others and start caring for yourself.* Center City, MN: Hazelden.

Bepko, C., & Krestan, J. A. (2002). *The responsibility trap: A blueprint for treating the alcoholic family.* New York, NY: Free Press.

Blumer, M., Hertlein, K. M., Smith, J., & Allen, H. (2014). How many bytes does it take?: A content analysis of cyber issues in couple and family therapy journals. *Journal of Marital and Family Therapy, 40*(1), 34-48.

Borhani, Y. (2013). Substance abuse and insecure attachment styles: A relational study. *LUX, 2*(1), 1-13.

Bradshaw, J. (1988). *Healing the shame that binds you.* Deerfield Beach, FL: Health Communications.

Bradshaw, J. (1996). *Family secrets: What you don't know can hurt you.* London: Bantam Press.

Braun-Harvey, D., & Vigorito, M. (2016). *Treating out of control sexual behavior: Rethinking sex addiction.* New York, NY: Springer Publishing Company.

Caspers, K. M., Yucuis, R., Trotman B., & Spinks, R. (2006). Attachment as an organizer of behavior: Implications for substance abuse problems and willingness to seek treatment. *Substance Abuse Treatment and Prevention Policy, 1*(1), 1-32.

Cravens, J. D., Hertlein, K. M., & Blumer, M. L. C. (2013). Online mediums: Assessing and treating Internet issues in relationships. *Family Therapy Magazine, 12*(2), 18-23.

Cullen, J., & Carr, A. (1999). Codependency: An empirical study from a systemic perspective. *Contemporary Family Therapy: An International Forum, 21*(4), 505-526.

Derbyshire, K. L., & Grant, J. E. (2015). Compulsive sexual behavior: A review of the literature. *Journal of Behavioral Addictions, 4*(2), 37-43.

Edwards, E. P., Eiden, R. D., & Leonard, K. E. (2004). Impact of fathers' alcoholism and associated risk factors on parent-infant attachment stability from 12 to 18 months. *Infant Mental Health Journal, 25*(6), 556-579.

Elliott, R. (1991). Five dimensions of therapy process. *Psychotherapy Research, 1,* 92-103.

Fals-Stewart, W., O'Farrell, T. J., & Lam, W. K. (2009). Behavioral couple therapy for gay and lesbian couples with alcohol use disorders. *Journal Substance Abuse Treatment,* (4), 379-387.

Finzi-Dottan, R., Cohen, O., Iwaniec, D., Sapir, Y., &, Weizman, A. (2003). The drug-user husband and his wife: Attachment styles, family cohesion, and adaptability. *Substance Use and Misuse, 38*(2), 271-292.

Flores, P. J. (2001). Addiction as an attachment disorder: Implications for group therapy. International *Journal of Group Psychotherapy, 51*(1), 63-81.

Flores, P. J. (2004). *Addiction as an attachment disorder.* Lanham, MD: Jason Aronson, Inc.

Galea, S., Nandi, A., Vlahov, D. (2004). The social epidemiology of substance use. *Epidemiologic Reviews, 26*(1), 36-52.

Galvin, K. M., Bylund, C. L., & Brommel, B. J. (2007). *Family communication: Cohesion and change* (7th ed.). Boston, MA: Pearson A and B.

Griffiths, M. (2005). A 'components' model of addiction within a biopsychosocial framework. *Journal of Substance Use, 10*(4), 191-197.

Hazan, C., & Shaver, P. (1987). Romantic love conceptualized as an attachment process. *Journal of Personality and Social Psychology, 52*(3), 511-524.

Hertlein, K. M., & Blumer, M. L. C. (2013). *The couple and family technology framework: Intimate relationships in a digital age.* New York, NY: Routledge.

Höfler, D. Z., & Kooyman, M. (1996). Attachment transition, addiction and therapeutic bonding – An integrative approach. *Journal of Substance Abuse Treatment, 13*(6), 511-519.

Inaba, D., & Cohen, W. E. (2007). *Uppers, downers, all arounders: Physical and mental effects of psychoactive drugs* (6th ed.). Medford, OR: CNS Productions.

Jaeger, E., Hahn, N. B., & Weinraub, M. (2000). Attachment in adult daughters of alcoholic fathers. *Addiction, 95*(2), 267-276.

Johnson, S. M., Makinen, J. A., & Millikin, J. W. (2001). Attachment injuries in couple relationships: A new perspective on impasses in couples therapy. *Journal of Marital and Family Therapy, 27*(2), 145-155.

Juen, F., Arnold, L., Meissner, D., Nolte, T., & Buchheim, A. (2013). Attachment disorganization in different clinical groups: What underpins unresolved attachment? *Psihologija, 46*(2), 127-141.

Juhnke, G. A., & Hagedorn, W. B. (2006). *Counseling addicted families: An integrated assessment and treatment model.* New York, NY: Routledge/Taylor Francis.

Karila, L., Wery, A., Weinstein, A., Cottencin, O., Petit, A., Reynaud, M., & Billieux, J. (2014). Sexual addiction or hypersexual disorder: Different terms for the same problem? A review of the literature. *CPD Current Pharmaceutical Design, 20*(25), 4012-4020.

Knudson, T. M., & Terrell, H. K. (2012). Codependency, perceived interparental control, and substance abuse in the family origin. *The American Journal of Family Therapy, 40*(3), 245-257.

Kuss, D. (2013). Internet gaming addiction: Current perspectives. *Psychology Research and Behavior Management, 6,* 125-137.

LaBrie, J. W., & Sessoms A. E. (2012). Parents still matter: The role of parental attachment in risky drinking among college students. *Journal of Child and Adolescent Substance Abuse, 21,* 91-104.

Liddle, H. (1999). Theory development in a family-based therapy for adolescent drug abuse. *Journal of Clinical Child Psychology, 28*(4), 521-532.

Liddle, H. A., & Rowe, C. L. (2003). Multidimensional Family Therapy for adolescent drug abuse: Making the case for a developmental-contextual, family-based intervention. In D. W. Brook & H. I. Spitz (Eds.), *The group psychotherapy of substance abuse* (pp. 275-292). Washington, DC: American Psychiatric Association Press.

Liddle, H. (2010). Treating adolescent substance abuse using multidimensional family therapy. In J. Weisz & A. Kazdin (Eds.), *Evidence-based psychotherapies for children and adolescents* (2nd ed., pp. 416-432). New York, NY: Guilford.

Lorenz, V. C., & Shuttlesworth, D. E. (1983). The impact of pathological gambling on the spouse of the gambler. *Journal of Community Psychology, 11*(1), 67-76.

McArdle, J. J., Ferrer-Caja, E., Hamagami, F., & Woodcock, R. W. (2002). Comparative longitudinal multilevel structural analyses of the growth and decline of multiple intellectual abilities over the life-span. *Developmental Psychology, 38,* 115-142.

Minkoff, M. (2003). *Dual diagnosis: An integrated model for the treatment of people with co-occurring psychiatric and substance disorders* [workshop]. Anchorage, AK: Annual School on Addictions.

Molnar, D. S., Sadava, S. W., Decourville, N. H., & Perrier, C. P. (2010). Attachment, motivations, and alcohol: Testing a dual-path model of high-risk drinking and adverse consequences in transitional clinical and student samples. *Canadian Journal of Behavioural Science / Revue Canadienne Des Sciences Du Comportement, 42*(1), 1-13.

Morgenstern, J., & Mckay, J. R. (2007). Rethinking the paradigms that inform behavioral treatment research for substance use disorders. *Addiction, 102*(9), 1377-1389.Moser, R. P., & Jacob, T. (1997). Parent-child interactions and child outcomes as related to gender of alcoholic parent. *Journal of Substance Abuse, 9*, 189-208.

O'Farrell, T. J., & Clements, K. (2011). Review of outcome research on marital and family therapy in treatment for alcoholism. *Journal of Marital and Family Therapy, 38*(1), 122-144.

Petry, N. M., Rehbein, F., Gentile, D. A., Lemmens, J. S., Rumpf, H., Mößle, T., & O'brien, C. P. (2014). An international consensus for assessing internet gaming disorder using the new DSM-5 approach. *Addiction, 109*(9), 1399-1406.

Quinn, P. D., & Fromme, K. (2011). Alcohol use and related problems among college students and their noncollege peers: The competing roles of personality and peer influence. *Journal of Studies on Alcohol and Drugs, 72*(4), 622-632.

Rathus, S. A., Greene, B., & Nevid, J. S. (2006). *Abnormal psychology in a changing world* (6th ed.). Upper Saddle River, NJ: Prentice Hall, Inc.

Real, T. (1997). *I don't want to talk about it: Overcoming the secret legacy of male depression*. New York, NY: Scribner.

deRick, A. D., & Vanheule, S. (2007). Attachment styles in alcoholic inpatients. *European Addiction Research, 13*(2), 101-108.

Roberts, L. J., & McCrady, B. S. (2003). *Alcohol problems in intimate relationships: Identification and intervention. A guide for marriage and family therapists*. Alexandria, VA: National Institutes of Health, and Dept. of Health & Human Services.

Schindler, A., Thomasius, R., Sack, P., Gemeinhardt, B., Küstner, U., & Eckert, J. (2007). Attachment and substance use disorders: A review of the literature and a study in drug dependent adolescents. *Attachment & Human Development, 7*(3), 207-228.

Selzer, M. L. (1971). The Michigan alcoholism screening test: The quest for a new diagnostic instrument. *American Journal of Psychiatry, 127*(12), 1653-1658.

Smith, J. M., Twist, M. L. C., & Hertlein, K. M. (2015). Exploration of female-specific clinical programming for adolescent substance use. *Journal of Feminist Family Therapy: An International Forum, 27*(3-4), 101-115.

Stanton, M. D., & Todd, T. C. (1982). *The family therapy of drug abuse and addiction*. New York, NY: Guilford Press.

Stanton, M. D., Todd, T. C., Heard, D. B., Kirschner, S., Kleiman, J. I., Mowatt, D. T., & Deusen, J. M. (1978). Heroin addiction as a family phenomenon: A new conceptual model. *The American Journal of Drug and Alcohol Abuse, 5*(2), 125-150.

Stosny, S. (1995). *Treating attachment abuse: A compassionate approach*. New York, NY: Springer Publishing Company.

Substance Abuse and Mental Health Administration [SAMSHA]. (2010). *Five million Americans attend self-help groups*. PsycEXTRA Dataset.

Wegscheider-Cruse, S. (1981). *Another chance: Hope and health for the alcoholic family*. Palo Alto, CA: Science and Behavior Books.

White, L. W. (1996). *Pathways from the culture of addiction to the culture of recovery: A travel guide for addiction professionals*. Center City, MN: Hazelden.

Widyanto, L., & Griffiths, M. D. (2006). Internet addiction: A critical review. *International Journal of Mental Health and Addiction, 4*, 31-51.

Williams, Q., & Edison, R. (2009). *Culture of addiction and the culture of recovery*. Bloomington, IL: Dawn Farm Education Series.

World Health Organization [WHO]. (2010). Retrieved from www.who.int/reproductivehealth/topics/sexual_health/sh_definitions/en/

Wyrzykowska, E., Głogowska, K., & Mickiewicz, K. (2014). Attachment relationships among alcohol dependent persons. *Alcoholism and Drug Addiction, 27*(2), 145-161.

Appendix

Focused Genogram Questions

This appendix provides questions from both editions of the *Focused Genograms* (FG) texts along with the *Attachment-Based Focused Genogram Workbook*.

The Basic Genogram

The Basic Genogram (BG) identifies the client system, organizing names, dates, descriptors of family members, marriage and divorce patterns, birth order, occupations, health problems, and other important areas of life. The focused questions of the BG yield a tremendous amount of data for the practitioner to consider as the treatment process proceeds. Each aspect of BG (and those topics not included here) can be explored in greater detail through the construction of the appropriate FGs.

Family Functioning Questions

1   Who would you list as the most important people for you in your family system? This can include very close friends who might also be considered family.
2   What are the patterns of expressing both positive and negative emotions?
3   How do family members provide support, security, and encouragement to one another?
4   What are the patterns of time spent together?
5   What kinds of established alliances, coalitions, cutoffs exist between and among family members?
6   Do people in your family respond quickly to help one another? How? Who reaches out? Does anyone hold back?
7   Describe family beliefs, feelings, and actions with regard to individual uniqueness, needs, motives and group identity for members of the family.
8   How does the family system celebrate rituals of connection: family meals, rising and retiring, coming and going, going out and going away, couple rituals?
9   How does the family system observe these rituals of celebration and community: special person rituals, community and religious rituals, rites of passage?
10   What abilities and resources do family members use in coping with crises?
11   What are the client-system's (i.e., each individual, marital and/or partnered relationship, family as a unit) links to the wider community?

Marriage/Partnering, Divorce, and Dissolution Questions

1   What are the patterns of marriage and/or partnering (e.g., legal, spiritual, domestic, civil, plural, common-law marriages) and dissolutions (e.g., divorce, separation, dissolution) in the family system?
2   If there are dissolutions, what are the known circumstances surrounding the ending of the relationship?
3   What types of partnerings are there in the family system?
4   Have family members participated in premarital counseling or marital/couples therapy?

5   What kinds of stresses have resulted in the family if there has been dissolution?
6   How have parents worked out custody and visitation?

Birth Order Questions

Sibling position and role, often referred to as birth order, affects individual development and personality in a number of ways, as well as future involvement in relationships. The questions that follow focus attention on this area of family life.

1   What is your birth order in your family of origin?
2   What is the spacing between siblings? Was spacing planned? Were there large periods of time between siblings?
3   Are there half-siblings, step-siblings, and blended family siblings?
4   What is the gender of each sibling? Was there an expressed preference for specific gender of a child?
5   What are the similarities and differences among siblings?
6   Which siblings are more emotionally close to one another and which are more emotionally distant from each other?
7   Who is like one's parent(s), grandparent(s), aunt, uncle, or any other family member(s)?
8   How did you experience favoritism in your family?
9   Was there sibling rivalry or conflict that was experienced? How was this managed by the siblings? By parents?
10 Was there sibling support or encouragement that was experienced? How was this expressed by the siblings? By parents?
11 What is the birth order of your parent(s)? What effect do you think that has had on them?
12 What is the birth order of your partner(s)? What effect do you think this has had on your relationship?

Adoption Questions

Adoption is another facet of birth order, as well as the overall family dynamics. The following are questions to consider when examining the effects of adoption.

1   What information is known about the biological donors? What beliefs exist about their circumstances, if known?
2   What are the differences and similarities between the culture of the adopted family and the culture of the biological donor family?
3   If infertility was a factor, how was it addressed?
4   What was the decision-making process? Were family reactions explored?
5   What kind of process (e.g., open, semi-open, private, closed, public, etc.) around adoption has taken place?
6   Were there difficulties with other children in the family (e.g. school problems, secrecy, inheritance issues, behavior problems)?
7   What was the age of adopted members at the time of adoption?
8   How has the family managed any stigmatization around the adoption?
9   With regard to the adoption, what were some of the positives experienced within the family?
10 What are the history and family patterns around adoption?

Health Questions

1   What are the patterns of illness (mental, genetic, physical) in the family? Did your parents' health affect the way they related to you? To others?
2   What messages did you receive from family members about illness in general, and/or certain medical diagnoses?
3   What are the known causes of death? Are there mysteries about how family members died?

4 Who was regarded as afflicted (sick or ill) in your family? Who believed themselves to be affected?

5 What were the attitudes of family members to those who were or are affected?

6 What is the meaning of doing something different regarding the genetic risks in your family (e.g., having or not having testing, terminating a pregnancy)?

7 What about the meaning of doing something different regarding the environmental risk factors in your family (e.g., eating less red meat, exercising, drinking less alcohol)?

8 What health conditions do you have if any, and what are the consequences for you?

9 Do you have health fears or concerns for your mortality?

10 Is your health affecting the way you relate to others?

Socioeconomic Questions

Social class is an important aspect of American life, yet it is frequently overlooked in the clinical setting. Yet socioeconomics cut across all aspects of one's life and their intergenerational story. Thus, questions around socioeconomics are essential to include in BG construction.

1 What did you learn from your parents about social class? With what class did your parents identify themselves? How did this fit or not fit with what they modeled for you by their behavior, where they lived, whom they associated with, and so forth?

2 Would your parents agree or disagree with your perceptions? How important was social class to them and to your siblings in the neighborhood in which you grew up?

3 Do you think your family was more or less concerned about social class than other families? How might things have been different in your family if different economic possibilities had been available to it?

4 Do different members of your family belong to different social classes? Have members of your family changed class (up or down) due to marriage, making or losing money, illness, or bad luck?

5 When you were growing up, what messages did your peers pass on about social class? What ideas about social class do you want to pass on to the next generation? How are these the same or different from what your parents taught you?

6 Think back to when you first visited, lived in, worked in a neighborhood of a different social class. How did you think about social class differently/act differently, after that?

7 How have recessions affected your family of origin? Family of procreation? Family of choice? Neighborhood? Community?

8 What are the family-of-origin and procreation experiences with relocation and moving? What have been the reasons behind the moves? Have the moves been within a state, across states, across countries, etc.?

9 How might things have been different in your family if different economic possibilities had been available to it?

10 What ideas about social class do you want to pass on to the next generation? How are these the same or different from what your parents taught you?

Questions about Culture

Culture is part of the Contextual Domain and comprises the outer domain of the Intersystem Approach and explores a variety of themes that include a variety of considerations including immigration, religion, and other topics.

1 What were the migration patterns of the group or groups that constitute your family? How do family members define themselves racially and how do you define yourself?

2 If other than Native American, under what conditions did different family members (or their descendants) enter the United States? In which year did they arrive? If they came as a family, who in the family wished to emigrate, and who did not? Were there ties to the homeland? Where and how were they maintained?

3 What were or are the group's experiences with oppression? What were or are the markers of oppression?

4   What issues divide members within the same group? What are the sources of intragroup conflict?

5   Describe the relationship between the group's identity and your national ancestry. (If the group is defined in terms of nationality, please skip this question.)

6   What significance do race, skin color, and hair play within the group?

7   What are the dominant religions of the group? What role does religion and spirituality play in the everyday lives of members of the group?

8   What role does regionality and geography play in the group?

9   How are gender roles defined within the group? How is sexual orientation regarded?

10   What prejudices or stereotypes does this group have about itself? What prejudices and stereotypes do other groups have about this group? What prejudices and stereotypes does this group have about other groups?

11   What role (if any) do names play in the group? Are there rules, mores, or rituals governing the assignment of names?

12   How is social class defined in the group?

13   What occupational roles are valued or devalued by the group?

14   What is the relationship between age and the values of the group?

15   How does the group define family?

16   How does this group view outsiders in general, mental-health professionals, and other professions?

17   How have the organizing principles of this group shaped this family and its members? What effect have they had on the client?

18   What are the ways in which pride and shame issues of each group manifested in the family system?

19   If more than one group makes up the culture of origin, how were the differences negotiated in the family? What were the intergenerational consequences?

Religion, Spirituality, and/or Life Philosophy Questions

In order to enhance the power of the religious-orientation genogram, additional questions can be asked about family traditions and rituals.

Careful assessment in these areas may uncover hopeful and helpful supports or guidance for the individuals and the family as they work together at problem-solving and decision-making.

1   How important is religious or spiritual practice or affiliation?

2   What religious or spiritual affiliations exist within the family?

3   Is there conflict within the family about religious or spiritual practices?

4   How do religious, spiritual, and/or life philosophy beliefs influence self-esteem, partnering, marriage, parenting, sexuality, and familial responsibilities and loyalties?

5   What are the unique features of the religious, spiritual, or philosophical orientation(s) of the family?

6   Have family members married outside the family faith or belief system? What were the consequences?

7   Is religious, spiritual, or philosophical affiliation a source of strength in the family system or a source of conflict?

8   How is family membership defined by the family's religious, spiritual, or philosophical orientation?

9   To what extent does the family's religion, spirituality, and/or life philosophy influence the degree of permeability of the family's boundaries with the neighborhood, community, and outside environment?

10   To what extent does the family's religion, spirituality, and/or life philosophy emphasize tradition, stability, and order?

11   How does the family system celebrate rituals of connection: family meals, rising and retiring, coming and going, going out and going away, couple(s) rituals?

12   How does the family system observe the rituals of celebration and community, special-person rituals, community rituals, lifespan rituals, religious rituals, rites of passage rituals, etc.?

13   How important is religious practice or affiliation? What religious affiliations exist within the family?

14   Is there conflict within the family about religious practices?

15   How do religious beliefs influence self-esteem, marriage, parenting, sexuality, and familial responsibilities and loyalties?

16 What are the unique features of the religious orientation of the family?

17 Have family members married outside the family faith? What were the consequences?

18 Is religious affiliation a source of strength in the family system or a source of conflict?

Questions about *Family Rituals and Traditions*

Family rituals and traditions have various levels of importance within family systems and often are tied to religious beliefs among different traditions.

1 How does the family system celebrate rituals of connection: family meals, rising and retiring, coming and going, going out and going away, couple rituals?

2 How does the family system observe these rituals of celebration and community: special-person rituals (birthdays, Mother's Day, Father's Day), Thanksgiving, Christmas, community and religious rituals, and rituals of passage (weddings and funerals)?

The Attachments FG

The Attachments Genogram examines the psychological bonds within the family system and links family-of-origin experience, marital dynamics and interactional patterns within the family.

Questions about *Attachment*

Attachment behaviors and styles are an integral part of human relationships.

1 Do you find it easy to get close to others or difficult to get close to others? How is this pattern for other members of the family?

2 Do you worry that others do not really care about you? Do other members of your family have these worries or fears?

3 Would you describe your mother and father (or other caregivers) as warm and consistent, as unavailable and rejecting, or as attentive but out-of-sync with you? Were they different with you at different times in your life? Describe these different times.

4 Do people in your family respond quickly to one another? How? Who reaches out? Does anyone hold back?

5 Is independence applauded and encouraged within your family? By whom? How?

6 Does your family tend to be compliant, unresponsive, or demanding with each other? Are there differences between the generations?

7 Were you described by your parents or caregivers as easily comforted, difficult to soothe, or angry and demanding?

Questions about *Touch and Bonding*

Because tactile communication is an important form of nonverbal communication in family systems as well as important in bonding and holding, these patterns are closely examined in the Attachments Genogram.

1 How were you comforted as a child? How were others comforted? Were there similarities or differences in the way you were comforted compared with your cousins or other family relatives?

2. Were you rejected, were there separations or losses? Were there rejections, separations, or losses for others in the family? What were the circumstances?

3 Is your family physically affectionate? In what ways? Are you affectionate with other relatives? Describe any differences among members.

4 Is touch comfortable in your family? Are some individuals in the family more comfortable with touch than others?

5 Are there inconsistencies in the kinds of holding and touch that goes on in family relationships?

6   Were there occasional or frequent negative or inappropriate touches?

7   Rate your family's touch comfort level in these areas:
    a)   Positive affect touches (including support, appreciation, sex, and affection)
    b)   Playful touches (playful affection and playful aggression)
    c)   Control touches (compliance, attention-getting, announcing a response)
    d)   Ritualistic touches (greeting and departure)
    e)   Hybrid touches (greeting-affection and departure-affection)
    f)   Task-related touches (i.e., reference to appearance)
    g)   Accidental touches

8   What kinds of hugs (if any) are the norm in your family?

9   Are you or others in your family sensitive to certain kinds of clothing or touch, such as seams inside the toe or the sock or clothing tags at the neckline? Do these family members like to be "rough and tumble"?

Questions about Temperament

The Attachments Genogram would be incomplete without an assessment of temperament.

1   Would you describe yourself as easy going, slow to warm, cautious, or difficult? How would you describe other members of the family?

2   Rate yourself and your family members in these areas on a scale of 1–10 (10 being the greatest): activity level, intensity, distractibility, moodiness/sulkiness, irregularity, smiling and laughter, fear, soothability, and comfort with extended interpersonal contact. What are the patterns of temperament for you and your family members?

The Fairness FG: A Contextual Therapy Perspective

B. Janet Hibbs, MFT, PhD, Special Contributor, *Focused Genograms*, 2nd Edition (2017).

The Fairness Genogram was a new addition to the FG and to the mental health field. Trustworthiness is key to attachment security among all the IA domains – the individual, the couple, and the family/intergenerational systems. We propose that Contextual Theory is at heart grounded in attachment theory, but from a unique theoretical construct based on the virtue of justice. This chapter, contributed by B. Janet Hibbs, provides a new FG that will help practitioners further explore and apply contextual therapy within the IA. – Rita DeMaria, PhD, and Gerald Weeks, PhD.

Attachment Patterns and Relational Ethics

1   Who did you turn to as a child, then later as a teen or young adult? Whom did you depend on? Were you closer to one parent or another growing up?

2   Would you describe anyone in your family as a giver or a taker? Was there favoritism or scapegoating in your family? Were you ever asked to take sides with one parent against another?

Parental Expectations

3   What did your parents expect of you? Were you able to meet their expectations? What did that mean to you? Did you feel burdened by responsibility? Or were you babied, with few expectations? What happened if you disappointed your parents? What did you feel most valued or appreciated for?

4   Were family problems discussed or avoided? What happened if your feelings were hurt? If you hurt the feelings of a parent or sibling? Were there any problems that never got acknowledged or healed?

Communication Patterns

5   How often do you communicate with or visit your family members now? How similar or different is that from the prior generation? Is there any history of estrangement or cutoffs? How do you understand that?

6   What traditions from your family do you observe and continue now as an adult? What did you want to do differently in raising your children? Were you able to accomplish that? What regrets have your parents expressed to you? What regrets do you have or have you expressed to your children? To your parents?

7   Were there defining historical events that impacted you or your family over the past three generations, such as immigration? Did any relatives experience either physical or mental illness? Was there any family history of verbal, physical or sexual abuse, alcoholism or substance abuse? How did that affect members of your family? Was anyone in foster care? Was anyone adopted? Any history of separation or divorce?

The Gender FG

Questions about Family Impact on Current Gender Behavior

1   How close do you come to fulfilling your family's expectations of your gender?
2   How have you gone about trying to conform to or rebel against these expectations?
3   What positive or negative effects have these expectations had on your life?
4   How have you struggled to overcome the negative effects?
5   If you are married or in a serious relationship, how close do you and your partner come to meeting expectations of marriage, of being a husband or wife? How have family expectations regarding gender affected your relationship?
6   Under what circumstances do you have the most positive image of yourself in your relationship? The most negative? In what ways does your partner live up to your ideal wife, husband, or partner?

Questions about Peer Expectations

1   How have the standards of your peer group concerning male and female roles affected your life? Have there been different peer groups with different standards over the years to which you have related? When these groups are in conflict, which set of standards is most compelling to you?
2   How have you dealt with the pressure to conform to these standards?
3   Which standards do you consider desirable or undesirable?
4   How is your self-image affected if you fail to attain these standards?

Questions about Cultural Expectations

1   Who were your idols growing up (real or fictional)?
2   What did they model as desirable male or female qualities?
3   Which did you try to emulate, and how did this affect your life?
4   What effect did these models have on your expectations of relationships?
5   What impact are they having on your current relationship?
6   What is the effect of mass media (television, films, books, etc.) on your ideas about male and female roles and your current relationship?

The Addictions FG

The Individual Domain

The themes of the Individual Domain assess the biological and psychological aspects of substance use addiction. Although biological considerations are sometimes overlooked in the assessment of client-systems, the Addictions Genogram emphasizes a biological theme, as an important first step in assessing the individual domain.

Biological and Psychological Considerations and Addictions Question

1   Do you drink or use recreational, illicit, and/or prescription drugs? If so, exactly how often? (A journal will need to be kept if still using.)

2   Are you concerned about the amount of time and energy you devote to thinking about or doing drugs, and/or other behaviors that seem excessive?

3   Have you experienced any physical and/or psychological discomfort or pain in moments where you have not used a substance? If so, what was this experience like for you? How did you manage it? If not, why do you think this is the case?

4   Are other people, especially family members, concerned about the amount of time and energy you devote to thinking about or doing drugs or drinking?

5   Are there times when you do not want to use a substance, but do so anyway? What do you think causes you to use the substance in these instances where you do not resist doing so?

6   How does or has your substance use impacted you and your relationship with your partner(s)? How has or does your substance use impact you and your relationship with your child(ren)? How does your substance use affect your relationships with other family members?

7   How does your substance use affect you in your life -financially, emotionally, physically, socially, work/career/friendships? Does your substance use interfere with school, work, friendships, and/or other activities you have enjoyed?

8   Do other people tell you that your substance use is interfering in your relationship with them, your life, or your work?

9   Do you have family members who struggle with substance use addiction? What is your perspective on their problem?

10   How do you feel about using the substance(s) most of the time? Have you ever tried to not use the substances? If so, how was this experience? If not, how come?

11   Have you ever tried to get help for using substances? How, when, where, who? Do your family members, partner(s), friends, and/or fictive family members know that you are or have struggled with substance use?

Behavioral Addictions Questions

Questions around behavioral addictions include the following:

1   Do you struggle with behaviors like gambling, sexuality, and/or gaming? If so, how frequently?

2   Are you concerned about the amount of time and energy you devote to thinking about behaviors like gambling, sex, gaming, and/or other behaviors that seem excessive?

3   Are other people, especially family members, concerned about the amount of time and energy you devote to thinking about doing or actually doing things like gambling, having sex, and/or gaming?

4   Are there times when you do not want to engage in one of these behaviors, but do so anyway? What do you think causes you to do these behaviors in these instances where you do not resist doing so?

5   How do or have these behaviors impacted you and your relationship with your partner(s)? How have or do these behaviors impact you and your relationship with your child(ren)? How do these behaviors affect your relationships with other family members?

6   How do these behaviors affect you in your life - financially, emotionally, physically, socially, work/career/friendships? Are these behaviors interfering with school, work, friendships, and/or other activities you have enjoyed?

7   Do other people tell you that (name the problem) is interfering in your relationship with them, your life, or your work?

8   Do you have family members who struggle with controlling behaviors like gambling, sex, or gaming? What is your perspective on their problem?

9   How do you feel about your engagement in certain behaviors (e.g., gambling, sex, gaming, etc.) most of the time? Have you ever tried not to partake in these behaviors? If so, how was this experience? If not, how come?

10   Have you ever tried to get help for behavioral issues? How, when, where, who? Do your family members, partner(s), friends, and/or fictive family members know that you are or have struggled with behavioral issues like gambling, sex, and/or gaming?

Family Systems and Addictions Questions

In addition to the questions listed below regarding family systems and addictions.

1   Is substance use, and/or behaviors like gambling, sex, and technology use a problem in your family system, and/or for certain members within your family system? How widespread is the problem? If yes, how has the problem been addressed?

2   Have family members participated in any sort of treatment, therapy and/or counseling to get help for these kinds of problems (i.e., substance use, gambling, sex, technology)? If yes, how was this helpful (or unhelpful)? If not, how come?

3   Have any members of your family system ever attempted to control their and/or your substance and/or behaviorally related habits (e.g., switching types of alcohol, setting rules, promising to cut down, taking away one's smartphone, limiting one's Internet access, etc.)?

4   If someone has a problem in the family, how does everyone deal with it? If someone in the family is engaging in substance use and/or behavioral addiction behaviors, how does everyone deal with it? What is helpful and unhelpful about the way problems of any kind are dealt with in the family?

5   In cases where there is substance use and/or behavioral addiction is it kept a secret, ignored, a source of conflict, a mark of pride, a stressor for you and other family members, or something else?

6   To what extent do you feel you have a voice in your family system? When are times that you feel heard? To what extent are you are never heard by other family members or discounted in your thoughts and feelings?

7   How does your family communicate (also think about how people communicate in relation to substance use and/or behavioral habits)? Is communication calm, controlled, hostile, limited, confusing, or is there another word you would use?

8   How does your family deal with conflict (also think about how conflict in relation to substance use and/or behavioral habits is manifested and managed)? Do you resolve differences together? Is there one person in charge of solutions? Do some family members "go along to get along"? Do some "check out"?

Sociocultural Considerations and Addictions Questions

Questions regarding sociocultural considerations and addictions include the following:

1   What substances or addictive behaviors like gambling, sex, or gaming do your family, friends, work colleagues, and community use and/or engage in?

2   What attitudes do you think you have learned about substance use, and other addictive behaviors such as gambling, sex, online gaming from family, friends, and others?

3   When were you first exposed to substance use and/or behaviorally habitual experiences? By whom? Was it in secret or shared with others?

4   How is engagement in substance use and/or addictive behaviors viewed by you, your partner(s), family, friends, and community?

5   Are substance use and/or addictive behaviors seen as a part of "fitting in" to a group, or are they viewed negatively by members with whom you associate?

6   What values regarding your substance use and/or behaviors such as excessive gambling, sex, or use of technology (name behavior) guide your family and/or community? Do you think your use of one of the substances and/or behaviors is part of what is expected in your cultural group?

7   What consequences have been established in your community, your workplace, etc. for substance use and/or behaviorally habitual behaviors? How does the legal system attend to substance use and behavioral addictions?

8   What support systems exist for medical, psychological, family and social support in your community, particularly with regard to assistance in managing substance use and/or behavioral addictions?

Sexuality FG

Michele Marsh, PhD, CST, contributed the Sexuality FG in the *Focused Genograms*, 2nd Edition (2017) and is a new advance with a thorough incorporation of attachment theory. The Sexuality FG traces the development of the sexual genogram during clinical assessment.

Questions for Sexual FG

1 What are the overt and covert messages in this family regarding sexuality and intimacy? Regarding masculinity and femininity?
2 Who said or did what? Who was conspicuously silent or absent in the area of sexuality and intimacy?
3 Who was the most open sexually? Intimately? In what ways?
4 How were sexuality and intimacy encouraged? Discouraged? Controlled? Within a generation? Between generations?
5 What questions have you had regarding sexuality and intimacy in your "family tree" that you have been reluctant to ask? Who might have the answers? How could you discover the answers?
6 What were the "secrets" in your family regarding sexuality and intimacy (e.g., incest, unwanted pregnancies, or extramarital affairs)?
7 What do the other "players on the stage" have to say regarding these questions? How did these issues, events, and experiences have impact on them? Within a generation? Between generations? With whom have you talked about this? With whom would you like to talk about this? How would you do it?
8 How does your partner perceive your family tree or genogram regarding the previously mentioned issues? How do you perceive your partner's?
9 How would you change this genogram (including who and what) to meet what you wish had occurred regarding messages and experiences of sexuality and intimacy?
10 Were there inappropriate sexual behaviors by family members, for example, sexual fondling by relatives, nudity in the home when children reached adolescence, and detailed discussion of sexual preferences in the presence of small children?
11 Are any family members known homosexuals? How were they treated? How could one express nonsexual love for same-sex people?

Abuse, Violence, and Trauma FG

Briana Bogue, MFT, and Maisy Hughes, MFT, contributed to the Abuse, Violence, and Trauma (AVT) in Chapter 9.

Screening Questions for Disorganized Attachment in Childhood

Questions can be helpful in getting a sense of the presence of AVT in an individual's life and possible coping mechanisms that the individual has been using. These questions are not all-encompassing and do not represent a thorough trauma assessment. When clients have difficulty discussing or identifying emotions, asking what he/she/they are aware of in general may help get the process going. The more struggle the client has, the clearer it will be to the therapist that expression of emotion and self-soothing will be a challenge.

Threatening and Intimidation in the Family

1 What are your memories about anger and angry outbursts in your family?
2 How did your parents/other family members speak to you? Did you ever feel insulted, shamed, blamed, bullied, or put down by members of your family? Were you frequently cursed at?
3 Was anyone ever physically hurt when someone got angry?
4 Did you witness violence in your family? Between whom? Did you witness or participate in violence in your community?
5 Describe any and all experiences in your early life that felt abusive, emotionally, physically, and/or sexually?

Fear in the Family (Parental Figures Use of Corporal Punishment as a Method of Control)

1 Was corporal punishment used in your family? To what extent and how often?
2 Were there differences in the ways boys and girls in the family were punished?
3 Were there differences between the way the older children were punished compared with younger children?

4   Was corporal punishment used in the homes of cousins, other relatives, or friends?
5   Did you ever receive corporal punishment in school or any other setting outside your family?

Dissociation in the Family (Emotions and Behaviors Are Incongruent, Voice Changes, Frozen Postures, and Loss of Memory around Events)

1   Did parents sometimes not seem like themselves?
2   Did parental figures deny, avoid, or minimize abusive family experiences in their life?
3   Were you neglected physically or emotionally at times in your family?

Timidity in the Family (Includes Aggression and Oppression by Children on Parents and Caregivers)

1   Who ran the emotional climate in the home? Mother, father, children, or other caregivers?
2   What sibling rivalry experiences did you have with your siblings? How physical was the rivalry?
3   Who bullied whom in the family?

Inappropriate Intimate Touching (Includes Sexualized Touch)

1   Has anyone ever touched you in ways that made you feel uncomfortable?
2   Did you ever have any difficult or frightening sexual experiences? Did you have any childhood or adolescent sexual experiences that you think were wrong or were upsetting to you?
3   Has anyone in the family been sexually abused? What do you know about the circumstances?

Disorganized (Includes a Consistent Pattern or Contradictory or Unreliable Behaviors and Emotions)

1   Have you witnessed violence or child abuse? What were the circumstances and details?
2   Did child abuse ever take place in your family or your extended family? Was it reported to the authorities? Denied? What happened?
3   Have you shared difficult memories or experiences with anyone? How have you dealt with the memories/feelings from your past?

The AVT Assessment in the Couple Domain

Assessment of AVT in the couple domain begins with observation of the couple's attachment interaction patterns.

Questions for Disorganized Attachment for Adults and Their Intimate Relationships

1   How do your experiences of abuse and trauma play out in your current relationship? Have you had other relationships that included abuse or trauma?
2   Have you experienced intimidation or threatening behavior in your relationships?
3   Are you fearful when conflict escalates in your relationship?
4   Do you tend to placate your partner or try to "fix" the problem by yourself?
5   Does conflict in your relationship end up with sexual aggression, sexual intimidation, or sexual rejection?
6   Are there times in your relationship that you or your partner feel "out of it," disconnected, overwhelmed by fear, rage, or anguish?

Questions for Disorganized Attachment through the Family Lens

We suggest that the Family Control Map can be used specifically within this framework to observe the family presentation and assess for the presence of AVT. Other questions pertain to the events in the family history and experiences of AVT. These questions could be asked about family of origin, family of choice, other caregivers, foster families, and current families of procreation. If the client interviewed is a parent, we recommend asking these questions about the family of origin and the family of procreation/adoption to get a better understanding of how patterns of attachment and trauma may have been transmitted in the family of procreation through the parent (the client interviewed) and their partner.

1   Did you feel that your parent(s)/caregiver(s) were interested in you and/or enjoyed your presence? How did they show it?
2   Have you ever felt afraid in your family? Of whom, or what, in particular?
3   Were you ever frightened or threatened by other family members?
4   Has anyone in your family or neighborhood ever touched you in ways that made you uncomfortable or that you thought were wrong?
5   What did you think about the rules in your family? Did you feel like you had room to be yourself and make mistakes?
6   How is change dealt with in your family?
7   If you experienced personal trauma(s) or abuse, did you tell anyone in your family what happened to you? Did they find out another way? How did they react to the news?
8   If the person who hurt you is/was in your family, how did things change in the family after the incident(s)? How did things change after people found out (if they did)?
9   If someone else in your family experienced trauma, how did you react as a family member? How did it change your family? How is it still affecting your family today?
10 Are there any family members who are disconnected from the family? Do you know why or the circumstances? Is this a pattern in your family tree?

Questions for Exploring Attachment Impacts in the Community

These questions attempt to understand the traumas that are associated with the contextual and cultural identities a client may have. These questions focus on emotions associated with the culture and its particular trauma(s) as well as the history. They may need slight tweaking depending on what contextual factors and cultures are being explored. For instance, the word culture can be exchanged for neighborhood, religion, country, etc.

1   What are the cultural norms in your community that contribute to AVT? Has there been any abuse or trauma you have experienced that has felt unrecognized or invalidated by your culture? (e.g., discrimination on the basis of sexual orientation for religious reasons)
2   How is trauma dealt with in your culture? How does your culture support or disempower survivors?
3   Growing up, did you typically fit in with others in your/culture? If not, what stood out about you?
4   What kinds of traumatic experiences have you experienced outside your family?
5   Are there traumas in your family's cultural and/or contextual history that affect you?
6   Have you experienced trauma as a result of being different from others such as having a disease, disability, or being a member of a minority group?
7   Have you ever experienced war, poverty, discrimination, oppression, natural disaster or anything else that was traumatic for you?

The Emotions FG

The Emotions FG was included in *Focused Genograms*, 1st Edition (1999). The purpose of Emotions FG is to help the client become more aware of patterns of emotional expression in the family in terms of both pleasure and pain so that effective and satisfying emotional experiences can take place in the present.

General

1   What were the dominant feelings of each member of your family (the family you grew up with)?
2   What was the predominant feeling in your family? Who set the mood?

3 What feelings were expressed most often, most intensely?

4 What feelings were not allowed? How were members punished when an unallowed feeling was expressed?

5 What happened to the unexpressed feelings in the family?

6 Who knew or did not know about how others felt?

7 What happened to you when you expressed the taboo feeling or feelings?

8 How did you learn how to deal with these so-called unacceptable feelings?

9 Did others try to tell you how you should feel?

10 Did you ever see anyone lose control over his or her feelings? What would happen? Did anyone get hurt? How?

11 If corporal punishment was used in your family, what feelings did parents express? What feelings were allowable for children?

12 Do you find yourself having feelings that you cannot explain but seem like feelings you have had in the past?

Questions about Anger

1 How did your parents deal with anger and conflict?

2 Did you see your parents work through anger and conflict?

3 When members of your family (name each one) got angry, how did others respond?

4 What did you learn about anger from each of your parents? Would you identify any family members as type A personalities?

5 When a parent was angry with you, what did you do and feel?

6 When you got angry, who listened or failed to listen to you?

7 How did members of your family respond when you got angry?

8 Who was allowed or not allowed to be angry in your family?

9 What are your best and worst memories of anger in your family?

10 Was anyone ever physically hurt when someone got angry?

11 How were you punished as a child? How were siblings punished?

12 Did you witness violence in your family? Between whom?

13 Did you witness or participate in violence in your community?

14 What sibling rivalry experiences did you have with your siblings? How physical was the rivalry?

Questions about Sadness, Loss, and Grief

1 What are the patterns of loss in the family? What are the circumstances of these losses?

2 How was grief expressed or not expressed in the family and by whom?

3 Are there secrets surrounding any of the losses? Who has the information? How is it shared?

4 Are there any family or religious rituals for going through the grieving process? Were they followed?

5 Are both positive and negative feelings expressed about deaths or other losses? Are pictures, mementos, and stories shared openly, or are there no signs or perhaps "shrines" to someone who has died, abandoned, or been cutoff from the individual or the family?

6 Are there patterns of illness in the family?

More Questions about Grief

1 What were your experiences with grief in your family?

2 Who was allowed to grieve?

3 When was grief permitted (i.e., which losses are acknowledged as deserving grief)?

4 How was grief displayed and expressed in your family?

5 What were the family's attitudes about how long grief may last (i.e., what length of grieving is too long or too short)?

6 What does it mean to express grief differently than expected by your family?

7 How have children been involved in the grieving process?

8 How has the family viewed the use of outside support services such as support groups or mental health professionals?

Questions about Fear

1   What do you recall about being fearful in your life?
2   Did you experience traumatic events in your life? How was the fear expressed?
3   What frightened you as a child?
4   What frightens you today?
5   How do you react when you are frightened? How do you react when others are frightened?
6   What are your worries or phobias?
7   General screening for post-traumatic stress disorder (sexual abuse and severe posttraumatic symptoms are discussed in Chapter 8): Do you have particular fears or phobias; psychological numbing; difficulty concentrating; repetitive thoughts, feelings, or images; night terrors, waking in the night?
8   Did other family members suffer from traumatic events during their life? What happened? How did they deal with or express their fears?
9   Are there patterns of anxiety disorders within the family?

Questions about Pleasure

1   What kinds of creativity are evident in your family?
2   Are family members generally viewed as lovable and important? Is affection shown regularly?
3   Do people in the family participate in hobbies? Social activities? Sports? Community activities?
4   What kind of social network is available? Family? Friendship? Work or career associates? Social, religious, or civic memberships?
5   How are physical health and well-being addressed? What are the patterns of general health? What are the patterns of physical exercise and nutrition?
6   Do you have "fun" in your life? How? Do members of your extended family have "fun?" How?
7   Do you have a sense of humor? Do other members of you family have a sense of humor?
8   Do you set goals? Have a positive mental outlook? How about other members of the extended family, now and in the past?
9   Do you take vacations, short trips, and schedule activities? How often? Was this something your family did when you were growing up? How often?

Index

Note: **Bold** page numbers refer to tables; *italic* page numbers refer to figures and page numbers followed by "n" denote endnotes.